INCLUSION MATTERS

NEW FRONTIERS OF SOCIAL POLICY

INCLUSION MATTERS

THE FOUNDATION FOR SHARED PROSPERITY

THE WORLD BANK
Washington, D.C.

1818 H Street NW
Washington DC 20433
Telephone: 202-473-1000
Internet: www.worldbank.org

1 2 3 4 16 15 14 13

ISBN (paper): 978-1-4648-0010-8
ISBN (electronic): 978-1-4648-0011-5
DOI: 10.1596/978-1-4648-0010-8

Photo credits: All images require permission for further reuse. *Cover:* "Faces Blue" (n.d.), © Geoffrey Ernest Katantazi Mukasa/World Bank Art Program. *Part I opener:* detail from "Sin Título (Somos…)/Untitled (We are…)" (2008), © Andrés Asturias, courtesy of the artist. *Part II opener:* "I Be You You Be Me" (2007), © Victor Ekpuk/World Bank Art Program. *Part 3 opener:* "Solidarity" (n.d.), © Dolorosa Sinaga/World Bank Art Program.

Cover design: Naylor Design, Inc.

Library of Congress Cataloging-in Publication Data has been requested.

NEW FRONTIERS OF SOCIAL POLICY

In many developing countries, the mixed record of state effectiveness, market imperfections, and persistent structural inequities has undermined the effectiveness of social policy. To overcome these constraints, social policy needs to move beyond conventional social service approaches toward development's goals of equitable opportunity and social justice. This series has been created to promote debate among the development community, policy makers, and academia, and to broaden understanding of social policy challenges in developing country contexts.

The books in the series are linked to the World Bank's Social Development Strategy. The strategy is aimed at empowering people by transforming institutions to make them more inclusive, responsive, and accountable. This involves the transformation of subjects and beneficiaries into citizens with rights and responsibilities. Themes in this series include equity and development, assets and livelihoods, citizenship and rights-based social policy, and the social dimensions of infrastructure and climate change.

Titles in the series:

- *Assets, Livelihoods, and Social Policy*
- *Building Equality and Opportunity through Social Guarantees: New Approaches to Public Policy and the Realization of Rights*
- *Delivering Services in Multicultural Societies*
- *Inclusion Matters: The Foundation for Shared Prosperity*
- *Inclusive States: Social Policy and Structural Inequalities*
- *Institutional Pathways to Equity: Addressing Inequality Traps*
- *Living through Crises: How the Food, Fuel, and Financial Shocks Affect the Poor*
- *Social Dimensions of Climate Change: Equity and Vulnerability in a Warming World*
- *Societal Dynamics and Fragility: Engaging Societies in Responding to Fragile Situations*

CONTENTS

I. FRAMING THE ISSUE

II. TRANSITIONS, TRANSFORMATIONS, AND PERCEPTIONS

Boxes

Figures

Tables

FOREWORD

In every country, certain groups—whether illegal immigrants, indigenous people, or other minorities—confront barriers that prevent them from fully participating in their nation's political, economic, and social life. These groups are branded by stereotypes, stigmas, and superstitions. They often live with insecurity. And such disadvantages not only preclude them from capitalizing on opportunities to lead a better life, they also rob them of dignity.

In many countries, excluded people have organized to right a lifetime of wrongs. These newly active citizens include victims of violence who are demanding justice, or members of growing middle classes demanding greater voice in their countries' political processes. They come armed or simply angry, protesting in Brazil or India, and occupying Wall Street or Tahrir Square. Taken together, their outrage demonstrates a global crisis of inclusion.

At the World Bank Group, we have realized that confronting the need for social inclusion will prove vital if we are to meet our goal of building shared prosperity for all people. While great strides have been made in reducing extreme poverty, in country after country, groups remain excluded from development gains. A rising tide does not necessarily lift all boats.

Acknowledging this, in May 2013, the United Nations (UN) Secretary-General's High-Level Panel of Eminent Persons on the Post-2015 Development Agenda called for designing development goals that focus on reaching excluded groups. "Leave no one behind," they urged the Secretary-General, adding, "We should ensure that no person—regardless of ethnicity, gender, geography, disability, race, or status—is denied universal human rights and basic economic opportunities."

Including the excluded is a complex challenge. At the World Bank Group, we begin where we always do: by surveying, sifting, and analyzing the evidence. The result of that work is this evidence-based study of social inclusion. It is the first of its kind for the Bank Group. We believe it represents one of the most comprehensive reviews of social inclusion available. While more work is needed, our research allows us to say a few things with confidence:

Ostracized groups exist in all countries, rich and poor, democratic and not. They are often hidden from public censuses, made invisible by their fear of reprisal. Still, they can be found. In Vietnam, for example, where poverty reduction has been impressive, indigenous people are less likely to be covered by health programs or receive essential vaccinations. In the United States, African Americans were twice as likely as whites to be unemployed during the recent financial crisis. In Bolivia, ethnic minority Quechua-speaking women are 28 percentage points less likely to complete secondary school than Spanish-speaking Bolivian men.

Excluded groups are denied opportunities. Excluded groups are significantly less likely to receive the benefits of development investments. In Uganda, for example, where electricity coverage is low, almost half of respondents from the Buganda group reported having electricity, compared to less than 5 percent of the minority Lugbara and Ngakaramajong populations. The same breakdown appears in terms of access to clean water. Some excluded groups have been denied opportunities for hundreds of years, such as Native Americans in the United States.

Poverty and exclusion are not the same. In some societies, even the rich can be excluded, as might be the case with wealthy homosexual men in some African countries. The protest movements in the Middle East have been fueled in part by demands among middle-class citizens for greater inclusion in public decision making and accountability from political leaders.

Exclusion is costly. Measuring the cost of exclusion has methodological challenges, but the costs—whether social, political, or economic—are likely to be substantial. Occupational segregation can restrict the free movement of talent and resources, resulting in productivity losses to an entire economy. One study found that exclusion of the ethnic minority Roma cost Romania 887 million euros in lost productivity. Studies in Bolivia estimate that ethnic exclusion reduces agricultural productivity by up to 36 percent.

Most importantly, we find abundant evidence that inclusion can be planned and achieved. Education represents an unparalleled agent for stimulating inclusion. Religious leaders and other champions of change can help excluded groups acquire voice and confidence. The march towards greater inclusion, however, is not linear. Expanding the rights of formerly oppressed people risks triggering a backlash from historically dominant groups, who see their interests threatened. The process of fostering inclusion is incremental. It requires time and unwavering commitment. Still, the benefits of persistently striving for inclusion are at once striking and numerous. Examples can be seen around the world, from the overthrow of apartheid in South Africa, to China's outlawing of foot binding, to the growing support that Brazilian police now provide to victims of rape. Exclusion is far from immutable.

Solving the problem of social exclusion is urgent. Tensions are rising around the world, due to demographic shifts, migration, food price shocks, and economic volatility. People fleeing war and extreme poverty often become the most excluded groups in host countries. In the future, moreover, climate change will likely result in mass migrations, as cities and countries confront extreme drought, storms, heat waves, and sea-level rise. Longstanding prejudices may result in excluded groups receiving blame for growing societal tension and competition for resources.

To move ahead wisely, we need a clear research agenda. We need better tools to measure the costs of exclusion and for diagnosing its root causes. We must also develop more sophisticated analyses of which strategies are most likely to foster social inclusion, and mechanisms for gauging when inclusion efforts are working and when they are not.

We offer this report with the hope that it will stimulate research, action, and a broader debate on social inclusion. Increased understanding of this crucial topic will strengthen efforts to deliver better results for the world's poor, and help achieve our shared goals of ending extreme poverty and building shared prosperity for all people.

Jim Yong Kim
President
The World Bank Group

ACKNOWLEDGMENTS

This report was prepared by a team led by Maitreyi Bordia Das, Social Development Department (SDV), under the guidance of Rachel Kyte, Vice President of the Sustainable Development Network (SDN) and Cyprian Fisiy, Director of the Social Development Department (SDV).

The core team comprised Sabina Espinoza, Gillette Hall, Soumya Kapoor-Mehta, Kamila Kasprzycka, Maria Beatriz Orlando, Juan Carlos Parra Osorio, Maira Emy Reimão, Lisa Schmidt, Sonya Sultan, Emcet Oktay Taş, and Ieva Žumbytė. In addition, Sabina Espinoza, Soumya Kapoor-Mehta, and Emcet Oktay Taş were part of the main writing team. Special thanks are due to Elizabeth Acul, Colum Garrity, Kyung Min In, Nona (Anju) Sachdeva, Syed Abdul Salam and Cristy Tumale from SDV for their outstanding support.

Background inputs were prepared by Taaka Awori (independent consultant), Sabina Espinoza, Patricia Fernandes, Roberto Foa (Harvard University), Rasmus Heltberg, Surinder Jodhka (Jawaharlal Nehru University, New Delhi), Soumya Kapoor-Mehta, Kamila Kasprzycka, Sadaf Lakhani, Rachel Marcus (independent consultant), Roberto Miranda (Inter-American Development Bank), Simon O'Meally, Maria Beatriz Orlando, Juan Carlos Parra Osorio, Beata Plonka (independent consultant), Graeme Ramshaw (independent consultant), Maira Emy Reimão, Audrey Sacks, Lisa Schmidt, Hilary Silver (Brown University), Li Shi (Beijing Normal University), Sonya Sultan, Emcet Oktay Taş, Francesco di Villarosa (independent consultant), Maria Cecilia Villegas, Xiaolin Wang (International Poverty Reduction Center in China), and Ieva Žumbytė.

The team would like to thank peer reviewers Dan Banik (University of Oslo and China Agricultural University), Francisco Ferreira, Arjan de Haan (International Development Research Centre, Canada), Jesko Hentschel, Andrew Norton (Overseas Development Institute), Dena Ringold, and Carolyn Turk for their insightful comments and for participating in the review meetings. Marianne Fay (Chief Economist, SDN), Elisabeth Huybens (Sector Manager, SDV when this report was conceived; now Sector Manager, Social Development, Europe and Central Asia Region) and Susan Wong (Sector Manager, SDV) also provided valuable comments and guidance.

Constructive comments were received at various stages of the review process from Motoko Aizawa, Beatrix Allah-Mensah, Ian Bannon, Kaushik Basu, Tara Beteille, Ana Maria Muñoz Boudet, Franck Bousquet, Charles Cormier, Maria Correia, Alberto Coelho Gomes Costa, Anis Dani, Pyush Dogra, Mariana Felicio, Varun Gauri, Elena Glinskaya, Helene Grandvoinnet, Asli Gurkan, Sara Gustafsson, Bernard Harborne, Karla Hoff, Naila Kabeer (School of Oriental and African Studies, University of London), Sarah Keener, Jeni Klugman, Markus Kostner, Paul Kriss, Angela Nyawira Khaminwa, Andrea Liverani, Alexandre Marc, Robin Mearns, Bala Menon, Sarah Michael, Ambar Narayan, Deepa Narayan (international advisor), Claudia Nassif, Sarah Nedolast, John Newman, Clarence Tsimpo Nkengne, Asta Olesen, Pedro Olinto, Mario Picon, Hans-Otto Sano, Rodrigo Serrano, Ulrich Schmidt, Jordan Schwartz, Sudhir Shetty, Iain Shuker, Varun Singh, Emmanuel Skoufias, Rob Swinkels, Sarah Twigg, Paolo Verme, Varalakshmi Verumu, Chaogang Wang, Gregor Wolf and Michael Woolcock.

The Social Development Sector Board helped to refine many of the ideas in this report. Discussions with Junaid Ahmad, Mariana Cavalcanti (Getúlio Vargas Foundation, Rio de Janeiro, Brazil), He Hsiaojun (International Poverty Reduction Center in China), Ricardo Paes de Barros (Secretariat of Strategic Affairs of the Presidency of Brazil), Dewen Wang, and Xiaoqing Yu helped in crafting the story line. Early findings of the report were presented at meetings and seminars organized by the Organisation for Economic Co-operation and Development (OECD), Swiss Agency for Development and Cooperation (SDC), United Nations Educational, Scientific and Cultural Organization (UNESCO), International Poverty Reduction Center in China (IPRCC), Institute for Studies on Labor and Society (IETS), and Overseas Development Institute (ODI), and participants provided valuable inputs.

The report drew upon a range of operational and analytical engagements that were supported by staff based in the World Bank country offices of Afghanistan, Brazil, China, Ghana, Poland, and Uganda. The support from the Nordic Trust Fund (NTF) and the Multi-Donor Trust

Fund for Poverty and Social Impact Analysis (PSIA-MDTF) is gratefully acknowledged.

Finally, Fionna Douglas, Hendrik Barkeling, Doreen Kibuka-Musoke, and Ewa Sobczynska provided valuable support and advice. Bruce Ross-Larson facilitated a writers' workshop and Dick Thompson provided editorial support for the overview.

ABBREVIATIONS

ABEC	Alternative Basic Education Centre
ADA	Americans with Disabilities Act
AIDS	acquired immune deficiency syndrome
ARV	antiretroviral
BDP	Botswana Democratic Party
BRAC	Bangladesh Rural Advancement Centre
CDD	community-driven development
EEOC	Equal Employment Opportunity Commission
EPAG	Economic Empowerment of Adolescent Girls and Young Women
EU	European Union
GDP	gross domestic product
GEM	Gender Empowerment Measure
GHI	Global Hunger Index
HIV	human immunodeficiency virus
HOI	Human Opportunities Index
ICERD	International Convention on the Elimination of All Forms of Racial Discrimination
ICESCR	International Covenant on Economic, Social and Cultural Rights
ICT	information and communications technology
IOM	International Organization for Migration
KDP	Kecamatan Development Program
LGBT	lesbian, gay, bisexual, and transgender
LiTS	Life in Transition Survey
MDG	Millennium Development Goal
MPM	Multidimensional Poverty Measure
MSM	men who have sex with men
NFHS	National Family Health Survey

NGO	nongovernmental organization
OECD	Organisation for Economic Co-operation and Development
OSCE	Organization for Security and Co-operation in Europe
PARSP	Post-Accession Rural Support Project
PCA	Principal Components Analysis
PMTCT	prevention of mother-to-child transmission
PSIA	Poverty and Social Impact Analysis
TAC	Treatment Action Campaign
TFR	total fertility rate
UDHR	Universal Declaration of Human Rights (1948)
UN	United Nations
UNAIDS	Joint United Nations Programme on HIV/AIDS
UNDRIP	United Nations Declaration on the Rights of Indigenous Peoples
UP	Union Parishad
UPP	Unidades de Polícia Pacificadora
WHO	World Health Organization

Social Inclusion

- The process of improving the terms for individuals and groups to take part in society
- The process of improving the ability, opportunity, and dignity of people, disadvantaged on the basis of their identity, to take part in society

Overview

The World Bank Group's focus on social inclusion began with the observation that even within countries, development investments produced unequal benefits. Further assessments revealed that groups with certain distinguishing characteristics consistently failed to benefit from a nation's progress. These groups were among the poorest in a nation, but they were not consistently the poorest. They were often, but not always, minorities. What set them apart was that they were members of excluded groups—indigenous people, new immigrants, people with disabilities, people with different skin tones, people who spoke the official language imperfectly. These were people branded by stigmas, stereotypes, and superstitions. They confronted unique barriers that kept them from fully participating in their country's political and economic life. They were excluded.

One of the world's greatest development efforts is coming to a close. The year 2015 marks the endpoint for achievement of the Millennium Development Goals (MDGs). In assessing the MDG response and charting a course for the next era of development, the United Nations Secretary-General's High-Level Panel of Eminent Persons on the Post-2015 Development Agenda (UN 2013) called for designing development goals that focus on reaching excluded groups. "Leave no one behind," it advised. "We should ensure that no person—regardless of ethnicity, gender, geography, disability, race, or status—is denied universal human rights and basic economic opportunities."

Along with global developments, the World Bank Group has announced two ambitious goals for itself: ending extreme poverty and promoting shared prosperity. Underlying the goals is the notion of "sustainability." A sustainable path for development and poverty reduction is defined as one that manages the resources of the planet for future generations, ensures social inclusion and adopts fiscally responsible policies that limit future debt burden (World Bank 2013b). As a recent World Bank Group publication notes:

> A sustainable path toward ending extreme poverty and promoting shared prosperity would also involve creating *an inclusive society*, not only in terms of economic welfare but also in terms of the voice and empowerment of all groups. An inclusive society must have the institutions, structures, and processes that empower local communities, so they can hold their governments accountable. It also requires the participation of all groups in society, including traditionally marginalized groups, such as ethnic minorities and indigenous populations, in decision-making processes. (World Bank 2013b, 33, emphasis added)

Social inclusion matters for itself. But it also matters because it is the foundation for shared prosperity and because social exclusion is simply too costly. There are substantial costs—social, political, and economic—to not addressing the exclusion of entire groups of people. The Arab Spring may have been the most costly recent reaction to the exclusion of educated youth—from labor markets but also, and perhaps mainly, from political decision making and accountability. Although there are significant methodological challenges in measuring the cost of exclusion, some efforts have been made. A World Bank report on the Roma (an ethnic minority in Europe) estimates annual productivity losses caused by their exclusion. It suggests that these costs could range from €231 million in Serbia to €887 million in Romania (de Laat 2010).

Exclusion has deleterious consequences for human capital development as well. For instance, a recent report finds that children with disabilities are less likely to start school than children without disabilities and have lower rates of staying in school (WHO and World Bank 2011). Similarly, women in India who experience spousal violence are less likely to receive antenatal care and more likely to have a terminated pregnancy or still birth, and their children are more likely to be stunted than are children of mothers who have not been abused (World Bank 2011a).

This report provides a frame of reference to help understand and move toward social inclusion. It is intended for policy makers, academics, activists, and development partners—indeed, anyone who is curious about what inclusion can mean and how it can be addressed in a world that is in the throes of formidable transitions. Although it does not provide definitive answers, it offers a definition and a framework to help advance the agenda of social inclusion. It builds on the Bank's previous analytical work on themes that have touched upon social inclusion. It also draws on a review of relevant literature, analysis of survey data, some new qualitative work, and policy engagement with select countries.

This report is the Bank's first comprehensive examination of inclusion. It is certainly incomplete. It is hoped that this first effort prods and inspires further research by social scientists to broaden the understanding of the causes, consequences, and remedies of exclusion.

There are seven main messages in this report:

1. Excluded groups exist in all countries.
2. Excluded groups are consistently denied opportunities.
3. Intense global transitions are leading to social transformations that create new opportunities for inclusion as well as exacerbating existing forms of exclusion.
4. People take part in society through markets, services, and spaces.
5. Social and economic transformations affect the attitudes and perceptions of people. As people act on the basis of how they feel, it is important to pay attention to their attitudes and perceptions.
6. Exclusion is not immutable. Abundant evidence demonstrates that social inclusion can be planned and achieved.
7. Moving ahead will require a broader and deeper knowledge of exclusion and its impacts as well as taking concerted action.

Clarifying Concepts

Although there is general agreement that social inclusion matters, there are few terms as abstract and political as *social inclusion*. It is notoriously many things to many people. Although it is true that the term is more political than analytical (Øyen 1997), it is also true that it has its roots in identifiable models of welfare and in principles of social justice and human dignity.

This report proposes defining social inclusion in two ways. The first is a broad sweep to guide policy makers. It states that social inclusion is

> The process of improving the terms for individuals and groups to take part in society.

A second, sharper definition takes into account how the terms of social inclusion can be improved and for whom. It articulates social inclusion as

The process of improving the ability, opportunity, and dignity of people, disadvantaged on the basis of their identity, to take part in society.

People often find it easier to explain what social exclusion is. Yet even social exclusion is often lumped with the related concepts of poverty and inequality. Social inclusion may well be about reducing poverty—but it is often about more than poverty, and in some cases, it is not about poverty at all. Take the case of a homosexual man living in a rich neighborhood in any of several African countries. He may not be poor, but he is certainly excluded—and in some countries, at risk of death. Exclusion can intersect with poverty, deriving from a set of multiple, interrelated disadvantages that result in both economic and social deprivation (Silver n.d.). Understanding that "the poor" are not one homogeneous mass but are rather differentiated on the basis of occupation, ethnicity, place of residence, or race is central to developing effective inclusive policies.

Social inclusion takes poverty analysis beyond identifying correlates to uncovering its underlying causes. It asks questions such as *why* certain groups are overrepresented among the poor and *why* some people lack access to education, health, and other services or receive poorer-quality services. It exposes the multidimensional nature of chronic deprivation arising from social exclusion, which plays a key role in driving the more readily observable correlates of poverty (lack of schooling, poor health, and constrained labor market returns). It underscores that deprivation arising from social exclusion tends to occur along multiple axes at once, so that policies that release just one of these axes of deprivation, such as improved access to education, will not unleash the grip of others. It draws back the curtain on the norms and belief systems that underpin this multifaceted exclusion, which may be overt norms, such as apartheid in South Africa, or the result of intangible belief systems handed down through history.

Social inclusion is also not the same as equality. The term *social inclusion* can add to the idea of equality, but much more importantly, it can explain why some inequalities exist or why some are particularly durable (Tilly 1999). There are many ways that people can achieve fuller participation and inclusion, even if they lack an equal share of resources. At the same time, even people at the higher end of the income distribution may face social exclusion through political persecution or discrimination based on age, gender, sexual orientation, or disability (Warschauer 2003). So exclusion can be horizontal, affecting several members of a group, whether poor or rich. It is a process, of which inequality is sometimes, but not always, an outcome.

Practitioners of development, who sometimes consider social inclusion too esoteric an idea, often ask how it could be quantified. How would one know when exclusion takes place and when inclusion is achieved? Such measurement is indeed important to establish the extent and depth of exclusion and to monitor progress toward inclusion.

There has been considerable progress in the area of measurement of human well-being, if not social inclusion, more directly. In fact, "happiness-based" conceptualizations of societal progress go back to the writings of Bentham and Mill. But over time, attention moved away from happiness to the measurement of real production (Galbraith 1998; Sen 2000). In recent years, there have been several significant initiatives to measure societal progress more comprehensively, and many have incorporated subjective reports of well-being.

The test of moving toward social inclusion is to move forward from the metrics to *ask why* certain outcomes obtain for certain groups, to focus on the drivers and processes of those outcomes. Doing so means persevering with questions, not being content, for instance, with the knowledge that certain groups are overrepresented among the poor or that some have worse human development outcomes, but rather *asking why* this is the case. It means building consensus around difficult answers that such questions will inevitably throw up. The narrative that is constructed as a result is the most important way in which social inclusion can have meaning.

Who Gets Excluded and How?

Individuals and groups are excluded or included based on their identity. Among the most common group identities resulting in exclusion are gender, race, caste, ethnicity, religion, and disability status. Social exclusion based on such group attributes can lead to lower social standing, often accompanied by lower outcomes in terms of income, human capital endowments, access to employment and services, and voice in both national and local decision making. Gaps between the attainment of males and females in a range of outcomes are well documented. People of African descent are still excluded in a variety of cultures. The caste system, peculiar to India and Nepal, stands out as an "ideal type" of exclusion, complete with an ideology and a hierarchy that has persisted through millennia. Religion continues to be a serious driver of exclusion. And indigenous people around the world continue to face exclusion that is rooted in large part in their displacement from their traditional lands (Hall and Patrinos 2012).

Some identities that were not acknowledged as sources of social exclusion or inclusion some decades ago are acknowledged as such today. They include sexual orientation, nationality, and HIV/AIDS. The lesbian, gay, bisexual, and transgender (LGBT) community, for instance, is targeted for exclusion in many, if not most, cultures. With huge waves of migration, both within countries and across them, the identity of migrant groups and individuals has come under special scrutiny, especially in developed countries, which are grappling with ways of integrating nonnatives.

Individuals are members of different groups at once and may be excluded through one of their identities but not another. The notion of "intersectionality" is based on the understanding that people are simultaneously situated in multiple social structures and realms (figure O.1). However, when they intersect, identities can produce a multiplication of advantage

Figure O.1 People Have Multiple, Intersecting Identities

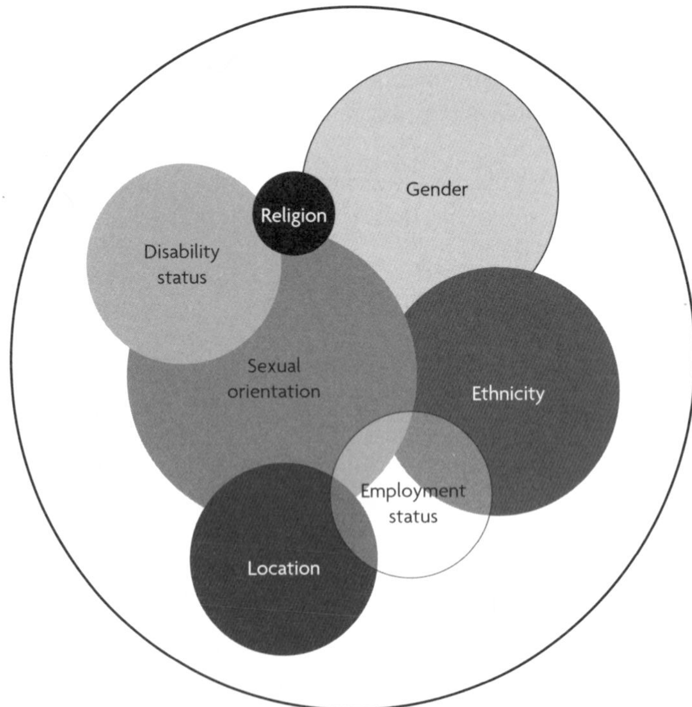

Note: Figure shows illustrative example of types of identities. The size of each bubble denotes the importance of an identity, which can vary across individuals, groups, and even the same individual over time.

or disadvantage. For instance, the intersection of gender, age, ethnicity, and place of residence can have significantly more deleterious effects than the effects of gender alone. Take the case of Bolivia, which has high levels of secondary school attainment. Figure O.2 shows that being a woman in Bolivia reduces the probability of completing secondary education by 5 percentage points, compared with being a Spanish-speaking man. If this Bolivian woman were a man who belonged to the Quechua people, the probability of completion would decline by 14 percentage points. If she were a Quechua woman, it would decline by 28 percentage points. Similarly, the intersection of social and spatial characteristics is a common marker of disadvantage.

Groups are heterogeneous, so exclusion within groups exists as well. Characteristics of some members of the group, such as socioeconomic status, place in the life cycle, or circumstances (such as widowhood), can also bestow advantage or disadvantage. Where social security systems are primarily informal, many elderly people are now at risk of ill treatment. Similarly, without concerted action on poverty, employment, and human development, countries with large youth cohorts are not being able to realize their "demographic dividend." Skin tone can matter as well; individuals within the same race or ethnicity (indeed even within the same family) who

Figure O.2 Intersecting Identities Transfer Cumulative Disadvantage: Secondary School Completion in Bolivia

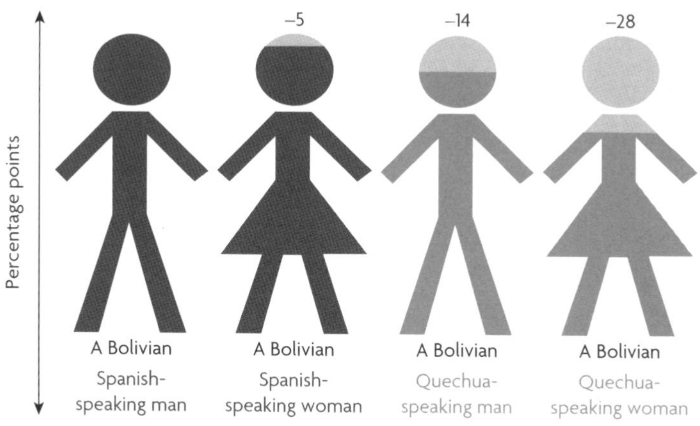

Source: World Bank, based on data from Minnesota Population Center 2011 and Bolivian National Institute of Statistics 2001.

Note: Figure shows secondary school completion marginal effects, using men and Spanish mother tongue as reference group, for people 25 years and older, controlling for age, age-squared, and urban/rural residence. All values are significant at the 1 percent level.

have lighter skin appear to have better outcomes, ranging from chances of getting married (especially of women) to employment (Hersch 2008; Jha and Adelman 2009; Villarreal 2010).

Exclusion plays out through both tangible and intangible practices and processes. Although it is most evident in differences in "tangible" outcomes, it is rooted in intangible social norms and beliefs, which in turn lead to stereotypes, prejudices, and stigmas. These intangible features are socially constructed and played out by both the excluder and the excluded. For example, stereotypes about groups can be so ingrained in the labor market that hiring managers or peers do not even realize that they have them (see Loury 1999; Deshpande and Newman 2007) or may not consider them stereotypes but facts. Stereotypes of "lazy" Roma or of women having low commitment to the labor market are so internalized by the majority that they are often regarded as truisms, even though they are not borne out by data on labor force participation (de Laat 2010). Sometimes the words that describe certain practices say a lot about the social acceptance of exclusion. For instance, the term *eve teasing* is used in South Asia as a flippant euphemism to signify sexual harassment of women in public places, and both the term and the practice are treated with the same indulgence.

Inclusion in What and How?

This report provides an illustrative set of interventions, but any policy or program can be designed and implemented using a social inclusion lens.

Individuals and groups want to be included in three interrelated domains: markets, services, and spaces (figure O.3). The three domains represent both barriers to and opportunities for inclusion. Just as different dimensions of an individual's life intersect, so do the three domains. Intervening in one domain without consideration of the others is likely to be one of the most important reasons for the limited success of inclusion policies and programs.

Markets

In their day-to-day interactions, people engage in society through four major markets—land, housing, labor, and credit—all of which intersect at the individual and the household level. Land, for instance, has been a historical driver of exclusion. The roots of exclusion of indigenous populations around the world, for instance, lie, in significant part, in the appropriation

Figure O.3 Propelling Social Inclusion: A Framework

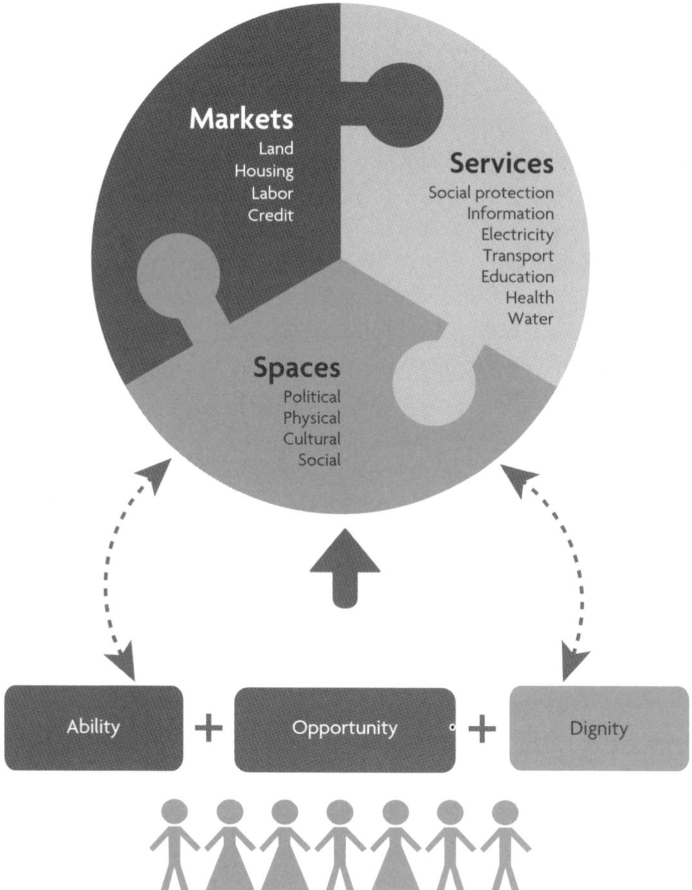

of their lands by their colonizers or by other nonindigenous groups. Major social upheavals have been caused by unequal agrarian relations, which at once straddle land and labor markets. In many parts of the world, women's historical lack of access to land has underpinned their lack of enforceable property and other rights. Exclusion from access to land affects both rural and urban populations. Urban land markets are notoriously skewed in favor of the rich and powerful; laws that govern their use and sale have been, of late, the subject of considerable debate. One of the manifestations of exclusion from urban land markets is unequal access to housing, with negative externalities in other areas. On the side of inclusion, land ownership can confer status and security (see Deininger and Feder 1998; Carter 2000).

Like land markets, labor markets are crucial sites for the play of social relations. They reflect the existing and historical inequalities in a society and are tied up with social stratification (see Polanyi 1944). For instance, slavery was at its core an occupational division of labor, with slaves working on farms and plantations. Caste, similarly, is a system of occupational segregation that became a form of social stratification, systematically excluding certain groups.

Disparity in labor market outcomes is most visibly demonstrated by the gap in earnings between preferred and excluded groups. In a study of 18 Latin American countries, Ñopo, Atal, and Winder (2010) find sizable gender and ethnic wage gaps between indigenous and nonindigenous populations. Occupational segregation by race, ethnicity, and gender is pervasive and contributes to the exclusion of certain groups from preferred jobs.

Land and labor markets are intricately linked to credit markets, especially in developing societies. The most extreme form of coalescence between the three types of markets is forced labor, which still persists in many countries. In Nepal, for instance, as part of the Kamaiya and Haruwa/Charuwa systems, indebted families, often from the historically disadvantaged castes, pledge themselves or their children to work because they cannot pay debts to moneylenders, who are often also landowners. Such labor arrangements involve agricultural workers agreeing to bondage in return for advance payments of salary from landlords at rates far below minimum wages or in lieu of loans at very high interest rates. Workers attached to the labor market through bonded labor mechanisms are rarely able to accumulate sufficient savings to repay the bond and are thus effectively in serfdom for the remainder of their lives. The transition from bonded labor to greater labor freedom is fraught with risk, because freedom severs connections with former "employers," who are also "patrons," who in addition to providing employment provide housing, protection, and in-kind transfers (World Bank 2011b).

The global push toward "financial inclusion" may be overtly about the penetration of financial instruments into untapped markets, but it is equally about social inclusion. Social assistance and wages, even for unskilled workers, are increasingly being channeled through banks and other formal payment mechanisms. Under these circumstances, lack of access to financial systems becomes an important axis of exclusion. Financial services are, moreover, increasingly tied up with access to digital technology, such as smart cards and automatic teller machines, which may create an additional layer of exclusion for individuals and groups that are either uneducated or otherwise already disadvantaged. Only 15 percent of adults in fragile and conflict-affected states have bank accounts (Demirgüç-Kunt, Klapper, and Randall 2013). In more developed financial markets, too, broad economic shocks and poor access to credit can hurt minorities disproportionately, as evident in the mortgage crisis in the United States, where African Americans and Latinos were disproportionately affected relative to their share of mortgage originations (Bocian, Li, and Ernst 2010).

Services

Access to services is essential to improving social inclusion. Health and education services enhance human capital. Social protection services cushion vulnerable groups against the effects of shocks and promote their well-being. Transport services enhance mobility and connect individuals to opportunities. Water and sanitation are essential for good health. Access to energy is important for livelihoods and for human capital. And information services enhance connectedness and allow individuals to take part in the "new economy."

Overall, subordinate groups tend to have lower access to basic services. In rural areas of the Lao People's Democratic Republic, for example, estimates suggest that a higher proportion of women from the excluded community (non-Lao-Tai) never attended school (34 percent compared with 6 percent of Lao-Tai women). Men from the excluded group fare better than women but still worse than the majority group: 17 percent of non-Lao-Tai men never attended school compared to 4 percent of Lao-Tai men. Disparities are also visible in access to health services. In Vietnam, where poverty reduction has been impressive, indigenous peoples are less likely to be covered by health programs or receive vital vaccinations, despite impressive improvements in overall access to health (Hall and Patrinos 2006, 2012). Data from African countries show that groups that speak minority languages as their mother tongue typically have lower access to services such as water and electricity. In Uganda, for instance, where electricity coverage is low in general, almost half the Muganda respondents in the 2011 Demographic and Health Survey (UBOS and ICF 2012) reported having electricity, but less than 5 percent of the Lugbara and Ngakaramajong did (figure O.4). Similar results show up in self-reported water insecurity from the Afrobarometer: the Langi, the Ateso, and the Alur report the highest incidence of having experienced water insecurity "most or all the time," and the Mutooro, Mukiga, and Munyankole are most likely to report never having experienced such insecurity.

Figure O.4 Access to Electricity Varies by Ethnicity in Uganda, 2010

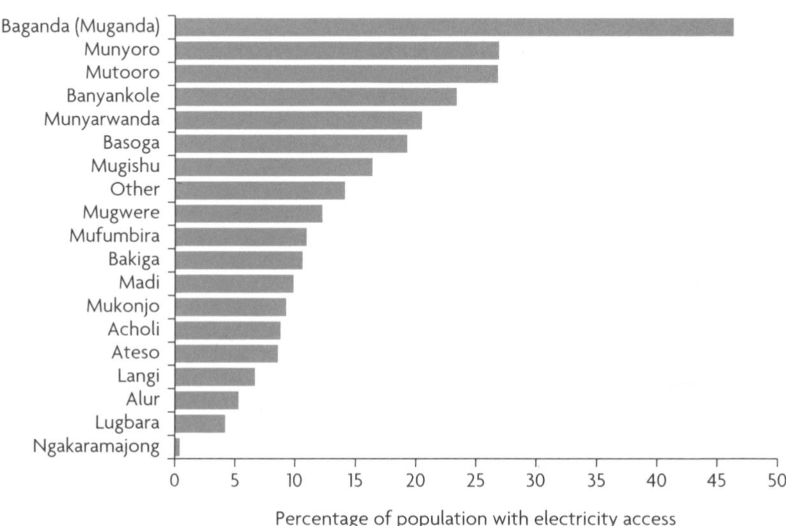

Source: World Bank, based on data from the Uganda Demographic and Health Survey 2011 (UBOS and ICF 2012).
Note: Names of ethnic groups appear as they are in the survey.

Spaces

Physical spaces have a social, political, and cultural character that solidifies systems and processes of exclusion. The most overt example of exclusion is when physical spaces are reserved for dominant groups, such as whites-only clubs during apartheid in South Africa or during slavery in the United States. The literature suggests a subculture created by dominant groups in the United States to implicitly exclude minorities even when they can afford to buy homes in their neighborhoods. Neighborhoods thus become "white" or "black"; the term "white flight" is used to document the departure of white families when black people start to move into their neighborhoods. Black neighborhoods are often considered poor or "bad" or unsafe, reflecting at once a judgment on their social and economic character. Similarly, there is evidence to suggest that Dalits in India and Nepal are still sometimes barred from entering temples and other physical spaces that are considered "pure."

Excluded groups can react to their disadvantage by claiming certain spaces. Clustering in certain geographical areas can serve as opportunity enclaves for the excluded, who, when excluded from the primary market, concentrate in markets for the excluded and use them for social and economic mobility (Wilson and Portes 1980; Portes and Jensen 1989). This phenomenon has been documented, for instance, for Cubans in Miami and other immigrants, who skirt labor market discrimination by consolidating their positions in clusters of the excluded. Not all strategies of clustering necessarily lead to social mobility, however. The perverse impact of clustering is illustrated in differential child mortality patterns in Ghana, where the Ga have higher levels of mortality than other ethnic groups. Weeks and his colleagues (2006) found a close association between differences in child mortality (by ethnicity) and residential clustering in Accra.

Because social inclusion is also at its core about accountability of the state to its citizens, it is as much about occupying political space as it is about having an equitable share in markets and services. It is not just poor people or traditionally excluded groups that demand greater political space and voice. Increasingly, educated people who feel excluded from a range of spaces are clamoring for greater participation. Poverty and minority status often compound the lack of access to political space. Many countries have seen a rolling back of state power since the 1980s, accompanied by a widening of economic opportunities. Yet state power continues to underpin many processes of exclusion and inclusion, and rent-seeking becomes an important process of exclusion. For instance, the power to award mining leases or to sit in positions that can influence public sector hiring offers ample scope for consolidating social, political, and economic space. Although politicians do not necessarily or exclusively favor their own ethnic or cultural group, groups with little or no political representation risk their interests being excluded from consideration (Marcus et al. 2013).

Enhancing Social Inclusion by Improving Ability, Opportunity, and Dignity

Ability

This report uses the ideas of ability, opportunity, and dignity and applies them to excluded groups. Ability, for instance, is innate to individuals, but, when measured through achievement tests, it may not always be randomly distributed. Instead, it may be socially mediated. A child who performs poorly on standardized tests at an early age may be affected by a range of background processes. These processes can include the fact that she was born with low birthweight to a very young mother and may not have had the parental stimulation that her peers in more advantaged circumstances had. These cumulative disadvantages are often systematically distributed by race, ethnicity, or place of residence. The literature on early childhood education indicates that the brain starts to develop in utero, and although brains are elastic enough to compensate for maternal or other in utero deprivations, they may not be able to fully do so. In addition, when children are deprived of stimulation and nutrition in the early months and years of life, their development is permanently affected.

The ability of an individual is also affected by the people she sees around her and whom she regards as reference models. Borjas (1992) outlines the notion of "ethnic capital" to show that individuals who are members of high-performing groups tend to perform better. This report argues that reference groups and role models are important in the "capacity to aspire," to use Appadurai's term. When individuals from disadvantaged groups see others around them performing at a low level, they set a much lower bar for themselves than they would have if they had belonged to a high-performing group. In addition, they may internalize exclusion in such a way that they do not even bother to try for better outcomes, knowing that people from their group are discriminated against. Elmslie and Sedo (1996) propose the idea of "learned helplessness" to show that negative events, such as an episode of discrimination, can lead to a decrease in learning ability. Exclusion, therefore, can create resignation at both the group and the individual level, which in turn diminishes human capital, constrains effort, and becomes somewhat of a self-fulfilling prophecy.

Opportunity

Inequality of opportunity is one of the major constraints to the realization of human potential. Recent work on the Human Opportunities Index (HOI) underscores this and focuses policy attention on investments that equalize opportunities at the beginning of the life cycle. The underlying assumption is that equalizing the supply of services will provide all individuals with an equal chance of translating their capabilities into enhanced well-being.

Providing full opportunity is not only an institutional challenge in many countries; the process of expanding opportunities can itself be exclusionary, constraining both the supply of and demand for opportunity.

Take the case of health facilities in remote areas where indigenous women live. The remoteness of their habitations means that providing them with the same quality and quantity of services as available to their urban counterparts is fiscally and institutionally challenging. The placement of health centers often depends on the political voice of the residents, and some of the most remote residents also have the weakest voice. Even if facilities are available, quality can be uneven, because medical staff are often absent. Finally, there is also "low demand" for facilities, for a number of reasons, including the indignity and humiliation meted out by service providers, which deter women from wanting to go to the facility.

Opportunity can also be mediated by special needs. For example, some groups may require remedial efforts to provide them with the same degree of opportunity, because of their initial conditions, which include their innate characteristics (for instance, disability status). An estimated 12–16 percent of all children in the United States come into the school system with a disability that hampers their ability to learn (AAP 2001). Children with disabilities who receive targeted support in addition to schooling are more likely to graduate, gain employment, and live independently (Shonkoff and Meisels 2000). Yet remedial services are often deficient, mirroring the wider social, economic, and political exclusion of people with disabilities (Yeo and Moore 2003). The situation for children with disabilities in less developed countries is even more adverse. What is the likelihood that they will be presented with equal opportunities?

Finally, opportunity changes over the life cycle. Equalizing opportunities at the beginning of life does not ensure the capacity for equal outcomes over time. There are critical junctures in the life cycle, such as entry into the job market from school and during future job searches for career advancement, where both demand and supply factors play an important role in reallocating opportunity. There are also catastrophic and unforeseen events, such as economic crises and natural disasters, which work to reallocate opportunity, with unequal impacts on population subgroups. In the recent financial crisis in the United States, for instance, black people were twice as likely to become unemployed than whites, and it took them much longer to regain employment (Lynch 2012). At the individual level, events such as accidents or a death in the family can forever alter access to opportunity.

Dignity

This report brings the idea of dignity into the lexicon of the World Bank Group. The idea that dignity matters for individuals and groups is not new for development theory. The word *dignity* is mentioned in several human rights covenants and charters. Amartya Sen's idea of capabilities encompasses the notion of human dignity.

Dignity as it relates to social inclusion is intrinsically linked to notions of respect and recognition. When, through their institutions and norms, dominant cultures and processes actively disrespect individuals and groups who are considered subordinate, those individuals and groups can either opt out, submit, or protest.

The lack of recognition can render some individuals and even entire groups "invisible" in official statistics. For instance, in many cultures, a disabled member of the household is not reported in the household roster when survey personnel conduct interviews. In other cases, people such as refugees who cross borders without documents may actively avoid official contact. Other unrecognized people include stateless people and even legal citizens who lack documents to prove their residency or eligibility for various benefits. In still other cases, such as the Roma in many European countries, the excluded group hides itself from official surveys and censuses so that it can meld into the statistics of the majority. In figurative terms, dignity and recognition are linked to the way subordinate groups are treated by dominant groups and by the state. This treatment includes contempt for their cultures and practices and intentional or unintentional stereotyping that prevents them from fully taking part in society.

Tools are being developed to measure when individuals are being accorded dignity or treated without it. The empirical literature on dignity has been led by medical ethicists and advocates of respectful treatment of patients, especially the terminally ill, the elderly, and people with significant physical and cognitive impairments, at the hands of medical providers. For example, using data from the Commonwealth Fund 2001 Health Care Quality Survey of 6,722 adults living in the United States, Beach et al. (2005) analyze the association between two measures of respect (involvement in decisions and treatment with dignity) and patient outcomes (satisfaction, adherence, and receipt of optimal preventive care). After adjusting for respondents' demographic characteristics, they find that people who were treated with dignity had a higher probability of reporting satisfaction. As measures of dignity are still being developed, the terms *dignity, respect,* and *recognition* are often used interchangeably.

A recent survey in China of 128,000 migrants in urban areas asked respondents whether they thought migrants were "always looked down on" in the cities in which they lived. Between one-third and one-fourth of respondents thought they were always looked down on by locals—a finding that varied little with age or education level (figure O.5). Feelings of being looked down on increased with length of stay, suggesting that migrants encountered unpleasant behavior if they stayed long enough and interacted with more people (Shi 2012).

Figure O.5 Migrants in Urban China Speak of "Being Looked Down on" by Locals, 2011

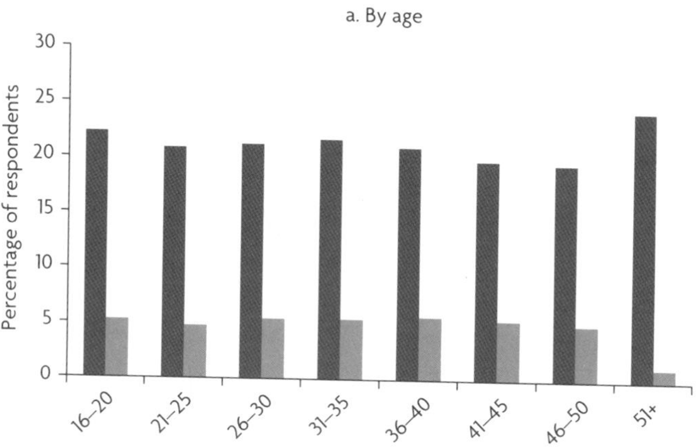

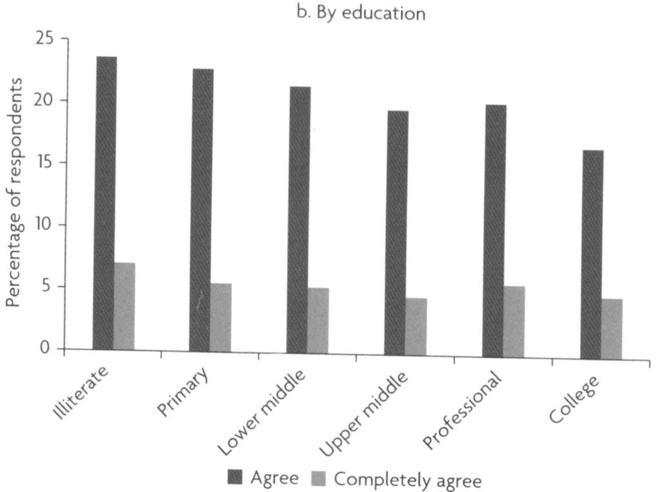

Source: Shi 2012.
Note: Based on responses to the question, "Do you agree with the view that migrants are always looked down on by locals?" in the 2011 Migrant Survey conducted by the National Health and Family Planning Commission of the People's Republic of China.

The Changing Context for Social Inclusion

Much of today's global political upheaval can be linked to demographic, spatial, economic, and knowledge transitions that are transforming societies. The cumulative impact of the transitions of the past several decades has changed the profile of the global community and reshaped some of the social inclusion issues. The cumulative impact of these large-scale transitions has changed the context for inclusion by creating new opportunities for both inclusion and exclusion.

Complex demographic transitions have significant social impacts. Lower fertility and mortality rates are transforming age structures and living arrangements. Increasing numbers of the elderly mean that countries have to provide new ways of dealing with a large new cohort. Globally, the youth cohort is the largest in history, living mostly in developing and conflict countries. Population "pyramids" (box O.1) are history. Consequently, reaping the demographic dividend requires concerted action to include young people in markets, services, and spaces, as well as skillful management of the political economy.

Additionally, current trends suggest that migration is likely to become a more dramatic and volatile demographic process than fertility or mortality. Europe is the largest hosting region. Its fertility rate is below replacement levels, indicating that unless birth rates rise over a sustained period, it will continue to have to import labor.

Migration within countries is also becoming larger in size and significance. The ongoing internal migration in China, for example, is the greatest and fastest movement of people in history, creating, among other things, shortages of urban services. Simultaneously, natural disasters, war, human trafficking, and economic recession are affecting migration patterns. All of these trends have a bearing on inclusion. For example, some countries and regions are witnessing high levels of hostility and resistance to migrants.

Urbanization was one of the most dramatic transitions of the previous century, and it will continue to unfold in the present one. At the individual and household level, urbanization offers the possibility for social mobility through a range of new opportunities. Migrants from rural areas move to cities and towns seeking new jobs, business opportunities, and education. Cities and towns also offer a different social milieu. Old norms and values give way to new and more diverse ones. However, not all social processes in urban areas are necessarily positive for excluded groups.

BOX O.1

Population Pyramids Are History

Transitions in fertility and mortality and uneven migration patterns will make population pyramids extinct by 2050, in all except the very high fertility countries. Figure BO.1.1 shows age structures of three very different contexts: Uganda, where the fertility transition has been slow and late; Poland, which has very low fertility and low mortality; and the Arab Republic of Egypt, which falls in between these two scenarios. The pyramids show that by 2050, half of Uganda's population will be below 20 years of age; Egypt's population, which is young now, will be older and replaced by a much smaller cohort of young people; and Poland will have a full-fledged aging crisis. Each of these three scenarios underscores the need for planning and vision.

Figure BO.1.1 Population Pyramids in Uganda, Poland, and the Arab Republic of Egypt, 1950, 2010, and 2050

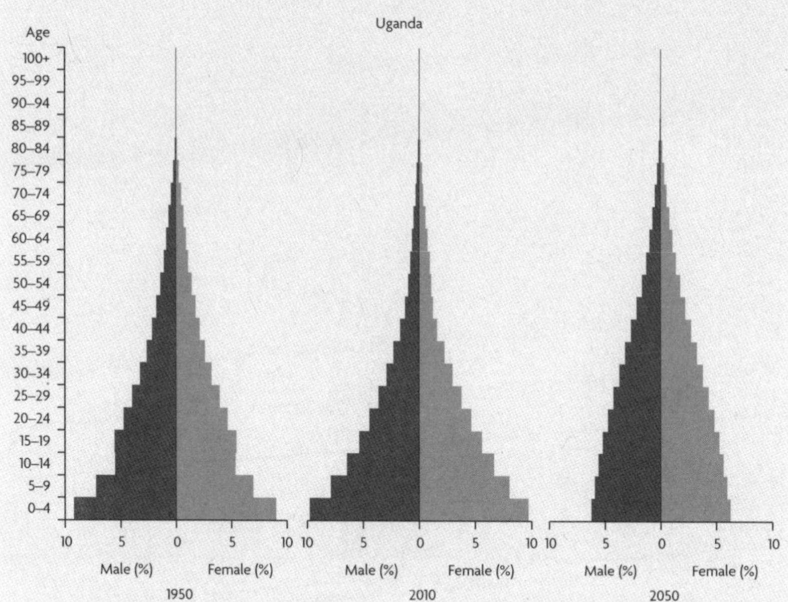

(*continued next page*)

BOX O.1 *(continued)*

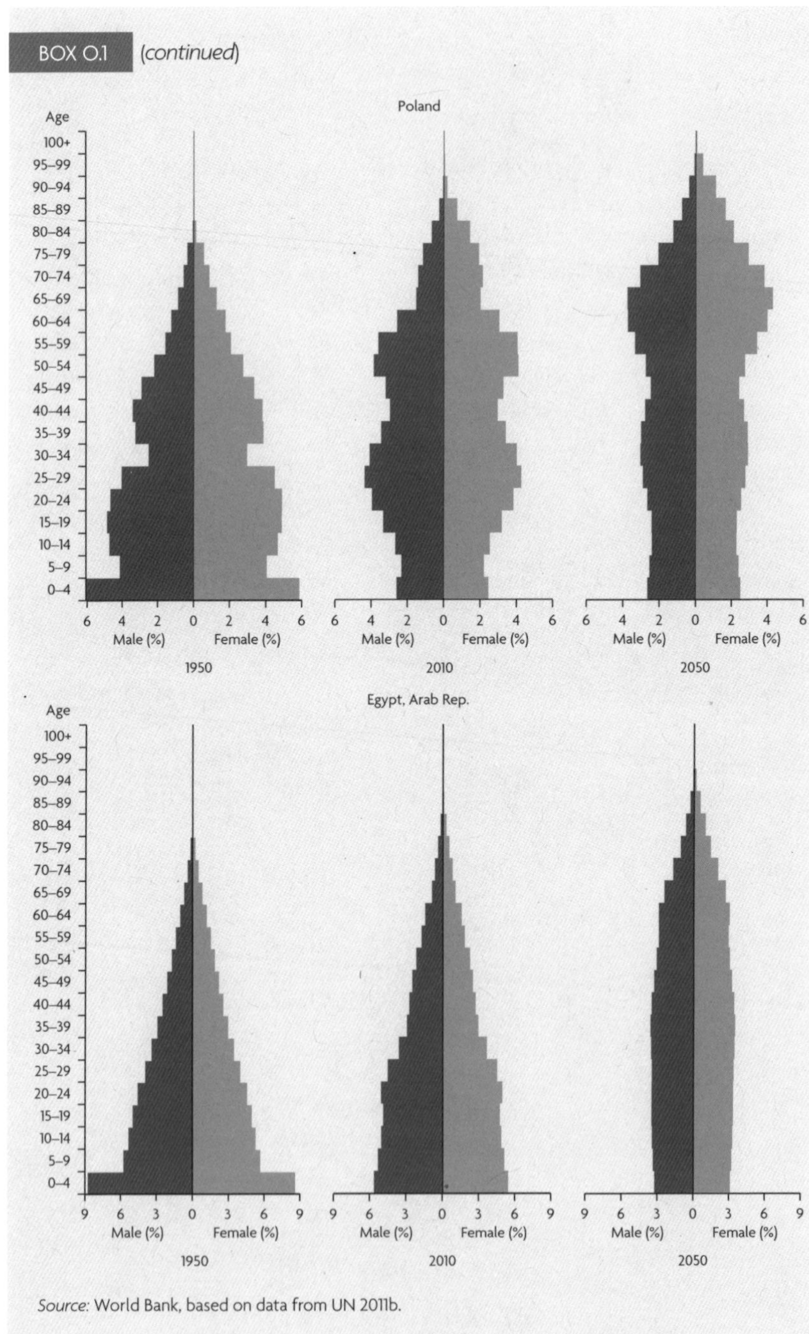

Source: World Bank, based on data from UN 2011b.

Cities are increasingly polarized between people who have access to basic services and people who do not.

The slums in Brazil, known as *favelas*, are a case in point. Recognizing that *favelas* are a visual testimony to the country's inequality, Brazil adopted a mantra of moving from "divided cities" to "integrated cities."

Inequality within cities is also one of the root causes for the crime that has beset many cities. Over time, violence can become institutionalized, making it difficult to dismantle. Governance challenges in urban areas contribute to some groups feeling left out and having few opportunities for voice and redress. Core government functions can be taken over by land mafia, drug lords, and other extortionists. Mental health issues, substance abuse, and poor security all affect individuals more negatively in urban areas. Excluded groups live in areas that expose them to these negative factors more intensely.

One of the most profound transitions of this century is occurring as a result of climate change. It is already having rapid and catastrophic consequences on livelihoods, crops, and ecosystems. A recent report portends a scenario of a world that will be 4°C warmer in 2100 than in preindustrial times, leading to catastrophic heat waves, droughts, and floods in many regions (World Bank 2013a). Periods of climate-related stress, such as a drought, affect food availability, with people in conflict-affected areas hit hardest. Sen (2001) argues that food insecurity during periods of climatic stresses is higher in countries affected by conflict, because, unlike peaceful countries, regimes in conflict end up spending more on the military than on social programs and have poorly functioning markets and services. Conflict can affect agricultural production, for instance, by blocking the ability to import (UN 1993), by preventing access to farmlands and removing men from farming. These fragile populations often take refuge in countries with greater food security, but their presence can exacerbate tensions.

In tandem with, and underlying, other transitions over the last few decades are deep economic transitions. Globalization and regional integration, coupled with substantial reforms at the national level, have led to impressive growth and poverty reduction across the globe. As a consequence, a large cohort has now "graduated" to the middle class (Dadush and Shaw 2011; Kharas and Gertz 2011; Ferreira et al. 2013), implying a change in societal values and aspirations. The middle class is often the harbinger of change. Its support is critical to achieving the goals of social inclusion, partly because the relationship of the middle class to the state is quite different from that of the poor to the state. The middle class demands voice and accountability as a right; the poor can often be reduced to a supplicant by a strong state. Simultaneously, revolutions in knowledge, social networking, and citizen action have shown that aspirations, when unfulfilled, can create unique challenges for governments. Although inequality trends are highly heterogeneous across countries, income inequality is growing in the most populous countries like China and India. Finally, food security remains a challenge for most developing countries, with excluded groups and people who live in remote areas at greatest risk.

Education is another powerful force that is also changing the social context. Education is the unparalleled agent of social change and one that has expanded across the board, even in the poorest countries. A new cohort of young people has attainments, aspirations, and hopes that are quite different from those of their parents' generation.

In Sub-Saharan Africa, for instance, there was a fivefold increase in gross secondary school enrollment, from 7 percent to 36 percent, between 1970 and 2009 (WDI database). At the global level, the corresponding figure nearly doubled, from 36 percent to 68 percent. Education changes relationships of power within society and within households. Groups that were considered subordinate acquire voice and confidence when they are educated. They tend to be more assertive in holding the state and service providers accountable and in demanding dignity and respect from groups that were considered dominant. At the household level, educated young women have greater say in decision making and are able to access opportunities outside their homes in ways that their mothers never did. Their education changes intrafamily power relations.

A large body of literature focuses on the enormous impact that education can have on women's inclusion into markets, services, and spaces. When young women in Bangladesh were asked during focus group discussions how education had changed their lives, they poignantly described "being able to speak" as the most important gain (World Bank 2008). Yet ensuring decent quality of education remains a challenge. Additionally, educational institutions can be important spaces of exclusion.

Attention to Attitudes and Perceptions Is Important in Addressing Social Inclusion

Attitudes and perceptions matter for social inclusion because people act on the basis of how they feel. Their feelings of being included and respected are central to the opportunities they access and the ways in which they take part in society. Conversely, which groups get included and excluded, and on what terms, is shaped by people's attitudes about each other and about themselves.

The importance of attitudes and perceptions also spills over to levels above the individual. A large body of literature shows that prejudices, stereotypes, and misperceptions affect the way policy is implemented and even designed. This report shows that attitudes play a key role in the treatment of individuals and groups, both by other members of the society and by the state. Attitudes and perceptions also mediate social inclusion and shine a light on the processes through which exclusion takes place. Perceptions of unfairness and injustice and frustration with social and political institutions or with the society at large often reflect individuals' feelings of powerlessness. Feelings of fairness, justice, and "being part of society" can be manifestations of how much the society recognizes, respects, and listens to its members.

People's attitudes are often related to outcomes. Attitudes toward women's education, access to jobs, and leadership positions have a strong association with poor outcomes for women. Analysis of the World Values Surveys data conducted for this report, for instance, finds an inverse relationship between gross tertiary school enrollment rates for women and negative attitudes toward higher education for women. In Australia, New Zealand, and some Scandinavian countries, tertiary school enrollment among women is almost universal, and discriminatory attitudes toward access to higher education are very low. Attitudes regarding women's access to jobs are far less favorable in countries that have the lowest female labor force participation rates (less than 20 percent), including Egypt, Iraq, Saudi Arabia, Pakistan, Algeria, Jordan, and the Islamic Republic of Iran (figure O.6). There also seems to be a relationship between attitudes toward women taking up leadership positions and their becoming leaders. Countries where fewer respondents say that men will make better political leaders are also the ones with the highest share of women parliamentarians (for example, Andorra, Sweden, Canada, Finland, Argentina, and the Netherlands).

Attitudes and perceptions are shaped by history, culture, and the way institutions have evolved over time. Take the case of perceived inequality and its acceptance in societies. Analysis of the World Values Surveys data conducted for this report suggests a nonlinear relationship between the extent of aversion to inequality and observed inequality. Australia and

Figure O.6 Countries and Areas Where People Say Men Have More Right to Jobs Also Have Lower Labor Force Participation Rates for Women, 2005–08

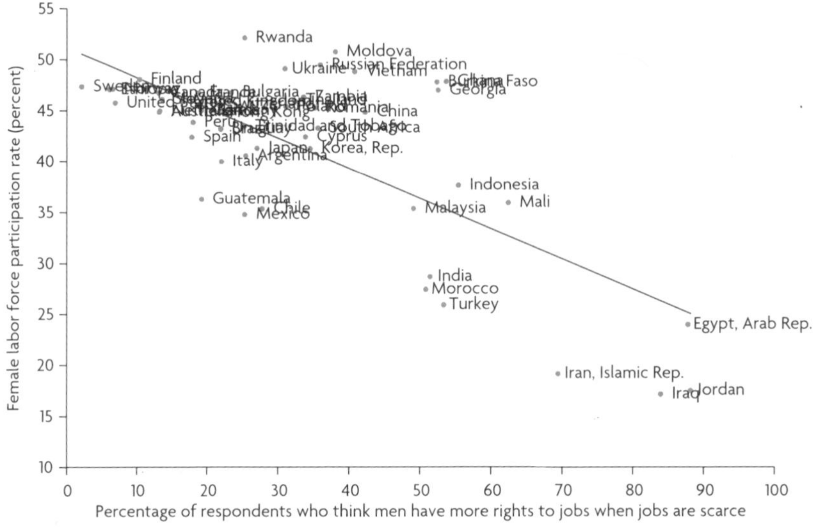

Sources: World Bank, based on data from World Values Surveys 2005–08 (attitudes) and World Development Indicators 2005–08 (female labor force participation).
Note: Values correspond to data that were available for both variables within a span of two years. Data are latest available between 2005 and 2008.

many countries in Europe have both low inequality and a low appetite for it. Some countries in Latin America (for example, Chile, Argentina, Uruguay, and to some extent Brazil) have high levels of measured inequality, but their aversion to it looks quite similar to other countries with much lower levels of inequality.

Citizens' views about the extent of fairness in their country often reflect deeper issues of inclusion and exclusion in society. This report finds, for instance, based on data from the Afrobarometer, that a majority of citizens in African countries feel that their country treats people unequally. This finding may be indicative of the fact that exclusion is a problem for many, rather than a few, and that the state is perceived as catering to the needs of a small section of society.

Perceptions about unfairness in Africa are substantiated by other trends in some countries. Africa's economic growth over the past decade was driven largely by mineral extraction, with the benefits concentrated among a few. Economic power is closely related to political power and representation in decision making, which in turn affects the allocation of public expenditure and can lead to disparities in opportunities. Income inequality, for example, has risen considerably in the last three decades throughout Sub-Saharan Africa. In 2010, Africa was the second most unequal region in the world (after Latin America), and 6 of the world's 10 most unequal countries worldwide were located in Southern Africa (AfDB 2012). Perceptions about inequality in non-African contexts may be shaped, similarly, by underlying trends in those contexts.

Social Inclusion Can Be Achieved

This report is an unequivocal statement that change is possible, that policy makers, activists, development partners, and others who care about justice and shared prosperity can steer change toward social inclusion. Exclusion is not embedded in culture and is not immutable. Change may happen by stealth or by design. It may happen through discrete events or through gradual processes that culminate over time.

Change is rarely linear. Attempts to make change inclusive may involve tradeoffs, creating both winners and losers. There can be push-back from the dominant groups when previously subordinate groups feel included and break the norms. Push-back can come with active retaliation, setting back the process of change.

Examples of change toward inclusion abound in history. South Africa, for example, moved from institutionalized segregation toward an ideal of a "rainbow nation" in a matter of two decades. Foot-binding, an ancient tradition in China, was curtailed and eventually disappeared following an intense social campaign and prohibition by law. The articulation of social exclusion in Brazil that started with a widespread belief in a "racial democracy" came to accept that discrimination on the basis of race has held some groups back. The exclusionary system of informal local justice in Bangladesh, the *shalish*, has been transformed by greater voice and participation. In a region where women's role in society is confined to the private sphere, higher educational attainment among women in Jordan has become the rule rather than the exception.

The state has the preeminent role in promoting change toward inclusion, but other actors play important roles too. In fact, it is the interplay of state and nonstate actions that leads to inclusion. Catalysts and champions of change toward social inclusion, for instance, often come from the elite.

The abolition of slavery in the United States, the end of foot-binding in China, and the end of apartheid in South Africa were all the product of social movements led by elites. Some of them came from excluded groups, as in the case of South Africa; others came from dominant groups, as in the case of the United States. In many countries, the role of religious leaders in both resisting and propelling change has been considerable. The role of business leaders in promoting social inclusion is also well recognized. Finally, civil society movements and collective action by excluded groups have historically pushed agendas for social inclusion by taking up specific "wrongs" that society needs to correct. More recently, the media has been known to play a significant role in changing mindsets and creating awareness against exclusion (Trujillo and Paluck 2012).

Moving from exclusion to inclusion does not happen overnight; it is important to have a long-term view. Social inclusion requires overcoming negative beliefs and stereotypes about excluded groups, which cannot be undone in a few years of "inclusive policy." Timing is therefore of the essence; the impacts of some changes may be felt years into the future or may well be the unintended consequences of policy or other developments. Similarly, the impact of change on groups can vary, and what is considered costly for some groups today may have positive outcomes in the future or vice versa.

Countries that are successful in addressing social exclusion usually have strong institutions. The strength of institutions lies in large part in their agility and malleability in addressing new needs of social inclusion. Take the case of Sweden, often held up as a shining example of social inclusion. Today the country is grappling with the challenges of immigration. Its institutions, which have historically responded positively to social and economic challenges, now need ways to accommodate a more heterogeneous population than Sweden has been used to. Institutions, in turn, are influenced by historical circumstance and can often be intractable to change as a result.

What Can Policies and Programs Do to Enhance Social Inclusion?

How do policies that are effective in addressing social exclusion differ from ordinary social policies? In essence, social inclusion policies are policies that do not necessarily do more but that do things differently. No single set of policies or programs can be classified as "social inclusion policies" or "social inclusion programs." In fact, depending on the "wrong" that needs to be addressed or the "right" that needs to be deepened, a range of interventions could be employed. This report provides a few examples of interventions within the broad typology of markets, services, and spaces, but any policy or program can be designed and implemented with a social inclusion focus.

Often the same policy or program can cut across different domains—market, services, and spaces. Policies toward social inclusion need to be connected or cross-sectoral. Social exclusion is a multidimensional process in which practices in one domain lead to or reinforce exclusion in another domain. Policies to address social exclusion therefore require what Silver (2013) calls "a dynamic sequence of interventions." Illustrating her argument with the case of the homeless, she argues that their inclusion in society requires a "continuum of care" starting from transitional housing, labor market training, and (possible) drug and alcohol treatment to (eventually) permanent housing, perhaps with long-term supportive services to help them stay housed. This report categorizes interventions into the domains of markets, services, and spaces, realizing that the domains overlap and that intervening in one domain can have effects in others.

Policies and programs can intervene in a range of markets. Take the case of land reforms. Although land reforms are not by themselves a panacea for exclusion or inequality, societies that have carried them out tend to be more inclusionary. Land titles to women and de facto recognition of the communal land use patterns of indigenous populations can be effective in creating opportunity and enhancing dignity. Women in many societies do not traditionally own land. Making them joint landholders in land redistribution or resettlement projects or reserving land use quotas can increase their access to opportunities while also empowering them. Deininger, Goyal, and Nagarajan (2010), for instance, find that coparcenary rights for women in property can have a positive effect on the education of girls within the household. Programs offering child care can enhance women's labor market outcomes. Both women's labor force participation rates and their wages are lower than men's, even after controlling for a range of individual and household level factors (World Bank 2012, 2013c). Many women cannot work because of their family responsibilities, yet child care in most places is costly and scarce. Programs providing subsidized child care not only can help women improve their labor market outcomes, they also can have other positive externalities as well.

Access to services that take into account the special needs of excluded groups can go a long way in enhancing social inclusion. Subsidized fares targeted to excluded groups and accessible transport services can help connect these groups to markets, services, and spaces. The city of São Paolo has chosen flat fares as an alternative to distance-based fares in order to cross-subsidize the poor. Fares are valid across multiple modes/trips on one journey. Some groups, such as women and people with disabilities, face additional barriers to using transport (for example, inadequate street lighting leading to concerns around safety, transport that is inaccessible to people with disabilities, and so forth). Here, too, countries are experimenting with innovative methods to address the challenges these groups face in physical mobility.

The manner in which services are provided matters almost as much as the technical design of the service. Stereotypes that are often ingrained in service providers can have a damaging effect on the way they treat their clients, but these issues are not insurmountable. A growing practice focuses on "cultural competencies" among service providers. This practice is particularly advanced in health and social work and is growing in education and other sectors. Holding providers accountable not merely for their presence and their technical skill but for cultural competence as a performance indicator is likely to go a long way toward ensuring that cultural minorities feel comfortable in accessing services.

According recognition to excluded and "invisible" groups is an important step toward their overall inclusion. For instance, many countries have weak systems of birth and death registration. Initiatives to improve these systems may not immediately conjure up images of social inclusion, but without such registration a child can often not be admitted to school and family members not permitted access to the property of the deceased. The poorest or most excluded groups cannot access benefits because they do not have identification or any means to prove that they indeed exist. Such literal recognition can come from initiatives that provide identity cards or create electronic databases or make special efforts to count people at risk of remaining invisible. Brazil's efficiency in implementing the Bolsa Familia and related cash transfer programs stems partly from the existence of the Cadastro Único, an electronic database of program participants.

Language is an important aspect of identity and claim to political and cultural space. Language policy can thus be an important driver of both exclusion and inclusion. The status of certain languages as official languages for government or education has symbolic, political, and practical consequences. Symbolically, official status suggests that certain ethno-linguistic groups and their cultures are more valuable than others.

Practically, according some languages official status can disadvantage those who are unable to communicate in them. The disadvantage may compound over generations, with children of linguistically excluded groups facing an additional barrier to access learning and jobs, public services, and democratic spaces.

Interventions that work at the cusp of social and physical space can be transformative. The city of Medellín, Colombia, stands as a unique and innovative example of how cities can become inclusive for their citizens through both infrastructure planning and citizen engagement. Infamously known for its drug cartel, which used the city as a base for operations, the city undertook wide-ranging police and military action between 2003 and 2006 that resulted in the dismantling of the cartel and a significant decline in the number of homicides (Muse 2012). Under a new mayor, it transformed its transportation system, with cable cars running between *comunas* (municipalities or councils) previously at war (Romero 2007). Among the different urban development initiatives undertaken was the creation of new public spaces—for example, the Parque Biblioteca España and new museums—to encourage social interaction. A large part of Medellín's municipal budget is now spent on social investments, which target vulnerable sections of the population, including older people. Several programs work on organizing youth and older adults into community action groups. These groups, which come with elected positions, help the vulnerable put forth their interests to municipalities (especially at the time of budgetary planning) and enable them to hold government entities accountable.

There is a long-standing tension between policies and programs that seek to provide universal access and those that target specific groups. Targeting can range from area-based approaches (often called "geographical targeting") to the targeting of certain individuals or groups. Targeting criteria can include poverty status, age, disability status, gender, minority status, or a mix of these criteria. Affirmative action policies can be viewed as a form of targeting in which certain groups, by virtue of their historical exclusion, are given special treatment to enable them to catch up with the average in the population. Affirmative action can come in various forms; quotas are just one example of affirmative action. Laws that ensure equal opportunity in employment, credit, housing, and education are another form of affirmative action. In addition, the constitutions of several countries—such as Bolivia, India, Malaysia, Nepal, South Africa, and Uganda—allow for preferential policies for excluded groups to redress historical imbalances. Intended to enhance opportunities and level the playing field, these policies reserve places in public educational institutions, public employment, or legislative bodies.

Preferential policies often create a range of dilemmas and concerns. One dilemma is whether countries want to name groups, thereby "affirming" the divide. In Brazil, for instance, the establishment of quotas for Afro-Brazilians was preceded by an intense debate over whether such quotas would mean implicit recognition of race as a marker of discrimination—an idea that ran contrary to Brazil's construct of a racial democracy. France has opted for geographical targeting of socioeconomically deprived areas rather than naming ethnic groups living in those areas. China has made impressive advances in reducing poverty and social exclusion by good geographical targeting. In the European Union accession countries, the Roma are not specifically acknowledged in affirmative action legislation but are subsumed under the overarching term of "disadvantaged groups" (Silver 2013).

A second dilemma is how to ensure that entrenched elites do not skim the benefits of quotas when resources are scarce. A related dilemma is how to prevent perverse incentives for other groups to show "weakness" and hence entitlement in order to qualify for affirmative action. A final concern is that positive discrimination policies build resentment among dominant groups, who may question the qualifications of candidates who receive preferential treatment, thereby intensifying those candidates' stigma.

Community-driven development (CDD) is an approach that gives community groups control over planning decisions and investment resources for local development projects. Recent evidence on the impact of CDD programs suggests that when implemented well, these programs can improve service delivery in sectors such as health and education, improve resource sustainability, and help communities build lower-cost and better-quality infrastructure (Wong 2012; Mansuri and Rao 2013). Furthermore, by virtue of targeting mostly the poor and vulnerable, these programs can help bring the voice of such groups to the policy table. An impact evaluation of Indonesia's Kecamatan Development Program (KDP), for instance, finds widespread participation of beneficiaries in program meetings, with poorer and female-headed households as likely to attend as others (Barron et al. 2009). Several CDD programs have succeeded in improving access to spaces for the poor and building social capital. CDD programs also have the advantage of being able to innovate more readily, because they are founded on the principle of community mobilization. They thus have the advantage of flexibility and community voice that encourages the generation of new ideas.

Sometimes the impact of programs far exceeds the original intent, which may be to enhance coverage or benefits. Take the case of social protection programs. Many of these programs can also enhance the self-esteem of subordinate groups, as well as the attitudes of others toward them. In Lesotho, for example, recipients of social pensions indicated an increase in respect for them in society once the national social pension was introduced. The pension also contributed to greater self-esteem, because recipients were able to contribute more financially to their grandchildren's upbringing and education. In Nicaragua, similarly, a conditional cash transfer program reports unforeseen positive impacts on women's leadership (Makours and Vakis 2009).

Social grants and transfers can play a role in reducing historical disparities. In apartheid South Africa, the beneficiaries of social grants were primarily white and "colored" people; blacks received a minor share of the benefits. The postapartheid government instituted reforms such that social grants would be targeted to blacks, who were hugely overrepresented among the poor but were not receiving transfers (Leibbrandt, Woolard, and Woolard 2007). Mexico's well-targeted Oportunidades, in addition to benefiting a much larger proportion of the population in indigenous than in nonindigenous municipalities, also decreased gender gaps in employment and reduced levels of domestic violence.

Just as some programs can have benefits that exceed their intent, others can have costs that were unforeseen. For instance, differential retirement ages for men and women in the Chinese civil service are meant as a concession to women workers, as are laws in many countries that are meant to protect young female migrants from abuse overseas by enforcing a minimum age for their departure. But both policies may have negative consequences—by excluding older Chinese women from the labor market or creating conditions for poor young women to migrate without documentation (see Das 2008, 2012).

The Right Question

The report takes on one intractable problem—that of poor maternal health outcomes among indigenous groups—and argues that change toward social inclusion needs to start with the right diagnosis. It needs to "ask why" (figure O.7).

Figure O.7 How to Include: Addressing the High Numbers of Maternal Deaths among Tribal Women in India

Diagnose: "Ask why?"

- Why do a large majority of tribal women say they don't think it's necessary to give birth in health facilities?
- If the reason is poverty, why are these women overrepresented among the poor?
- If the reason is lack of knowledge, why are they not better informed?
- If the reason is remoteness, why are they not connected?

Through:

- Conducting innovative ex ante analysis
- Holding meaningful consultations, including through the use of information and communications technology (ICT) to allow women to respond to questions anonymously

Design action

- Provide vouchers, grants, and culturally appropriate incentives
- Launch education/awareness campaigns in local language and idiom
- Register births and deaths
- Involve the community in health surveillance
- Use tribal systems of knowledge of health
- Establish links to other programs
- Make innovative use of private providers, including private transport agencies
- Hire more female staff from tribal communities
- Require cultural competency training for service providers
- Hold providers accountable for their behavior as well as technical skills
- Create incentives for providers to reside in remote areas

Monitor progress

- Establish a monitoring framework that can be accessed by tribal people
- Create community monitoring mechanisms
- Establish third-party monitoring mechanisms
- Use social audits and hold public meetings
- Conduct "verbal autopsies"
- Mandate citizen report cards
- Publicly disclose results of monitoring, including through electronic channels
- Use ICT to solicit anonymous feedback

Create avenues for recourse and feedback

- Establish an empowered ombudsman-like institution that enforces tribal rights
- Empower tribal women through legislation and provide them with legal assistance
- Create independent help lines
- Establish local tribal health committees with access to district administration
- Form empowered grievance redress committees
- Establish systems to report back to communities on action taken

Tribal women in India do not, for the most part, give birth in health centers. When they are asked why, the overwhelming majority of them say they do not think it necessary. Health practitioners then blame their poor health outcomes on low demand for formal health care. Continuing to ask *why*, however, reveals that low demand may reflect an assertion of dignity and a rejection of humiliation by excluded groups, in this case tribal women, who resent being treated badly by service providers.

Underlying the proximate reasons for poor outcomes are complex phenomena that are not immediately visible. Overall, the poor health of a tribal woman is rooted in the low power she has relative to almost everyone else in the country. Issues of land and forests are central to her situation. Once viewed in this way, it is clear that a supply-side push for better health facilities is a relatively blunt instrument with which to address high levels of maternal mortality.

Asking the right questions is likely to lead to a different design of a social program. Questions can include the following:

- What is the "wrong" or intractable problem being addressed, or what went "right" that needs to be deepened?
- Whom does the intervention or service seek to include, and who is at risk of being left out?
- Why are those groups or areas at risk of being left out? What are the channels through which inclusion can take place?
- What innovations can be put in place to ensure inclusion? What can be done differently?

Concluding Reflections

Although the contribution of this report to the world of ideas is an important objective, the report will be a larger public good only if it influences the world of research, policies, programs, and projects. What are the potential contributions of this report to the design and implementation of policies, programs, and projects? How does it highlight a new agenda for social inclusion?

It is hoped that this report speaks to practitioners in the following broad ways:

- It is an exhortation to both policy makers and researchers to use the term *social inclusion* with careful attention to meaning and boundaries.

- It brings some new ideas from philosophy and theory into the realm of practice.
- It highlights gaps in the understanding of social inclusion and potential areas for additional work through piloting new initiatives and undertaking new empirical analysis.
- It underscores the importance of additional work in measuring social inclusion.
- It emphasizes the importance of *asking why* poor outcomes continue to persist for some groups, before designing the instruments with which to combat exclusion.
- It stresses that building social inclusion is about building alliances and social consensus.
- It draws attention to the fact that monitoring change toward social inclusion needs innovation and that such innovation needs to be incorporated into practice.
- It is a call for greater participation of researchers to provide policy makers with the knowledge that will be essential for the wise design of social inclusion policies and programs.

References

AAP (American Academy of Pediatrics). 2001. "The Continued Importance of Supplemental Security Income (SSI) for Children and Adolescents with Disabilities." *Pediatrics* 107 (4): 790–93.

AfDB (African Development Bank) Group. 2012. "Income Inequality in Africa." Briefing Note 5, AfDB, Tunis-Belvedère, Tunisia. http://www.afdb.org/fileadmin/uploads/afdb/Documents/Policy-Documents/FINAL%20Briefing%20Note%205%20Income%20Inequality%20in%20Africa.pdf (accessed April 5, 2013).

Barron, P., M. Humphreys, L. Paler, and J. Weinstein. 2009. "Community-Based Reintegration in Aceh: Assessing the Impacts of BRA-KDP." Indonesian Social Development Paper 12, World Bank, Jakarta.

Beach, M. C., J. Sugarman, R. L. Johnson, J. J. Arbelaez, P. S. Duggan, and L. A. Cooper. 2005. "Do Patients Treated with Dignity Report Higher Satisfaction, Adherence, and Receipt of Preventive Care?" *Annals of Family Medicine* 3 (4): 331–38.

Bocian, D. G., W. Li, and K. S. Ernst. 2010. *Foreclosures by Race and Ethnicity: The Demographics of a Crisis*. CRL Research Report, Center for Responsible Lending, Durham, NC.

Borjas, G. J. 1992. "Ethnic Capital and Intergenerational Mobility." *Quarterly Journal of Economics* 107 (1): 123–50.

Carter, M. R. 2000. "Ownership Inequality and the Income Distribution Consequences of Economic Growth." Working Paper 201, United Nations University–World Institute for Development Economic Research (UNU-WIDER), Helsinki. http://www.wider.unu.edu/publications/working-papers/previous/en_GB/wp-201/_files/82530864866142466/default/wp201.pdf.

Dadush, U. B., and W. Shaw. 2011. *Juggernaut: How Emerging Markets Are Reshaping Globalization*. Washington, DC: Carnegie Endowment for International Peace.

Das, M. B. 2008. "Minority Status and Labor Market Outcomes: Does India Have Minority Enclaves?" Policy Research Working Paper 4653, World Bank, Washington, DC.

———. 2012. "Stubborn Inequalities, Subtle Processes: Exclusion and Discrimination in the Labor Market." Background paper for *World Development Report 2013*, World Bank, Washington, DC.

Deininger, K., and G. Feder. 1998. "Land Institutions and Land Markets." Policy Research Working Paper 2014, World Bank, Washington, DC. http://documents.worldbank.org/curated/en/1998/11/438636/land-institutions-land-markets.

Deininger, K., A. Goyal, and H. Nagarajan. 2010. "Inheritance Law Reform and Women's Access to Capital: Evidence from India's Hindu Succession Act." Policy Research Working Paper 5338, World Bank, Washington, DC.

de Laat, J. 2010. "Roma Inclusion: An Economic Opportunity for Bulgaria, Czech Republic, Romania and Serbia." Policy Note, World Bank, Human Development Sector Unit, Washington, DC.

Demirgüç-Kunt, A., L. Klapper, and D. Randall. 2013. "The Global Findex Database. Financial Inclusion in Fragile and Conflict-Affected States." Findex Note 07, World Bank, Washington, DC. http://inec.usip.org/resource/global-findex-database-financial-inclusion-fragile-and-conflict-affected-states.

Deshpande, A., and K. Newman. 2007. "Where the Path Leads: The Role of Caste in Post-University Employment Expectations." *Economic and Political Weekly* 42 (41): 4133–40.

Elmslie, B., and S. Sedo. 1996. "Discrimination, Social Psychology, and Hysteresis in Labor Markets." *Journal of Economic Psychology* 17 (4): 465–78.

Ferreira, F. H. G., J. Messina, J. Rigolini, L. López-Calva, M. A. Lugo, and R. Vakis. 2013. *Economic Mobility and the Rise of the Latin American Middle Class*. Washington, DC: World Bank.

Galbraith, J. K. 1998. *The Affluent Society*. New York: Houghton-Mifflin.

Hall, G., and H. A. Patrinos, eds. 2006. *Indigenous Peoples, Poverty, and Human Development in Latin America*. New York: Palgrave Macmillan.

———. eds. 2012. *Indigenous Peoples, Poverty, and Development*. Cambridge, U.K.: Cambridge University Press.

Hersch, J. 2008. "Skin Color, Immigrant Wages, and Discrimination." In *Racism in the 21st Century: An Empirical Analysis of Skin Color*, ed. R. E. Hall, 77–90. New York: Springer.

Jha, S., and M. Adelman. 2009. "Looking for Love in All the White Places: A Study of Skin Color Preferences on Indian Matrimonial and Mate-Seeking Websites." *Studies in South Asian Film and Media* 1: 65–83.

Kharas H., and G. Gertz. 2011. *The New Global Middle Class: A Cross-Over from West to East*. Brookings Institution, Wolfensohn Center for Development, Washington, DC. http://www.brookings.edu/~/media/Files/rc/papers/2010/03_china_middle_class_kharas/03_china_middle_class_kharas.pdf (accessed April 19, 2013).

Leibbrandt, M., I. Woolard, and C. Woolard. 2007. "Poverty and Inequality Dynamics in South Africa: Post-apartheid Developments in the Light of the Long-Run Legacy." Paper prepared for workshop sponsored by the International Poverty Centre and the David Rockefeller Center for Latin American Studies, Brasilia, January 11–13.

Loury, G. 1999. "Social Exclusion and Ethnic Groups: The Challenge to Economics." Paper presented at the Annual World Bank Conference on Development Economics, Washington, DC, April 28–30.

Lynch, D. 2012. "First Black President Can't Help Blacks Stem Wealth Drop." *Bloomberg News,* September 5.

Makours, K., and R. Vakis. 2009. "Changing Households' Investments and Aspirations through Social Interactions: Evidence from a Randomized Transfer Program." Policy Research Working Paper 5137, World Bank, Washington, DC.

Mansuri, G., and V. Rao. 2013. *Localizing Development: Does Participation Work?* Washington, DC: World Bank.

Marcus, R., S. Espinoza, L. Schmidt, and S. Sultan. 2013. "Social Exclusion in Africa: Towards More Inclusive Approaches." Background paper draft, World Bank, Washington, DC.

Minnesota Population Center. 2011. Integrated Public Use Microdata Series, International: Version 6.1 (machine-readable database). University of Minnesota, Minneapolis.

Muse, T. 2012. "New Drug Gang Wars Blow Colombian City's Revival Apart." *Guardian,* April 10. http://www.theguardian.com/world/2012/apr/10/colombia-drug-gang-rivalry-medellin (accessed October 7, 2013).

Ñopo, H., J. P. Atal, and N. Winder. 2010. "New Century, Old Disparities: Gender and Ethnic Wage Gaps in Latin America." IZA Discussion Paper 5085, Institute for the Study of Labor, Bonn.

Øyen, E. 1997. "The Contradictory Concepts of Social Exclusion and Social Inclusion." In *Social Exclusion and Anti-poverty Policy: A Debate*, ed. C. Gore and J. B. Figuereido, 63–66. Geneva: International Institute for Labour Studies.

Polanyi, K. 1944. *The Great Transformation*. Boston: Beacon Hill.

Portes, A., and L. Jensen. 1989. "The Enclave and the Entrants: Patterns of Ethnic Enterprise in Miami before and after Mariel." *American Sociological Review* 54 (6): 929–49.

Romero, S. 2007. "Medellin's Nonconformist Mayor Turns Blight to Beauty." *New York Times*, July 15. http://www.nytimes.com/2007/07/15/world/americas/15medellin.html?pagewanted=all&_r=0 (accessed October 7, 2013).

Sen, A. 2000. "The Discipline of Cost-Benefit Analysis." *Journal of Legal Studies* 29 (S2): 931–52.

———. 2001. *Development as Freedom*. Oxford, U.K.: Oxford University Press.

Shi, L. 2012. "Migration and Social Inclusion: Analysis of the Well-Being of Rural Migrants in China." Background paper draft, World Bank, Washington, DC.

Shonkoff, J. P., and S. J. Meisels. 2000. *Handbook of Early Childhood Intervention*, vol. 2. Cambridge, U.K.: Cambridge University Press.

Silver, H. n.d. "Social Exclusion." In *Encyclopedia of Sociology*. Oxford, U.K.: Blackwell.

———. 2013. "Framing Social Inclusion Policies." Background paper draft, World Bank, Washington, DC.

Tilly, C. 1999. *Durable Inequality*. Berkeley, CA: University of California Press.

Trujillo, M. D., and E. L. Paluck. 2012. "The Devil Knows Best: Experimental Effects of a Televised Soap Opera on Latino Attitudes toward Government and Support for the 2010 U.S. Census." *Analyses of Social Issues and Public Policy* 12 (1): 113–32.

UBOS (Uganda Bureau of Statistics) and ICF International. 2012. *Uganda Demographic and Health Survey 2011*.Kampala, Uganda: UBOS; Calvert, MD, USA: ICF International.

UN (United Nations). 1993. *World Economic Survey 1993*. New York: United Nations.

———. 2011. *World Population Prospects: The 2010 Revision*. New York: United Nations Secretariat, Department of Economic and Social Affairs, Population Division. ST/ESA/SER.A/313 (vol. 1) and ST/ESA/SER.A/317 (vol. 2). http://esa.un.org/wpp.html.

———. 2013. *A New Global Partnership: Eradicate Poverty and Transform Economies through Sustainable Development. Report of the High-Level Panel of Eminent Persons on the Post-2015 Development Agenda*. New York: United Nations. http://www.un.org/sg/management/pdf/HLP_P2015_Report.pdf.

Villarreal, M. A. 2010. "US–Mexico Economic Relations: Trends, Issues, and Implications." Library of Congress, Washington, DC.

Warschauer, M. 2003. *Technology and Social Inclusion: Rethinking the Digital Divide*. Cambridge, MA: MIT Press.

WDI (World Development Indicators) (database). World Bank, Washington, DC. http://data.worldbank.org/data-catalog/world-development-indicators.

Weeks, J. R., A. G. Hill, A. Getis, and D. Stow. 2006. "Ethnic Residential Patterns as Predictors of Intra-Urban Child Mortality Inequality in Accra, Ghana." *Urban Geography* 27 (6): 526–48.

WHO (World Health Organization) and World Bank. 2011. *World Report on Disability*. Geneva: World Health Organization. http://www.refworld.org/docid/50854a322.html (accessed May 20, 2013).

Wilson, K. L., and A. Portes. 1980. "Immigrant Enclaves: An Analysis of the Labor Market Experiences of Cubans in Miami." *American Journal of Sociology* 86 (2): 295–319.

Wong, S. 2012. *What Have Been the Impacts of World Bank Community-Driven Development Programs? CDD Impact Evaluation Review and Operational & Research Implications*. World Bank, Sustainable Development Department, Washington, DC. http://www-wds.worldbank.org/external/default/WDSContentServer/WDSP/IB/2012/06/14/000386194_20120614062031/Rendered/PDF/695410WP0SW0CD00Box370017B00PUBLIC0.pdf.

World Bank. 2008. "Whispers to Voices: Gender and Social Transformation in Bangladesh." Bangladesh Development Series 22, World Bank, Dhaka.

———. 2011a. *Poverty and Social Exclusion in India*. Washington, DC: World Bank.

———. 2011b. "Social Safety Nets in Nepal." Draft report, World Bank, Washington, DC.

———. 2012. *World Development Report: Gender Equality and Development*. Washington, Washington, DC: World Bank.

———. 2013a. *Turn Down the Heat: Why a 4°C Warmer World Must Be Avoided*. Report for the World Bank by the Potsdam Institute for Climate Impact Research and Climate Analytics. Washington, DC: World Bank.

———. 2013b. *The World Bank Group Goals: End Extreme Poverty and Promote Shared Prosperity*. Washington, DC. http://www.worldbank.org/content/dam/Worldbank/document/WB-goals2013.pdf.

———. 2013c. *World Development Report: Jobs*. Washington, Washington, DC: World Bank.

World Values Surveys (database). World Values Survey Association. http://www.worldvaluessurvey.org.

Yeo, R., and K. Moore. 2003. "Including Disabled People in Poverty Reduction Work: Nothing about Us, without Us." *World Development* 31 (3): 571–90.

Introduction

Human progress is neither automatic nor inevitable. Even a superficial look at history reveals that no social advance rolls in on wheels of inevitability . . . Without persistent effort, time itself becomes an ally of the insurgent and primitive forces of irrational emotionalism and social destruction. This is no time for apathy or complacency. This is a time for vigorous and positive action.

—MARTIN LUTHER KING, JR., *STRIDE TOWARD FREEDOM: THE MONTGOMERY STORY* (1958)

The Issue and the Idea

The words *inclusive* and *inclusion* are high up in the global policy vocabulary. To some extent, it is about timing. The massive socioeconomic churning of the last few decades has catapulted the need for social inclusion onto national and global agendas, and policy makers and analysts need a frame of reference to explain it. That being said, there are few other terms as abstract as *social inclusion*. It is notoriously many things to many people. Although it is true, as Øyen (1997) says, that the problem with the concept is that it is more political than analytical, it is also true that it has its roots in identifiable theoretical paradigms of welfare that encompass political science, sociology, economics, and philosophy. For instance, its analytical foundations resonate with Amartya Sen's "capabilities" and "entitlements" approach, in which membership in a particular group limits individuals' "functionings" to acquire or use their capabilities. Sen (1999) calls the limits imposed by such membership the "relational roots of deprivation." The ideological tenets underlying social inclusion are ensconced in principles of social justice, which are in turn enshrined in multiple international conventions, such as the Universal Declaration of Human Rights 1948 (UDHR) and the International Covenant on Economic, Social and Cultural Rights (ICESCR).[1] Its empirical applications are often rooted in studies of discrimination, poverty, inequality, or inequity..

The urgency to better understand and address social inclusion is also prompted by the current global discourse toward the "post-2015" agenda. The year 2015 marks the endpoint for achievement of the Millennium Development Goals (MDGs). Although tremendous advances have been made, many countries still remain far from many goals. Slow progress on attaining the MDGs has prompted some collective soul-searching among development practitioners and thought leaders to understand why some countries and groups have been left behind. In parallel, new issues are being thrown up even as the world moves toward greater progress. Issues of inequality, sustainability, and the quality of services are center stage for rich and poor countries alike. These new global imperatives underscore the centrality of social inclusion—a message that comes through very clearly in the report of the United Nations (UN) Secretary-General's High-Level Panel of Eminent Persons on the Post-2015 Development Agenda (UN 2013).

In tandem with the new global imperatives, the World Bank Group is embarking upon an ambitious new strategy and has announced dual goals for itself: ending extreme poverty and promoting shared prosperity. Underlying the idea of shared prosperity is the notion of sustainability, an overarching theme that frames both goals. A sustainable path of development and poverty reduction is one that manages the resources of the planet for future generations, ensures social inclusion, and adopts fiscally responsible policies that limit future debt burden. As a recent World Bank Group publication notes:

> A sustainable path toward ending extreme poverty and promoting shared prosperity would also involve creating *an inclusive society*, not only in terms of economic welfare but also in terms of the voice and empowerment of all groups. An inclusive society must have the institutions, structures, and processes that empower local communities, so they can hold their governments accountable. It also requires the participation of all groups in society, including traditionally marginalized groups, such as ethnic minorities and indigenous populations, in decision-making processes. (World Bank 2013, 33, emphasis added)

Today, the world is at a conjuncture where issues of exclusion and inclusion are assuming new significance for both "developed" and "developing" countries. In a strange sense, the imperative for social inclusion has blurred the distinction between these two stylized poles of development. Countries that used to be referred to as "developed" are grappling with issues of exclusion and inclusion perhaps more intensely today than they did a decade ago. And countries previously called "developing" are grappling with both old issues and new forms of exclusion thrown up by growth. Nonlinear demographic transitions, global economic volatility, shifts in the international balance of power, and local political movements have had a large part to play in these shifting sands. These changes make social inclusion more urgent than it was even a decade ago.

What Does This Report Intend to Do?

This report tries to put boundaries around the abstraction that is "social inclusion." It is intended for policy makers, academics, activists, and development partners—indeed, anyone who is curious about what inclusion can mean and how it can be addressed in a world that is experiencing intense demographic, spatial, economic, and technological transitions. Placing the discussion of social inclusion within such global transitions and transformations, the report argues that social inclusion is an evolving agenda. It offers two easy-to-use definitions and a framework to assist practitioners in asking, outlining, and developing some of the right questions that can help advance the agenda of inclusion in different contexts.

Social inclusion is defined in two ways. The first is a broad sweep that defines it as

> The process of improving the terms for individuals and groups to take part in society.

A second, sharper definition takes into account how terms can be improved and for whom. It articulates social inclusion as

> The process of improving the ability, opportunity, and dignity of people, disadvantaged on the basis of their identity, to take part in society.

There are seven main messages in this report, with a set of key ideas embedded in them:

1. Excluded groups exist in all countries.
2. Excluded groups are consistently denied opportunities.

3. Intense global transitions are leading to social transformations that create new opportunities for inclusion as well as exacerbating existing forms of exclusion.
4. People take part in society through markets, services, and spaces.
5. Social and economic transformations affect the attitudes and perceptions of people. As people act on the basis of how they feel, it is important to pay attention to their attitudes and perceptions.
6. Exclusion is not immutable. Abundant evidence demonstrates that social inclusion can be planned and achieved.
7. Moving ahead will require a broader and deeper knowledge of exclusion and its impacts as well as taking concerted action.

The report is based on a number of sources. First, it reviews the relevant literature on social inclusion, both theoretical and empirical. Second, it relies on qualitative and quantitative evidence analyzed by the World Bank team or from background papers prepared for this report. Finally, it draws on ongoing policy engagement with a few of the countries with which the World Bank is partnering toward social reform.

This report builds on previous analytical work, especially by the World Bank, on themes that touch upon social inclusion, including multidimensional poverty, inequality, equity, social cohesion, and empowerment. Among the first *World Development Reports* to tackle the social aspects of poverty was *World Development Report 1990: Poverty*, which defined poverty in broad terms (comprising income poverty, literacy, and nutrition) and framed it as a situation arising out of multidimensional processes that interact with one another and are affected by social norms, values, and customs. It argued that reducing poverty was possible through labor market policies as well as the efficient provision of basic social services to the poor. *World Development Report 2000/01: Attacking Poverty* took forward the idea that empowerment of the poor through responsive institutions is a key driver of poverty alleviation. It was informed to a large extent by the World Bank's Voices of the Poor study, which revealed nonmaterial forms of poverty and drew attention to the role of social factors that trap people in deprivation. *World Development Report 2006: Equity and Development* made the case that leveling the economic and political playing field for disadvantaged groups is important not only as an end in itself but also for overall growth and development. Most recently, the idea of social inclusion is reflected in *World Development Report 2012: Gender Equality and Development* and *World Development Report 2013: Jobs.*

The 2012 report focuses on the well-being of the largest and most heterogeneous group that is often excluded: women. It posits that outcomes for women can improve through accumulation of endowments, economic opportunities that allow women to generate income, and women's own individual and collective agency. The 2013 report incorporates "social cohesion" as a pillar of its conceptual framework, arguing that societies flourish as jobs foster diversity and provide alternatives to conflict. The *World Development Report 2015: The Behavioral and Social Foundations of Economic Development* will look at the vital role that human psychology plays in development, emphasizing that norms and human cognition are malleable and can be influenced by policy.

In addition to the *World Development Reports*, recent work on measuring human opportunities also touches upon the idea of social inclusion. The Human Opportunities Index focuses policy attention on investments to equalize opportunities at the beginning of the life cycle.[2] In many ways, it is a response to evidence that the allocation of opportunities continues to be unequal and that the skewed nature of opportunity breaks down across gender, race, ethnicity, and other common dimensions of exclusion.

Roadmap of the Report

The report is divided into three parts. Part I comprises three chapters. Chapter 1 defines the problem of social exclusion and asks the following questions, among others: What are we seeking a solution to? Where is the evidence that social exclusion matters? How is social exclusion different from poverty and inequality? How does one measure inclusion and exclusion? Chapter 2 examines the axes along which exclusion is practiced and how they intersect. Chapter 3 shifts the conversation from social exclusion to inclusion and presents a framework to address it, by introducing the domains in which individuals and groups can be included in society.

Part II focuses on the changing context for social inclusion. It comprises two chapters. Chapter 4 looks at major transitions and transformations of the past several decades as a frame of reference to prognosticate on the drivers of exclusion or the potential for inclusion in the coming years. It focuses on transitions in four areas: demographic, spatial, economic, and knowledge and information-related. It argues that the cumulative impact of these large-scale transitions has changed the context for inclusion, either by creating new groups that deserve attention or by changing the forms of, and opportunities for, both inclusion and exclusion. Chapter 5 underscores that social and economic transformations affect attitudes and perceptions. As people act on the basis of how they feel, it is important to pay attention to these subjective accounts.

Part III includes three chapters. Chapter 6 is an unequivocal statement that change is possible and that policy makers, activists, development partners and other concerned stakeholders can steer change toward social inclusion. In doing so, the report provides a definitive shift away from the determinism of the view that exclusion is embedded in culture and norms that are immutable. Instead, it shows that change is political and incremental, but possible and within reach. Chapter 7 presents some examples of policies and programs that have tried to work toward inclusion. It illustrates social inclusion in practice by taking a development problem—maternal health in India's tribal areas—and walking the reader through the process of coming up with possible solutions. Chapter 8 sums up with some concluding reflections.

Notes

1. Principles of nondiscrimination, social justice, and fairness are core elements of social inclusion. There are several other conventions that address the exclusion of specific groups. They include the Convention on the Elimination of All Forms of Racial Discrimination (ICERD), the Convention on the Elimination of All Forms of Discrimination against Women (CEDAW), the International Convention on the Protection of the Rights of All Migrant Workers and Members of Their Families, and the United Nations Declaration on the Rights of Indigenous Peoples (UNDRIP).
2. The Human Opportunities Index places specific emphasis on children, given evidence that interventions to equalize opportunity early in life are the most cost-effective. The underlying assumption is that equalizing the supply of basic opportunities will give all individuals an equal chance of translating their capabilities into enhanced well-being (Molinas Vega et al. 2012).

References

Molinas Vega, J. R., R. Paes de Barros, C. J. Saavedra, M. Giugale, L. J. Cord, C. Pessino, and A. Hasan. 2012. *Do Our Children Have a Chance? A Human Opportunity Report for Latin America and the Caribbean*. Washington, DC: World Bank.

Øyen, E. 1997. "The Contradictory Concepts of Social Exclusion and Social Inclusion." In *Social Exclusion and Anti-poverty Policy: A Debate*, ed. C. Gore and J. B. Figuereido, 63–66. Geneva: International Institute for Labour Studies.

Sen, A. 1999. "The Possibility of Social Choice." *American Economic Review* 89 (3): 349–78.

UN (United Nations). 2013. *A New Global Partnership: Eradicate Poverty and Transform Economies through Sustainable Development*. Report of the High-Level Panel of Eminent Persons on the Post-2015 Development Agenda, New York. http://www.un.org/sg/management/pdf/HLP_P2015_Report.pdf.

World Bank. Voices of the Poor (research initiative). World Bank, Washington, DC. http://go.worldbank.org/H1N8746X10.

———. 2013. *The World Bank Group Goals: End Extreme Poverty and Promote Shared Prosperity*. Washington, DC. http://www.worldbank.org/content/dam/Worldbank/document/WB-goals2013.pdf.

PART 1

FRAMING THE ISSUE

CHAPTER 1

What Do We Mean by Social Inclusion?

A new and sweeping utopia of life ... where the races condemned to one hundred years of solitude will have, at last and forever, a second opportunity on earth.

—GABRIEL GARCÍA MÁRQUEZ, NOBEL ACCEPTANCE SPEECH

Where Does the Usage Come From?

During the 1960s, the terms *social exclusion* and *social inclusion* became integral parts of the social policy lexicon in Europe. The earliest usage is attributed to René Lenoir (1974), the French Secretary of State for Social Action in the Chirac government. Lenoir's "excluded" groups included people with disabilities, single parents, drug addicts, delinquents, and the elderly, all of whom he felt were excluded from social and economic participation and needed state help in the form of social insurance. These groups were vulnerable to uninsured risks; for them, poverty was a problem that economic growth could not resolve (Paugam 1993). Not including them would mean a "rupture in social bonds" that normally tie the individual to society (Silver 1994).

The idea of social inclusion was later incorporated into other political planks. It was important to the reelection of Tony Blair and to the New Labour agenda of the early 2000s (see Levitas 1998). Taking a leaf from the book of New Labour and from the concepts that Amartya Sen articulates, Australia created an entire cross-sectoral program devoted to enhancing "social inclusion." The focus on social inclusion as a moral imperative that enhances human dignity is evident in the policy statements and plans of many other countries as well.

Over the last few decades, the terms *social exclusion* and *social inclusion* have been widely used outside the Organisation for Economic Co-operation and Development (OECD) countries as well. In fact, the imperative for social inclusion blurs the distinction between "developed" and "developing" countries, because both have to grapple with these issues, probably more so today than in the recent past. Yet the usage in OECD and non-OECD contexts is quite different. The European discourse has historically defined social inclusion in terms of homelessness, unemployment, and chronic poverty, whereas the discourse in South Asia tends to focus on caste, ethnicity, and gender as the axes of exclusion. In Brazil, where social disparities intersect with regional disparities, "social integration" and "spatial integration" have become central policy preoccupations. In China, social inclusion is intrinsic to the notion of a "harmonious society." In Africa, where poverty intersects with other disadvantages, social exclusion is often about poverty and voice. Similarly, development agencies use the term *inclusion*, as either a noun or a modifier, very heterogeneously. Appendix A lists some of the ways in which the terms *social inclusion* and *social exclusion* are used.

Part I of this report sets up the problem of social exclusion and suggests a framework for thinking about social inclusion. This chapter is a reflection on concepts and measurement issues. It also makes the case that social inclusion is important not only as an end in itself but also because exclusion is too costly. Figure 1.1 illustrates the framework for social inclusion.

This report defines social inclusion in two ways. The first is a broad sweep that defines it as

> The process of improving the terms for individuals and groups to take part in society.

A second, sharper definition takes into account how those terms can be improved and for whom. It articulates social inclusion as

> The process of improving the ability, opportunity, and dignity of people, disadvantaged on the basis of their identity, to take part in society.

Contours around an Abstraction

The way social inclusion is articulated, and what constitutes exclusion, has a strong temporal dimension. Issues that may not have been framed in terms of social inclusion two decades ago may well be so framed now.

Figure 1.1 Propelling Social Inclusion: A Framework

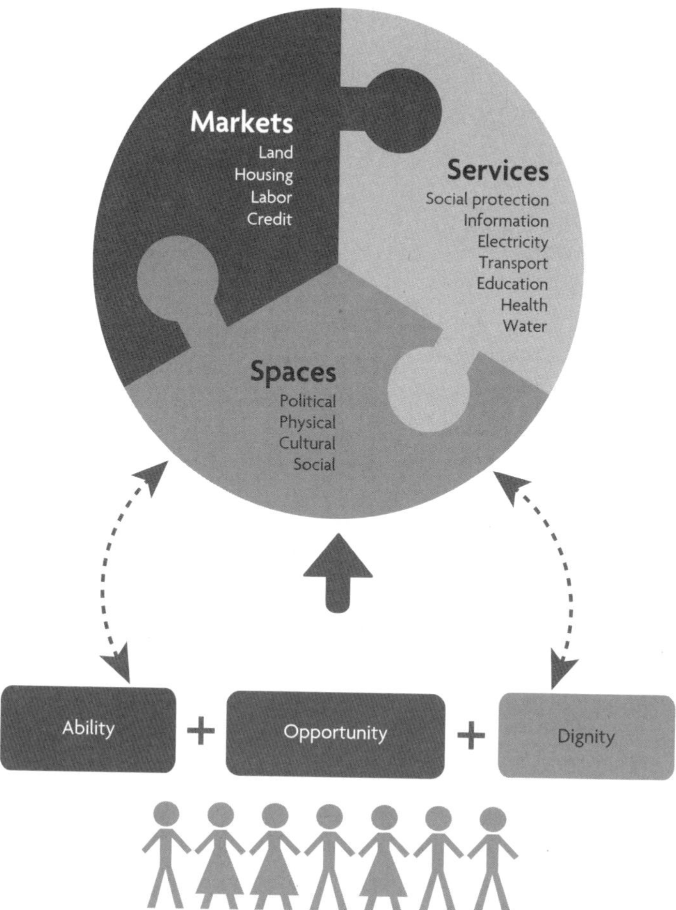

Who would have predicted a few decades ago, for instance, that same-sex marriage would be so central to the inclusion-exclusion agenda in OECD countries? And consider the case of a country like Nepal. The Rana oligarchy, which lasted nearly a century until the mid-1900s, intensified and consolidated caste as an axis of exclusion through laws and state-sponsored practices (Bennett 2005). But following incrementally deepening democracy and then the Maoist insurgency, the new state that came into being after the peace accord of 2006 embraced *samajik samaveshikaran*, or social inclusion, as the foundation of its social contract (World Bank 2011b). Similarly, issues of social inclusion that arise from different types of migration have become very important, as migration becomes more widespread and complex.

Quite often, the terms *social exclusion* and *inequality* or *social exclusion* and *poverty* are conflated. This report argues that inequality and poverty are outcomes, whereas social exclusion is both an outcome and a process. Social exclusion may well be about poverty, but it is often about more than poverty—and at certain times, it is not about poverty at all. At still other times, it helps explain the root causes of poverty. Exclusion can intersect with poverty, deriving from a set of multiple, interrelated disadvantages that result in both economic and social deprivation (Silver n.d.). It is also key to explaining why some groups remain trapped in poverty, failing to benefit fully from public investments in, say, education and health.

Understanding that "the poor" are not homogeneous but rather differentiated on the basis of occupation, ethnicity, place of residence, or race is central to developing effective policies. This insight, which originates with Sen (1981, as quoted in Hulme and Shepherd 2003), carries through mainstream work on chronic poverty.[1] A significant group among the poor, the chronically poor, are likely to remain constrained in their ability to benefit from growth without additional, different policy approaches to address the multiple factors that underpin their deprivation (Hulme and Shepherd 2003).

The concept of social inclusion takes poverty analysis beyond identifying correlates to uncovering its underlying causes. It asks questions such as *why* certain groups are overrepresented among the poor and *why* some people lack access to education, health, and other services or receive poorer-quality services. It exposes the interlocking, multidimensional nature of chronic deprivation arising from social exclusion, such as discrimination, peer effects, and adverse incorporation (see box 2.2 in chapter 2), which plays a key role in driving the simple and more readily observable correlates of poverty (lack of schooling, poor health, and constrained labor market returns).[2] It underscores that deprivation arising from social exclusion tends to occur on multiple axes at once, such that policies that release just one of these axes of deprivation (such as improved access to education) will not unleash the grip of others. It draws back the curtain on the norms and belief systems that underpin this multifaceted exclusion. These norms may be overt, such as apartheid in South Africa, or the result of intangible belief systems handed down through history. These underlying causes of poverty are largely invisible in standard empirical data and thus largely unexplored in standard poverty analysis and the design of poverty reduction strategies.

Sometimes social exclusion is not about poverty at all. Think of a hypothetical homosexual man living in a rich neighborhood in an African country. He may not be poor, but he is certainly excluded—and in some countries he may be at risk of death. Take also the case of Arab or South Asian Muslim men in the United States. They are not likely to be poor. In fact, they are quite likely to be well off, so they do not suffer the adverse consequences of income inequality. Yet in the events that followed 9/11, they clearly became a mistrusted and therefore excluded group. Similarly, Tunisia and the Arab Republic of Egypt, where poverty levels were lower than in many other countries, nevertheless saw expressions of protest driven by what can broadly be called social exclusion but not poverty.

Using cross-country data on feeling included and including others, Hochschild and Lang (2011) find, contrary to expectation, that a large proportion of rich people feel alienated or rejected by their country whereas many poor people are proud of and attached to theirs, suggesting that poverty does not necessarily drive feelings of exclusion. Take also the case of Poland, where residents of the poorer Eastern regions speak of exclusion less acutely than people in the more prosperous Western regions, which have a history of long-term unemployment triggered by the dismantling of state farms in the 1990s (Polish Ministry of Labor and Social Policy 2006; Plonka 2013).

Social inclusion is also not the same as equality. The term *social inclusion* can add to the idea of equality, but much more importantly, it can explain why some inequalities exist or why some are particularly durable (Tilly 1999). There are many ways that people can enjoy fuller participation and inclusion, even if they lack an equal share of resources. At the same time, even at the higher end of the income distribution, people may face social exclusion, through political persecution or discrimination based on age, gender, sexual orientation, or disability (Warschauer 2003). So exclusion can be "horizontal," affecting several members of a group, whether poor or rich. It is a process, of which inequality is sometimes, but not always, an outcome.

Social Inclusion Matters for Itself and Because Exclusion Is Too Costly

Social inclusion is about human well-being, shared prosperity, and social justice. There is an innate value to addressing the issue; policy makers and especially development practitioners should need no other reason to do so.

But there is also an instrumental value to addressing exclusion (see, for instance, Akerlof 1976; Scoville 1991). Social inclusion matters because exclusion is too costly. These costs are social, economic, and political and are often interrelated. Moreover, whereas these costs accrue most visibly to individuals and to specific segments, they can impose a cost on society as well. Stiglitz (2012), for instance, argues that income inequality hinders economic growth because it skews the economy toward rich households, who have a lower propensity to consume and spur aggregate demand than middle- and low-income households. Similarly, in their review of research linking inequality, democracy, and pro-growth institutions, Savoia, Easaw, and McKay (2010) conclude that inequality harms institutions that are good for growth and overall economic development. In particular, they draw a link between unequal distribution of economic assets (such as land and minerals) and elite capture, which may trap entire countries in low-development equilibriums.

The relationship between social exclusion and macro-level outcomes is difficult to separate out. Estimates of losses in productivity and economic growth as a result of social exclusion, although not precise as a result of methodological and data challenges, can be considered indicative. A World Bank report estimates the annual productivity losses caused by exclusion of the Roma, an ethnic minority in Europe (de Laat 2010). It suggests that these losses could range from €231 million in Serbia to €887 million in Romania. Zoninsein (2004) estimates that the Bolivian economy would have expanded by up to 36 percent in 1997 if the human capital and productivity gap between the majority and ethnic and racial minorities had been eliminated.

Occupational segregation can have similarly negative externalities. Segregating individuals and groups into specific occupations can stymie the free movement of talent, resulting in productivity losses for the entire economy. Rauch (1991) argues that if entrepreneurial ability is randomly distributed across the population, any barriers to entry to entrepreneurs from socially excluded groups may prevent new firms from developing and prospering. Finally, in financial and insurance markets, asymmetries of information can lead to poor access to credit and insurance products for some groups, stifling their productivity (World Bank 2006).

Widespread or long-term exclusion of certain groups can also lead to conflict, which in turn stifles economic development (Norton and de Haan 2012; World Bank Investment Climate Surveys). According to a series of social experiments conducted by the Inter-American Development Bank

(Cardenas, Chong, and Ñopo 2009), there may be a welfare loss of up to 22 percent as a result of lack of trust and cooperation among different ethnic groups in selected Latin American countries.

It is slightly easier to identify the channels through which social exclusion plays out in individual-level outcomes. Exclusion can have deleterious consequences for human capital development. A World Bank report on equality of opportunity for Latin American children measures disparity in access to education, health, and other public services based on predetermined characteristics, such as gender, ethnicity, education of the parents, and place of birth (Molinas Vega et al. 2012). A report on the Roma (de Laat 2010) estimates potential losses in earnings as a result of the Roma's inability to complete their education. It estimates that Roma who complete secondary education can expect to earn 52 percent more in Serbia, 83 percent more in Bulgaria, 110 percent more in the Czech Republic, and 144 percent more in Romania than Roma with only primary education. However, just 12.5 percent of working-age Roma in these countries are educated at or above the secondary level.

Although the effects of exclusion on education have been documented, the development literature has paid comparatively less attention to the costs of exclusion, especially on mental health. In the United States, the National School Climate Survey of self-reported sexual minority students shows that students who experienced high levels of in-school victimization based on their sexual orientation or gender expression also had poorer health and educational outcomes (Kosciw et al. 2012). These students had grade-point averages almost half a point lower than other students,[3] were less likely than other students to plan to pursue any postsecondary education, were about three times as likely to have missed school in the past month because of safety concerns, were less likely to feel a sense of belonging to their school community, and had lower levels of self-esteem and higher levels of depression and anxiety. Noh et al. (1999) find that Southeast Asian refugees in Canada who reported experiences of racial discrimination had a higher prevalence of depression than refugees who did not feel discriminated against.

The experience of being excluded can have long-term consequences for human and social capital. Research using neuroimaging techniques has found that the brain bases of social pain associated with exclusion are similar to those of physical pain, suggesting that the feeling of exclusion is literally a painful experience (Eisenberger et al. 2003). That brain growth continues well into adolescence suggests that negative images of one's own identity during this period can have lifelong consequences. Higher levels of perceived exclusion have also been shown to correlate with greater risk of health issues, including depression, disability, mental health problems, physical illness, and chronic disease (Berkman and Syme 1979). Such impacts are usually amplified when they are combined with impacts associated with individuals' and groups' behavioral responses to feelings of exclusion. Research from social psychology shows that excluded people can show even unprovoked aggression. They may also become defensive and uncooperative and then suffer from a range of negative consequences associated with these behaviors (Abrams, Hogg, and Marques 2005). In addition, excluded people may lack friends, social networks, and reserves of social capital to fall back on.

Violence against subordinate groups is a symptom of their intense exclusion, and lack of power and violence against women is very pervasive. There seems to be an association between spousal violence and women's health and the health of their children. Using data from the 2005/06 Indian National Family Health Survey, a World Bank report (2011a) finds that nearly one-third of Indian women experienced spousal violence at some point in their lives. The analysis shows worse outcomes for victims even after controlling for a number of household and individual characteristics, including ability to reach a health center and whether distance to a health center is a problem. Women who experienced violence were less likely to receive antenatal care and 1.5 times more likely to have terminated a pregnancy or had a stillbirth; their children were 1.14 times more likely to be stunted than children of mothers who had not been abused (figure 1.2). Garcio-Romano et al. (2005) and Morrison and Orlando (2006) find similar negative impacts of spousal violence in their research on other countries, using data from Demographic and Health Surveys and specialized victimization surveys.

Measure What You Value: The Challenge of Quantifying Social Inclusion

Practitioners of development, who sometimes consider social inclusion too esoteric an idea, may ask how it can be quantified. How would one know when exclusion takes place and when inclusion is achieved?

Measurement is indeed important to establish the extent and depth of exclusion and to monitor progress toward inclusion. There has also been considerable progress in measuring human well-being, if not social inclusion, more directly. In fact, "happiness-based" conceptualizations of

Figure 1.2 Indian Women Who Are Victims of Violence Have Worse Health Outcomes and Less Healthy Children

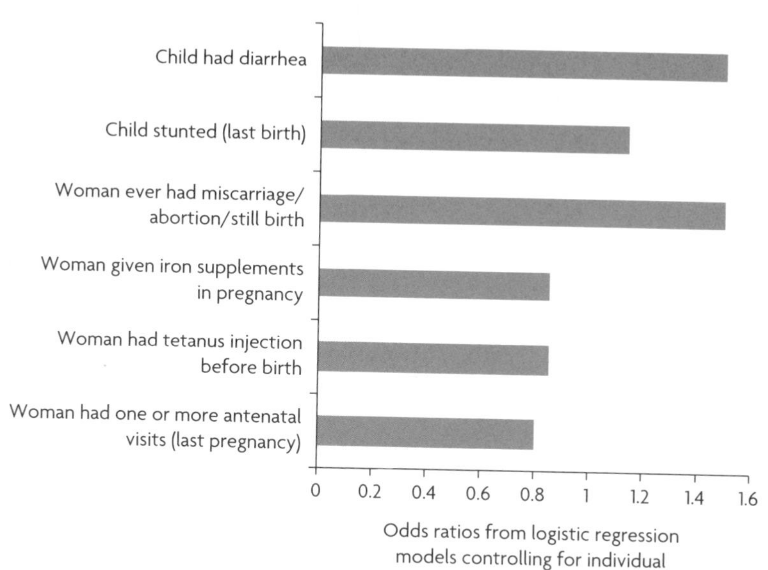

Source: Based on National Family Health Survey (NFHS) data 2005/06 (IIPS and Macro International 2007).
Note: The x-axis reports odds ratios from a logistic regression measuring the association between violence against women and their health outcomes and those of their children, after controlling for a number of individual and socioeconomic characteristics, including ability to reach a health center and whether distance to a health center is a problem.

societal progress go back to the writings of Bentham and Mill. But over time, attention moved away from happiness to the measurement of real production (Galbraith 1958; Sen 2000). As John Kenneth Galbraith wrote in *The Affluent Society* (1958, 214):

> The Benthamite test of public policy was "what serves the greatest happiness of the greatest number," and happiness was more or less implicitly identified with productivity. This is still the official test.... We have somewhat sensed though that we have not recognized the declining importance of goods. Yet even in its deteriorated form we cling to this criterion. It is so much simpler than to substitute the other tests—compassion, individual happiness and well-being, the minimization of community and other tensions—which now become relevant.

The "social indicators revolution" of the 1960s came as a reaction to measures that had weighted production and inputs too heavily (Atkinson 2005;

Noll 2005). The multidimensional nature of well-being gained greater recognition after Sen's seminal work framed development as the freedom to make choices (Sen 1999). The first *Human Development Report*, released by the United Nations in 1990, was the earliest systematic effort to measure multidimensional well-being, an effort that gained much wider currency after the World Bank's publication of the *World Development Report 1999/2000*.

As a result of these and other initiatives, many national and international policy circles are looking for ways to operationalize the idea that societal progress is not only about the functioning of the formal economic system but also about diverse experiences and living conditions of people. Appendix B lays out some recent efforts to measure well-being. These efforts can be adapted to measure social inclusion as well, although doing so requires careful consideration of the context and specific understanding of social inclusion in that context and of the processes and outcomes associated with it. Sometimes countries may choose to adopt multiple measures. Poland, for instance, measures social inclusion using the Laeken indicators, which cover inclusion along four areas: income, work, education, and health.[4] These indicators are based largely on the European Union's conception of social inclusion. To these measures, Poland adds "social participation" as an indicator of inclusion, well-being, and happiness (Szarfenberg 2008; Czapinski and Panek 2012).

In recent years, a surge of initiatives has sought to measure societal progress more comprehensively. Many of them have incorporated subjective reports of well-being. The OECD's Better Life indicators are a step forward in measuring well-being in ways that are feasible for data collection and comparability (*The Economist* 2011). Launched in 2011, the index is an interactive tool that allows people to compare countries' performances according to their own preferences in terms of what makes for a better life. The 11 dimensions of well-being span material living conditions and quality of life.

Another comprehensive measure of well-being is Alkire and Foster's Multidimensional Poverty Measure (MPM), a two-step method that first identifies the poor by considering the intensity of deprivations they suffer and then aggregates the dimensions along which they experience poverty (Alkire and Foster 2007; Alkire and Santos 2010). The MPM moves away from income-based definitions and allows for the application of the measure to different contexts.

Other efforts to measure well-being include the Index of Social Development, initiated at the World Bank and then taken forward by the Institute of Social Studies at The Hague, and the Social Progress Index, which is based on measures that encompass basic human needs, well-being, and opportunity (Foa and Tanner 2012; *The Economist* 2013).

Finally, perception surveys and subjective well-being indicators can also be used to measure social inclusion and exclusion. Perception surveys not only reflect societal norms, they can also include indicators that can be used as proxies for inclusion and exclusion. For example, overrepresentation of certain social groups in poor subjective well-being outcomes or perceptions of injustice/unfairness can reflect systematic patterns of exclusion. Perception-based indicators can supplement objective indicators to more accurately measure exclusion (box 1.1).

Drawing on recent efforts and keeping context specificity in mind, it is therefore possible to construct a measure or a set of indicators. There are two remaining challenges. The first, as discussed above, is to agree on what social inclusion means in a particular context, rather than skipping this step and moving too quickly to measurement. The second is to ensure cross-country comparability when talking about very context-specific and amorphous concepts.

The expectation is that this report will lead to the refinement and elaboration of measures of social inclusion and then to their application in practical policy situations. Regardless of the indicator or measure, it is important to emphasize that measures are merely symptoms or flags; the real test of moving toward social inclusion is to *ask why* certain outcomes obtain for certain groups and to focus on the drivers and processes of social inclusion. Doing so could mean, for instance, persevering with questions, not being content with the knowledge that certain groups are overrepresented among the poor or that certain groups have worse human development outcomes but rather *asking why* this is the case. The narrative that is so constructed is the most important way in which social inclusion can have meaning. According to Stiglitz et al. (2010), developing such a narrative requires a new vision that places the imperative of fostering economic growth within the broader context of societal progress.

Kaushik Basu, the current Chief Economist of the World Bank, aptly summarizes the complexity of measurement in a recent blog post: "To focus solely on measurement is to risk missing out on some essential features of life, which may be nebulous and not quite measureable, but nonetheless important" (Basu 2013).

BOX 1.1

Measuring Discrimination

They ask you how old you are; if you plan to have children, they will not hire you. They also do not employ women who are more than 35 years old, because younger women are quicker. I can iron 100 pieces, she can iron 10 pieces.

—Female focus group discussant in Azanja, Serbia, interviewed for the *World Development Report 2012*

Initially developed to test discrimination in the labor market, methods to measure discrimination have advanced considerably in recent years. The most common methods use labor market surveys and compare market outcomes, such as earnings, of different groups, controlling for productivity-related individual characteristics (such as human capital endowments). Studies traditionally focused mainly on race and gender as the axes of discrimination, but an increasing number of studies are now also testing for discrimination along other axes, including immigrant status, disability status, and ethnicity (see, for example, Ñopo, Saavedra, and Torero 2007, who introduce indicators to capture "degrees of whiteness" or "indigenousness'" to account for heterogeneity within the Peruvian mestizo population). They are also focusing on new arenas of discrimination, such as the marriage market.

In so-called correspondence tests, applications are submitted to job or housing advertisements in the name of two fictitious applicants. The applications are largely equivalent, with the only difference the potential marker of discrimination, such as a foreign surname. Discrimination is then assessed as the difference in call-back rates or invitations to personal interviews or property viewings the candidates receive. In audit studies, matched pairs of interviewees (actors) who differ with regard to the characteristic suspected to trigger discrimination (such as race or gender) attend interviews.

Another way of measuring discrimination is based on perceptions. Individuals are asked about personal experiences and views regarding unequal treatment. Such questions are included, for instance, in social surveys such as the European Social Survey, the Eurobarometer, and the General Social Surveys in Canada and New Zealand. Surveys may ask respondents about personal experiences of discrimination or more abstractly about whether they consider themselves members of a group that is discriminated against.

Sources: Daniel 1968; Jowell and Prescott-Clarke 1970; Yinger 1986; Neumark, Bank, and Van Nort 1996; Salkever and Domino 1997; Ñopo, Saavedra, and Torero 2007; Jha and Adelman 2009; Kuhn and Shen 2009; Das 2012; OECD 2012; World Bank 2012.

Notes

1. According to Sen, "a small peasant and a landless laborer may both be poor, but their fortunes are not tied together. In understanding the proneness to starvation of either we have to view them not as members of the huge army of 'poor,' but as members of particular classes, belonging to particular occupational groups, having different endowments, being governed by rather different entitlement relations. The category of the poor is not merely inadequate for evaluation exercises and a nuisance for causal analysis, it can also have distorting effects on policy matters" (Sen 1981, as quoted in Hulme and Shepherd 2003, 403).
2. The opposite of social exclusion is not always inclusion. One may be "included" in decision-making processes but have very limited say over outcomes; it is the terms of inclusion that matter. The concept of adverse incorporation suggests a situation where people are included but on highly adverse terms.
3. In the United States, grade-point averages are usually on a four-point scale.
4. The Laeken indicators are a set of common statistical indicators on poverty and social exclusion established at the European Council of December 2001 in the Brussels suburb of Laeken, Belgium. The indicators, which are disaggregated by criteria such as gender and age group, include the at-risk-of-poverty rate, the persistent at-risk-of-poverty rate, regional cohesion, the long-term unemployment rate, yearly school leavers not in education or training, and life expectancy at birth, among other indicators.

References

Abrams, D., M. A. Hogg, and J. M. Marques, eds. 2005. *The Social Psychology of Inclusion and Exclusion*. New York: Psychology Press.

Akerlof, George. 1976. "The Economics of Caste and of the Rat Race and Other Woeful Tales." *Quarterly Journal of Economics* 90 (4): 599–617.

Alkire, S., and J. Foster. 2007. "Counting and Multidimensional Poverty Measures." OPHI Working Paper Series 7, Oxford Poverty and Human Development Initiative, Oxford, U.K.

Alkire, S., and M. E. Santos. 2010. "Multidimensional Poverty Index." Research Brief, Oxford Poverty and Human Development Initiative, University of Oxford, Oxford, U.K.

Atkinson, A. B. 2005. "Measurement of UK Government Output and Productivity for the National Accounts." *Journal of the Statistical and Social Inquiry Society of Ireland* 34: 152–60.

Basu, K. 2013. "Targets and Measures, Poverty and Sharing." *Let's Talk Development* (blog), February 7. World Bank, Washington, DC. http://blogs.worldbank.org/developmenttalk/targets-and-measures-poverty-and-sharing.

Bennett, L. 2005. "Gender, Caste and Ethnic Exclusion in Nepal: Following the Policy Process from Analysis to Action." Paper presented at the Arusha Conference "New Frontiers of Social Policy," Washington, DC, December 12–15.

Berkman, L. F., and S. L. Syme. 1979. "Social Networks, Host Resistance, and Mortality: A Nine-Year Follow-Up Study of Alameda County Residents." *American Journal of Epidemiology* 109 (2): 186–204.

Cardenas, J. C., A. Chong, and H. Ñopo. 2009. "To What Extent Do Latin Americans Trust, Reciprocate, and Cooperate? Evidence from Experiments in Six Latin American Countries." *Economia* 9 (2): 45–94.

Czapinski, J., and T. Panek. 2012. *Social Diagnosis 2011*. Warsaw: Council for Social Monitoring.

Daniel, W. W. 1968. *Racial Discrimination in England*. Harmondsworth, U.K.: Penguin.

Das, M. B. 2012. "Stubborn Inequalities, Subtle Processes: Exclusion and Discrimination in the Labor Market." Background paper for *World Development Report 2013*, World Bank, Washington, DC.

de Laat, Joost. 2010. "Roma Inclusion: An Economic Opportunity for Bulgaria, Czech Republic, Romania and Serbia." Policy Note, World Bank, Human Development Sector Unit, Washington, DC.

Economist, The. 2011. "The Pursuit of Happiness." May 24. http://www.economist.com/blogs/dailychart/2011/05/well-being_and_wealth (accessed August 19, 2013).

———. 2013. "Beyond GDP." April 18. http://www.economist.com/blogs/feastandfamine/2013/04/social-progress (accessed August 19, 2013).

Eisenberger, N. I., M. D. Lieberman, and K. D. Williams. 2003. "Does Rejection Hurt? An fMRI Study of Social Exclusion." *Science* 302 (5643) 290–92.

Foa, R., and J. C. Tanner. 2012. "Methodology of the Indices of Social Development." Indices of Social Development, Working Paper No. 2012-4, International Institute of Social Studies, The Hague.

Galbraith, J. K. 1958. *The Affluent Society*. New York: Houghton-Mifflin.

Garcio-Romano, C., H. A. F. M. Jansen, M. Ellsberg, L. Heise, and C. Watts. 2005. *The WHO Multi-Country Study on Women's Health and Domestic Violence against Women: Initial Results on Prevalence, Health Outcomes and Women's Responses*. Geneva: World Health Organization.

Hochschild, J. L., and C. Lang. 2011. "Including Oneself and Including Others: Who Belongs in My Country?" *Annals of the American Academy of Political and Social Science* 634 (1): 78–97.

Hulme, D., and A. Shepherd. 2003. "Conceptualizing Chronic Poverty." *World Development* 31 (3): 403–23.

IIPS (International Institute for Population Sciences) and Macro International. 2007. *National Family Health Survey, 2005–06: India*. http://www.measuredhs.com/aboutsurveys/search/metadata.cfm?surv_id=264&ctry_id=57&SrvyTp=available (accessed August 10, 2013).

Jha, S., and M. Adelman. 2009. "Looking for Love in All the White Places: A Study of Skin Color Preferences on Indian Matrimonial and Mate-Seeking Websites." *Studies in South Asian Film and Media* 1: 65–83.

Jowell, R., and P. Prescott-Clarke. 1970. "Racial Discrimination and White-Collar Workers in Britain." *Race* (11) 4: 397–417.

Kosciw, J. G., E. A. Greytak, M. J. Bartkiewicz, M. J. Boesen, and N. A. Palmer. 2012. *The 2011 National School Climate Survey: The Experiences of Lesbian, Gay, Bisexual and Transgender Youth in Our Nation's Schools*. New York: GLSEN (Gay, Lesbian & Straight Education Network). http://glsen.org/download/file/MzIxOQ==.

Kuhn, P., and K. Shen. 2009. "Employers' Preferences for Gender, Age, Height and Beauty: Direct Evidence." NBER Working Paper 15564, National Bureau of Economic Research, Cambridge, MA.

Lenoir, R. 1974. *Les exclus: Un français sur dix (Excluded: One in Ten French)*. Paris: Le Seuil.

Levitas, R. 1998. *The Inclusive Society? Social Exclusion and New Labour*. London: Macmillan.

Molinas Vega, J. R., R. Paes de Barros, C. J. Saavedra, M. Giugale, L. J. Cord, C. Pessino, and A. Hasan. 2012. *Do Our Children Have a Chance? A Human Opportunity Report for Latin America and the Caribbean*. Washington, DC: World Bank.

Morrison, A., and M. B. Orlando. 2006. "The Cost and Impacts of Gender-Based Violence in Developing Countries: Methodological Considerations and New Evidence." Policy Research Working Paper 36151, World Bank, Washington, DC.

Neumark, D., R. J. Bank, and K. D. Van Nort. 1996. "Sex Discrimination in Restaurant Hiring: An Audit Study." *Quarterly Journal of Economics* 111 (3): 915–41.

Noh, S., M. Beiser, V. Kaspar, F. Hou, and J. Rummens. 1999. "Perceived Racial Discrimination, Depression, and Coping: A Study of Southeast Asian Refugees in Canada." *Journal of Health and Social Behavior* 40 (3): 193–207.

Noll, H.-H. 2005. "Conceptual Framework of the European System of Social Indicators." German Social Science Infrastructure Services, Mannheim, Germany. http://www.gesis.org/en/services/data-analysis/social-indicators/eusi/conceptual-frameworks (accessed October 7, 2013).

Ñopo, H., J. Saavedra, and M. Torero. 2007. "Ethnicity and Earnings in a Mixed-Race Labor Market." *Economic Development and Cultural Change* 55 (4): 709–34.

Norton, A., and A. de Haan. 2012. *Social Cohesion: Theoretical Debates and Practical Applications with Respect to Jobs*. Washington, DC: World Bank.

OECD (Organisation for Economic Co-operation and Development). 2012. *Settling In: OECD Indicators of Immigrant Integration 2012*. Paris: OECD.

Paugam, S. 1993. *La société française et ses pauvres* (*French Society and Its Poor*). Paris: PUF.

Plonka, B. 2013. "Social Inclusion in Poland." Background paper draft, World Bank, Washington, DC.

Polish Ministry of Labor and Social Policy. 2006. *Social Exclusion and Integration in Poland*. Warsaw.

Rauch, James E. 1991. "Productivity Gains from Geographic Concentration of Human Capital: Evidence from the Cities." NBER Working Paper 3905, National Bureau of Economic Research, Cambridge, MA.

Salkever, D. S., and M. E. Domino. 1997. "Within Group 'Structural' Tests of Labor-Market Discrimination: A Study of Persons with Serious Disabilities." NBER Working Paper 5931, National Bureau of Economic Research, Cambridge, MA.

Savoia, A., J. Easaw, and A. McKay. 2010. "Inequality, Democracy, and Institutions: A Critical Review of Recent Research." *World Development* 38 (2): 142–54.

Scoville, J. G., ed. 1991. *Status Influences in Third World Labor Markets*. New York: Walter de Gruyter.

Sen, A. 1981. *Poverty and Famines: An Essay on Entitlement and Deprivation*. Delhi: Oxford University Press.

———. 1999. "The Possibility of Social Choice." *American Economic Review* 89 (3): 349–78.

———. 2000. "The Discipline of Cost-Benefit Analysis." *Journal of Legal Studies* 29 (S2): 931–52.

Silver, H. 1994. "Social Exclusion and Social Solidarity: Three Paradigms." *International Labor Review* 133: 531–78. http://www.socialinclusion.org.np/new/files/Social_Exclusion_and_Solidarity_by_Hillary_SILVER_1336541445c29W.pdf.

———. n.d. "Social Exclusion." In *Encyclopedia of Sociology*. Oxford: Blackwell.

Stiglitz, J. E. 2012. The *Price of Inequality: How Today's Divided Society Endangers Our Future*. New York: W. W. Norton & Company.

Stiglitz, J. E., A. Sen, J. P. Fitoussi, and Commission on the Measurement of Economic Performance and Social Progress (France). 2010. *Mismeasuring Our Lives: Why GDP Doesn't Add Up: The Report*. New York: New Press.

Szarfenberg, R. 2008. "Pojecie wykluczenia spolecznego." Lectures, University of Warsaw, Warsaw, Poland.

Tilly, C. 1999. *Durable Inequality*. Berkeley, CA: University of California Press.

Warschauer, M. 2003. *Technology and Social Inclusion: Rethinking the Digital Divide*. Cambridge, MA: MIT Press.

World Bank. 2006. The *World Development Report: Equity and Development*. Washington, DC: World Bank.

———. 2011a. *Perspectives on Poverty in India: Stylized Facts from Survey Data*. Washington, DC: World Bank.

———. 2011b. "Social Safety Nets in Nepal." Draft report, Washington, DC. http://laurapaler.files.wordpress.com/2011/05/bhpw-bra-kdp-2010.pdf (accessed June 12, 2013).

———. 2012. *World Development Report 2012: Gender Equality and Development*. Washington, DC: World Bank.

———. Various years. *World Bank Investment Climate Surveys*. Washington, DC.

Yinger, J. 1986. "Measuring Discrimination with Fair Housing Audits: Caught in the Act." *American Economic Review* 76 (5): 881–93.

Zoninsein, J. 2004. *The Economic Case for Combating Racial and Ethnic Exclusion in Latin America and Caribbean Countries*. Research Report, Inter-American Development Bank, Washington, DC.

CHAPTER 2

Who Gets Excluded and Why?

The eyes of others our prisons, their minds our cages.

—VIRGINIA WOOLF, *AN UNWRITTEN NOVEL* (1921)

Individuals, Groups, and Their Identities

Identity is socially constructed and often forms the basis for inclusion or exclusion. An individual's identity is his or her affiliation with a group with whom he or she shares some attributes.

In reality, as discussed later, individuals have multiple identities (figure 2.1). These identities can be based on gender, occupation, caste, race, ethnicity, sexual orientation, religion, disability status, or citizenship. For instance, gender-based exclusion has historically disadvantaged females, but increasingly the literature documents the isolation and exclusion of certain males as well (Barker et al. 2012). Social exclusion based on certain group attributes can lead to lower social standing, often accompanied by worse outcomes in terms of income, human capital endowments, access to employment and services, and voice in both national and local decision making (table 2.1).

It is also important to keep in mind that minority status is not the only driver of exclusion: sometimes a minority can exclude the majority. Although this phenomenon is sometimes called "elite capture," in fact the state can be run by oligopolies that exclude the majority of the population. Economic, social, and political institutions similarly exclude women as an aggregate category from the labor market or from higher education or positions of power—excluding not a minority but half the population.

Figure 2.1 People Have Multiple, Intersecting Identities

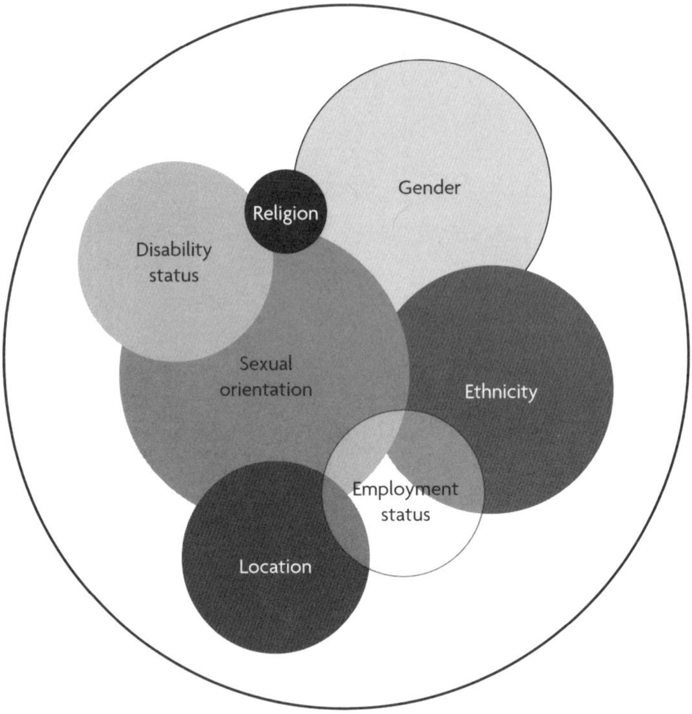

Note: Figure shows illustrative example of types of identities. The size of each bubble denotes the importance of an identity, which can vary across individuals, groups, and even the same individual over time.

Gender, race, ethnicity, and religion are among the most commonly discussed bases of disadvantage. But other identities—such as sexual orientation, disability status, and nationality—are also pervasive axes of exclusion. People of African descent are still excluded in a variety of cultures. This exclusion is grounded in historical circumstance; slavery in the Western world and apartheid in South Africa are two of the most extreme examples of how race, combined with economic subordination, rendered an entire people subservient. Research from the United States is among the most prolific in empirically documenting the disadvantage of people from African descent and, increasingly, Latino origin (box 2.1).

The caste system, peculiar to India and Nepal, warrants special mention, because it stands out as an ideal type of exclusion, complete with an ideology, clear rules and roles, and a hierarchy that has persisted

Table 2.1 Groups Eligible for Support under Indonesia's PNPM Peduli Facility

Adult and child victims of trafficking	Poor people in the state border area
Boatless fisherfolk	Poor women microentrepreneurs
Victims of drug abuse	Poor youth
Homeless and landless ethnic minorities	Scavengers/garbage collectors
Poor landless farm laborers	Sexual minorities
Male and female sex workers	Street beggars
Poor migrant workers	Street children
Orphans	Transgender people
People with HIV/AIDS	Victims of conflict
Plantation laborers	Victims of domestic or community abuse
Poor ethnic minorities	Youth in conflict with the law
Poor farmers	Child workers
Poor female-headed households	Victims of disaster
Poor indigenous people	Poor pedicab drivers

Note: Peduli means "to care." This relatively new initiative gives grants to civil society to work with "marginalized and invisible groups." The list of groups the program supports was created through a consultative process and reflects the framing of social inclusion. *State border area* refers to provinces that border other countries, such as Malaysia.

BOX 2.1

Domestic Workers in the United States: Working in the Informal Economy

The Help, a novel by Kathryn Stockett, paints a vivid picture of the mistreatment of African-American women working as house help in 1960s Mississippi. Today, there are millions of domestic workers in the United States. In 2008, for instance, about 3.2 million people worked as direct caregivers, a number that is expected to grow by more than a million by 2018. These workers continue to be in a very vulnerable position: a new report on their situation in the United States shows that many of them are paid less than the minimum wage and work in substandard conditions (Burnham, Theodore, and Ehrenreich 2012). Through a survey of 2,086 domestic caregivers, the report finds that 67 percent of live-in workers are paid below the state minimum wage. They rarely receive employment benefits; are uncovered by state social security; work long arduous hours; and often risk long-term exposure to toxic chemicals and verbal, psychological, and physical abuse.

(*continued next page*)

BOX 2.1 *(continued)*

Most domestic workers are thus excluded from the protection the formal labor market provides. They tend to come from precarious backgrounds and are often undocumented migrants, sometimes with limited language proficiency. More than 85 percent report that they would not complain about abuse for fear of losing their jobs or having their immigration status disclosed and used against them.

Sources: Burnham, Theodore, and Ehrenreich 2012; Covert 2013.

through millennia. It shows the hold of a social system that renders some groups (the erstwhile untouchables, who now call themselves Dalits) so excluded that they are outside the pale of the system of exclusion itself (outcaste). Lesbian, gay, bisexual, and transgender (LGBT) individuals are targeted for exclusion in many, if not most, cultures. In fact, homosexuality is still criminalized in many countries, and in some it is punishable by death.

Indigenous peoples across the world have faced historical exclusion, rooted in large part in their displacement from their traditional lands and forests. Over centuries, such exclusion has become so entrenched that although they make up roughly 4.5 percent of the global population, indigenous peoples account for about 10 percent of the global poor (Hall and Patrinos 2012). They also have worse human development outcomes than the average population. In Vietnam, the Hmong record the lowest female literacy rates; in Latin America, indigenous peoples have higher infant mortality levels (the highest levels are found among Mam speakers in Guatemala and the Quechua in Bolivia); in India, child mortality rates among the Adivasi (tribal groups that claim to be the original inhabitants of India) are significantly higher than rates among other social groups (Hall and Patrinos 2012).

The Roma, an ethnic minority in Europe, have historically led itinerant lives. Over the past decade or so, they have received more attention than in the past. The stereotyping and violence that the Roma historically faced and still face is increasingly being acknowledged and studied; it is also the subject of policy and programmatic intervention. Although governments in the European Union have indicated their support for integrating the Roma, laws and policies are often pretexts for victimizing them—sometimes inadvertently, though often deliberately. The Office for Democratic Institutions and Human Rights under the Organization for Security and Co-operation in Europe (OSCE 2009) documents recent developments in Italy, where laws and policies have adversely affected the Roma and Sinti ("gypsy" people of central Europe). These measures include emergency laws defining "nomads" as a public safety problem and permitting special measures of identification (including the fingerprinting of children) and deportation, for reasons of "national security."

Religion has historically been a rallying cry for generating support for the exclusion of people who do not belong. Exclusion based on religion often has other underlying drivers, such as competition for scarce resources or a history of claims on a geographical area. Entire groups have been treated with suspicion—for instance, because of pervasive anti-Semitism—and wars have been fought throughout history ostensibly to protect religion.

Religion continues to be an important driver of exclusion today. The negative stereotyping and profiling of young Muslim men in the post-9/11 era is part of a global current that views an entire religion negatively, leading to an atmosphere of mutual mistrust. Racial profiling of Muslims can lead to wrongful arrest and harassment in several domains of social life, among other things.

Disability is another axis of exclusion. The disadvantage faced by persons with disabilities is documented in the *World Report on Disability*, which estimates that more than a billion people around the world experience some form of disability (WHO and World Bank 2011). Despite actions to include persons with disabilities, evidence suggests that they face significant challenges in accessing infrastructure, services, information, and jobs. The report shows, for instance, that people with disabilities are more than twice as likely as people without disabilities to find health care provider skills inadequate to meet their needs. Children with disabilities are less likely than other children to start school and have lower rates of staying in school. Persons with disabilities are also treated with disrespect and often remain invisible at both the household and societal level, especially in developing countries.

Finally, with large waves of migration, both within countries and across them, the identity of migrant groups and individuals has come under special scrutiny. Chapters 4 and 5 discuss trends in migration and attitudes that have rendered migrants vulnerable to exclusion in recent years. Migrants are a very diverse group, and some are at greater risk of exclusion than others. For instance, migrants who lack documentation often lead lives as second-class citizens. Migrants who have been forced to move as a result of either war or disaster, both internally and externally displaced people, are especially unwelcome in their host areas.

A number of groups have been discussed in this section, several others have not. Depending on the context, various other groups can also face exclusion.

Groups Are Very Heterogeneous

In understanding the disadvantage or advantage that comes with social identity, it is important to recognize that groups are extremely heterogeneous. This heterogeneity means that exclusion within groups can be more salient than across groups. It can be driven by differential socioeconomic status, by the consolidation of elites within a group who exercise disproportionate power, or by the place in the life cycle. Women, for instance, make up half the world's population and in the aggregate do worse than men in the labor market. But they also usually live longer than men do, and rich women from a majority ethnic group may have better outcomes in many domains than poor men from minority ethnic groups. Even within countries, women from richer or poorer households or from different ethnic groups have very different outcomes.

Place in the life cycle is an important driver of heterogeneity. It can bestow either advantage or disadvantage, depending on the context. Although indigenous peoples are often excluded, the elderly among them have a special and important place in the group. The elderly in most parts of the world now also live much longer than they used to, imposing a new onus on their children's generation. Where social security systems are primarily informal, many elderly people are at risk of ill treatment.

Similarly, the existence of large youth cohorts in some countries does not immediately translate into certainty that the "demographic dividend" will be realized, as discussed in chapter 4. In many countries of the Middle East, the exclusion youth face has deleterious consequences at the individual, community, and societal levels (La Cava and Michael 2006; Silver 2007).

In some cases, a life-cycle event such as widowhood can lead to dire life-long consequences. There will be increasing numbers of widows going forward, as life expectancy increases overall but more for women than for men. In many Hindu communities, tradition regards widows as bringing back luck, which in turn leads to their exclusion from property, services, and dignity. It is less well known that widowhood is an axis of exclusion in Africa as well. The HIV/AIDS epidemic has been partly responsible for the large number of widows. These women are largely invisible in the data used to inform social policy. In Mali, for instance, households headed by widows have significantly lower living standards than other households across the country. Furthermore, the welfare difference persists even after their remarriage. These detrimental effects are in turn passed on to their children (van de Walle 2011).

Heterogeneity within groups can also be linked to other characteristics, such as skin tone. Individuals within the same race or ethnicity—even people within the same family—who have lighter skin appear to have better outcomes and opportunities, ranging from chances of getting married (especially of women) to employment. Villarreal (2010) finds that people in Mexico with darker skin tone have significantly lower levels of educational attainment and occupational status. Based on data from the New Immigrant Survey of 2003, Hersch (2008) shows that among new legal immigrants to the United States, those with the lightest skin color earn on average 17 percent more than comparable immigrants with the darkest skin, after controlling for education, English language proficiency, occupation in source country, family background, ethnicity, race, and country of birth. The importance of skin tone is also well recognized in Asia. Jha and Adelman (2009), for instance, empirically confirm a truism through an experimental study that shows that Indian men tend to veer toward lighter-skinned women in selecting a wife through arranged marriage. They also find that matrimonial websites tend to reinforce this preference for lighter-skinned brides.

Finally, it bears mention that identity is not constructed based only on others' conception of "them." It is equally constructed on the self-conception of groups. Self-reported identity is often the basis of census enumeration, but this technocratic descriptor can have underlying social and psychological foundations. Whether or not individuals consider themselves black, white, or indigenous depends to a large extent on the social milieu of which they are part. Elsewhere in this report, it is shown that African descendants in Brazil have begun to report themselves as "black" more often than in the past. Doing so is an assertion of their identity and also a reflection of their dignity, agency, and empowerment. They are no longer afraid or reticent about considering themselves as descendants of Africans.

In contrast, the Roma tend to hide their identity, fearing negative stereotyping. They do not yet have the collective confidence to declare their identity as an ethnic minority. In yet other cases, excluded groups act collectively to reject their descriptions by the majority, taking on new and more empowering descriptors and nouns. The term *Dalit* in India, for instance, means "the oppressed." Identifying themselves as such is a way to claim political and symbolic space, as well as a means to shake the dominant orthodoxy into accepting its responsibility for oppression. The same is true of the terms *Adivasi, Adibasi,* and *Janajati* in India, Bangladesh, and Nepal, which denote the preeminent and primordial rights of tribal peoples over their lands.

Take also the increasing use of the word *woman* in the United States, as opposed to the more value-laden term *lady*. It was propelled by the feminist movement, which rejected the patriarchal and class-based connotation of the term *lady*. This usage represents yet another example of assertion by a historically subordinate group. Hence, assertion or negation of identity by excluded groups is socially grounded and often has deep political and historical roots.

Individuals Have Overlapping Identities

Individuals are simultaneously members of different groups and may be excluded because of one of their identities but not another. The notion of "intersectionality" is based on the understanding that people are simultaneously situated in multiple social structures and realms, which interact in complex ways to influence human experiences, social relations, and outcomes. In Sen's words (2008, 6–7):

> A solitarist approach is, in general, a very efficient way of misunderstanding nearly everyone in the world. In our normal lives, we see ourselves as members of a variety of groups—we belong to all of them. The same person can be, without any contradiction, a Norwegian citizen, of Asian origin, with Bangladeshi ancestry, a Muslim, a socialist, a woman, a vegetarian, a jazz musician, a doctor, a poet, a feminist, a heterosexual, a believer in gay and lesbian rights.... Each of these identities can be of significance to the person, depending on the problem at hand and the context of choice, and the priorities between them could be influenced by her own values as well as by social pressures. There is no reason to think that whatever civilizational identity a person has—religious, communal, regional, national or global—must invariably dominate over every other relation or affiliation he or she may have.

Intersecting identities can produce an overlay or a multiplication of disadvantage or advantage. For instance, the intersection of gender, age, ethnicity, and place of residence can have significantly more deleterious effects than the effects of gender alone. Education and employment are documented in the literature as particularly salient mediators through which multiple disadvantages may play out. Take the case of Somali women and girls, who bear the brunt of long-term conflict. Almost one-third of Somali girls of primary-school age in Kenya are not enrolled in school, compared with only 9 percent of all girls in Kenya (Africa Progress Panel 2012). The Women's Refugee Commission (2012) shows that Somali women refugees in East Africa face multiple exclusions that stem from their ethnicity, religion, and refugee status, which are compounded by gender.

Multiple exclusions of some groups stand out in countries where average outcomes are quite good. Bolivia, for instance, has a high level of secondary-school attainment, with low gender differentials. Figure 2.2 shows the probability that an average Spanish-speaking Bolivian man (25 years of age or older) completes secondary education. If this Bolivian were a woman, the probability would be lower by 5 percentage points. If this Bolivian were a man who belonged to the Quechua people, the probability of secondary-school completion would be lower by 14 percentage points.

Figure 2.2 Intersecting Identities Transfer Cumulative Disadvantage: Secondary-School Completion in Bolivia

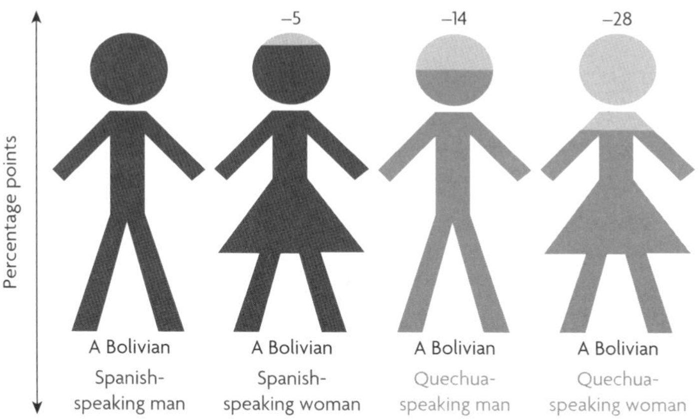

Source: World Bank, based on data from Minnesota Population Center 2011 and Bolivian National Institute of Statistics 2001.

Note: Figure shows secondary-school completion marginal effects, using men and Spanish mother tongue as reference group, for people 25 years and older, controlling for age, age-squared, and urban/rural residence. All values are significant at the 1 percent level.

If the person were a Quechua woman, she would have a 28 percentage point lower probability of completing secondary school than a Spanish-speaking Bolivian man. The qualitative literature on double and triple disadvantage for women and indigenous women documents this overlay of disadvantage very poignantly in a variety of settings.

The intersection of social and spatial characteristics is one of the most common markers of disadvantage. Take the case of Brazil, once considered the negative outlier on income inequality and today celebrated as a success story in reducing inequality. A large part of the decline in income inequality in Brazil is explained by convergence in outcomes between the historically poorest North and Northeast and the historically richest South and Southwest. Yet disparities in outcomes between the average Brazilian and minorities such as Afro-Brazilians or indigenous people persist.

Fertility is an outcome of interest, because it has a bearing on women's choice about how many children they will have, how they will control childbearing, and the timing of birth. Brazil has been a success in reducing fertility. The total fertility rate in Brazil is 1.9, putting it at below replacement level. Brazil has also been very successful in reducing teen fertility: in 2010, about 12 percent of women 15–19 had had a child, compared with 15 percent in 1991 and 18 percent in 1996 (World Bank 2013). At the national level, the indigenous population has much higher teen fertility rates, but the regional breakdown of differentials is even more instructive. The Southeast not only has the lowest incidence of teenage pregnancy, it also has the lowest differentials across racial groups, indicating that all women benefit from the relatively low rates of teenage pregnancy in the region (figure 2.3). In contrast, the overall incidence of teen pregnancy is only slightly higher in the Center-West, but indigenous women are disproportionately disadvantaged, with very high differentials between them and other women. Differentials in the South are also relatively high compared with other regions. The North has the highest incidence of teenage pregnancy, but the gap between indigenous and non-indigenous women is smaller, suggesting that all women face high rates of teenage pregnancy relative to the rest of the country. However, indigenous women who live in the North have lower teen fertility rates than their counterparts in the Center-West but comparable rates to their counterparts in the South. There could be many reasons for these patterns, but they serve to show that the interface between region and ethnicity creates particular advantages and disadvantages for social groups in terms of their human development outcomes.

Figure 2.3 Brazil's Teen Fertility Rate Varies by Race and Location

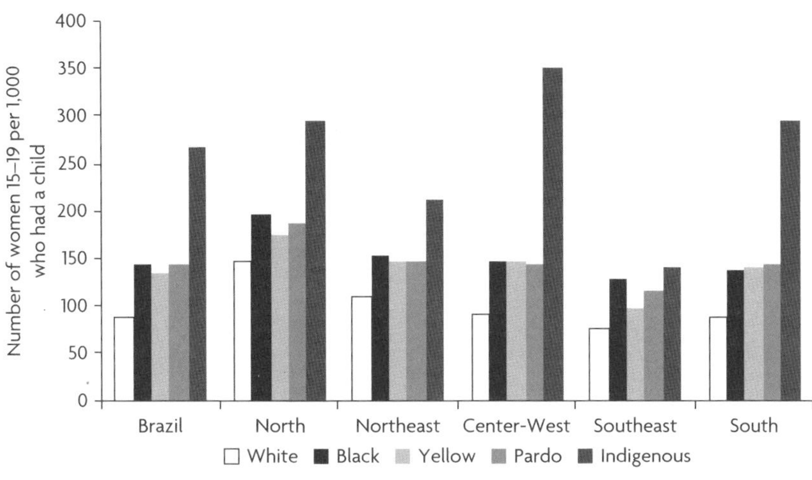

Source: World Bank, based on data from 2010 Brazilian census (IBGE 2012).
Note: Racial categories are translations from the Brazilian census.

How Exclusion Plays Out

Practices of Exclusion

Individuals and groups are excluded through behaviors and practices, including stereotypes, prejudices, and stigmas that are socially constructed and influence day-to-day interactions. These practices play out at different levels, often underpinned by sophisticated and ingrained social norms and the beliefs of both the excluder and the excluded.

The exclusion of less "valuable" members starts in the household and in family dynamics. It often mirrors the normative structure of society. For instance, in many families, the invisibility of a person with a disability mirrors his or her invisibility in society. The ostracism of widows in some societies plays out in their homes and families. Such practices continue at the community level, where they translate into exclusion by formal and informal institutions. In turn, institutions can also be the conduit for greater inclusion, this report argues.

Practices and processes of exclusion are not conspiracies, except under the most extreme circumstances. In many cases, the "code" is hidden even to the individuals who are executing the act of exclusion. For example, stereotypes about groups can be so ingrained in the labor market that hiring managers or even peers do not even realize that they have internalized them (see Loury 1999; Deshpande and Newman 2007), or they may not consider them stereotypes but facts. Stereotypes of the "lazy" Roma or of women as having low commitment to the labor market are so internalized by the majority that they are often regarded as truisms, even though they are not borne out by data on labor force participation (figure 2.4).

Employers find it easier to "connect" with employees who share their belief systems. Cornell and Welch (1996) show that employers are able to judge the qualities of job applicants better when candidates and employers belong to the same group, and the top applicant is likely to

Figure 2.4 Questioning the Stereotype of the Roma Being "Lazy": Labor Market Outcomes of Roma Men

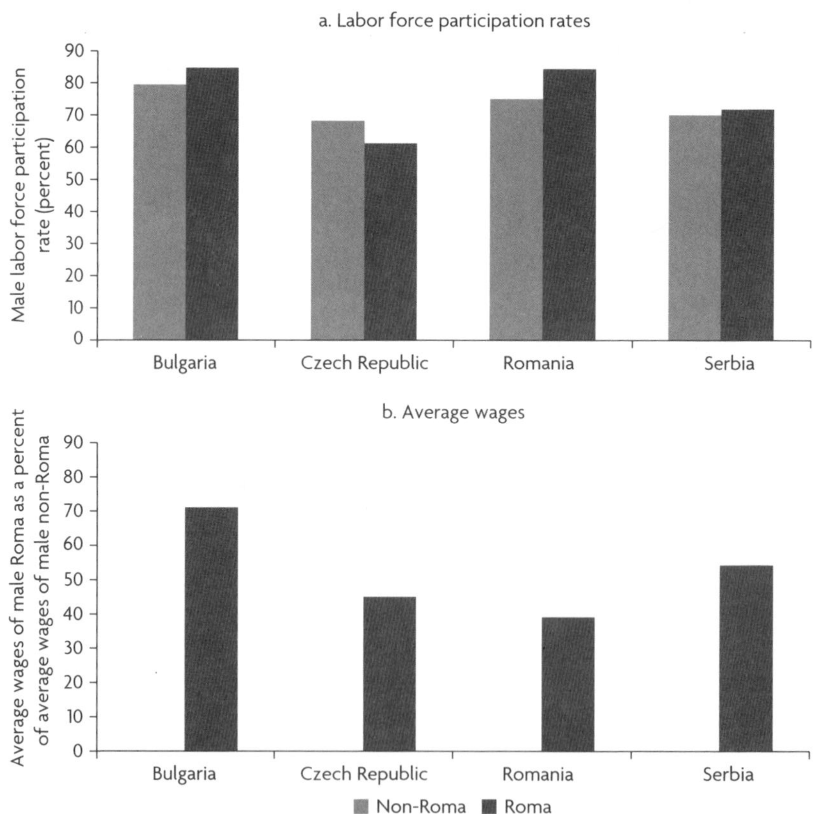

Source: de Laat 2010.

Note: Figures are for men 15–64 . Wages for Bulgaria, the Czech Republic, and Serbia are net; wages for Romania are gross. Data come from surveys carried out at different times between 2007 and 2009.

have the same background as the employer. They also point to some "reinforcing effects" of such screening discrimination. For instance, employers may infer the quality of applicants from the behavior of other employers, amounting to herd behavior, in which preferences expressed by third parties drive decisions. A recent book, *Blindspot: Hidden Biases of Good People*, suggests that there may be a part of the human brain that almost unknowingly favors certain kinds of people versus others (Banaji and Greenwald 2013). Such biases are shaped by a lifetime of exposure to attitudes and stereotypes about people, places, and things. Most important, the authors argue, it may be possible to change these blind spots.

Extreme stereotyping leads to stigma that deeply discredits some groups. Stigmatization combines social consensus about a specific target or group, a shared discontent against them by some members of the society, and a social justification or supportive ideology for their moral exclusion (Major and O'Brien 2005). People with HIV/AIDS—or earlier, leprosy—were stigmatized both literally and figuratively, because physical contact with them was considered polluting. In a survey of people receiving antiretroviral therapy in Botswana, more 50 percent of respondents said it was either equally or more difficult to cope with the social consequences of their HIV status than the medical ones (Ogden and Nyblade 2005). The Joint United Nations Programme on HIV/AIDS (UNAIDS) categorizes stigma as a primary obstacle in the fight against HIV/AIDS, because it prevents people from disclosing their sero-status, seeking medical information or treatment, adopting preventive behavior, and getting tested, even where services are available (DFID 2007). (Chapter 5 discusses attitudes toward certain commonly stigmatized groups.)

Language is a potent force for reinforcing excluded status and practices. This idea was most famously articulated by Bourdieu (1991), who outlined the notion of language as symbolic power. Name-calling and the use of pejoratives to describe individuals and groups with certain characteristics reinforce disrespect and exclusion. Examples include words used for black people in the United States, Dalits in India, women and sexual minorities in different languages, the Roma in Europe, and people with disabilities, among others. Sometimes the words that describe certain practices say much about the social acceptance of exclusion. Many egregious practices are described in playful or benign terms. For instance, the term *eve teasing* is used in South Asia as a flippant euphemism to signify sexual harassment of women in public places. Both the term and the practice are treated with the same indulgence. The practice has come under cynosure only after a horrific gang rape in Delhi in 2012 came to light. The same is true of the term *teasing*, which is common in schools across the world. Much of what was once thought of as innocuous teasing is now recognized as bullying, a process that succeeds in excluding students with certain characteristics. Both sexual harassment and bullying, which are about assertion of power, are also being recognized in the workplace; both are mechanisms that exclude (by threat) certain groups from active participation in social life.

Many exclusionary practices are upheld through elaborate ideologies, rules, religious tenets, and even dictats. Bourdieu (1989, 21) famously remarked that "objective relations of power tend to reproduce themselves in relations of symbolic power." Women, for instance, are assigned a place in the domestic sphere in most societies, a role endorsed by several religions. Caste in the Hindu hierarchy is a system of exclusion that sets clear roles and rules for groups, based on division of labor and ratified by religious texts. Castes are assigned their place in the economic, social, and religious orders. Other practices take on ritual significance because they are tied up with notions of honor that serve to keep groups excluded.

All of these practices have something in common: they create a web of norms that makes the most unequal and unfair practices seem normal. Hoff and Stiglitz (2010) cite the manner in which ideology shapes racial categories and perceptions, which in turn gives rise to "equilibrium fictions." In order to maintain an exclusionary equilibrium, dominant groups can generate elaborate "fictions." Dominant groups can also generate rules regarding who can do what. In feudal times, for instance, members of a group wore badges—epaulettes, logos, or other symbols—to indicate their status. Only members of the preferred group could use these symbols. In many societies, groups can be distinguished by their dress, headgear, or jewelry. These signs are one way of differentiating people socially; they are also a way of keeping lower-status groups in their "place" and maintaining the social distance between dominant and subordinate groups. Although many of these symbols and practices break down in urban areas, where anonymity trumps the maintenance of old forms of symbolic power, new intersections between power and space may occur.

The normative structure is not the only driver of social exclusion; both history and the quality of institutions matter. Slavery, apartheid, and caste are all systems of social stratification that have created institutions and processes that have solidified into divisions between dominant and subordinate groups. Many of these systems have changed over the years and continue to do so. Yet the inexorable depth to which they have seeped into institutions and processes has rendered their dismantling more intractable. Divisions between groups, and between ethnic groups, often reflect colonial legacies, because colonial governance was often organized along ethnic lines, giving ethno-linguistic differences a fixity and social significance they had previously lacked (Mamdani 1996). At other times, ethnic or regional representation among key political power-holders often leads to some being considered "insiders" and others "outsiders."

Laws, policies, and programs can propel change, but they may also have unintended consequences. Thus, differential retirement ages for men and women in China are meant as a concession to women workers, as are laws meant to protect young female migrants from abuse overseas by enforcing a minimum age for their departure. But both can have potentially negative consequences—excluding older women from the labor market and creating conditions for poor young women to migrate without documentation (Das 2008, 2012).

Another study (Ebenstein 2010) links China's high ratios of males to females to the enforcement of its One Child Policy. It uses census data to show that fertility is lower and sex ratios higher among couples who are put under stricter fertility control. By exploiting regional and temporal variation in fines levied for "unauthorized births," it finds that higher-fine regimes discourage fertility but are associated with higher ratios of males to females.

Take also the case of child molesting in the United States. In a bid to be tough on child molesters, several states and local governments passed zoning laws prohibiting sex offenders from living within close proximity to schools, parks, playgrounds, day care centers, and other places where children congregate. Levenson and Hern (2007) show that these residence restrictions had adverse consequences for long-term integration of the offenders into family and society, ranging from housing instability to limited accessibility to employment opportunities, social services, and social support. Young adult offenders were especially affected, because residence restrictions limited affordable housing options and often prevented them from living with family members.

Some unintended consequences of policies and programs are the result of service providers' prejudices and preferences. For instance, service providers can reinforce and even exacerbate negative gender norms in the way they deal with patients or school children. The American Psychological Association (APA 2012) reports that teachers in the United States tend to perpetuate gender stereotypes in academic achievement, with lower expectations for boys' general academic skills, even after controlling for actual academic performance. African American boys are referred for disciplinary infractions more often than girls and nonminority children. This discipline gap appears to be related to behaviors that involve subjective interpretations; there are few ethnic and racial differences in referrals for behavior problems that are objectively identified, such as physical altercations and possession of weapons in schools.

Internalization of Exclusion

Negative stereotypes can have insidious effects when they are internalized in the belief systems of the excluded. They can, for instance, lead to low self-esteem, low aspirations, and potential group discouragement. The social psychology literature shows that people who maintain affiliations with a particular group echo the beliefs of that group, comply with its norms, and mimic the behavior of its members (Fiske 1998; Abrams and Hogg 1998).

A set of field experiments in the Greater Accra region of Ghana primed participants to make religious identity more salient and then measured the impact on altruism, trust, and trustworthiness. It found that increased salience of religious affiliation results in less altruism, trust, and trustworthiness toward members of other religions (Parra, Joseph, and Wodon 2013). Such internalization can also have insidious effects on the behavior of stigmatized individuals and groups, who may, for example, internalize stigma as a strategy of self-defense in the face of ostracism (Major and Eccleston 2005). This internalization may in turn perpetuate the same beliefs among their excluders that led to the exclusion in the first place.

There is now increasing evidence that exclusion, often conflated with "discrimination," can affect the performance of excluded groups. Perceived discrimination can alter both the expectations of jobseekers from the labor market and their future labor supply decisions (Goldsmith et al. 2004). Members of excluded groups may therefore become discouraged and drop out of the labor force.

Similar effects of "giving up" are evident in education. Students who know they will face discrimination may not bother to apply to higher-level institutions (Leonhardt 2013). Using controlled experiments with junior high school (grades 6 to 8) students from the historically most disadvantaged caste in a village in Uttar Pradesh, India, Hoff and Pandey (2006) find that beliefs shaped by a history of prejudicial treatment can have a significant impact on children's cognitive performance when opportunities are presented to them. Elmslie and Sedo (1996) use the concept of learned helplessness to show that negative events, such as an episode of discrimination, can lead to a decrease in learning ability. Exclusion therefore can create helplessness and resignation at both the group and the individual level, which in turn diminishes human capital, constrains effort, and becomes somewhat of a self-fulfilling prophecy. As Loury (1999, 17) notes:

> A psychological externality can occur when individuals draw on their own encounters with the market, and on the encounters of others to whom they are socially connected, to reach conclusions about, say, the extent to which effort accounts for market rewards—as opposed to ability or luck. In this scenario, the degree to which an individual believes that bad personal outcomes are a result of inadequate personal "effort" can depend on the aggregate experience of other members of the group.

A significant strand of the literature on policy preference places the onus of participation on the excluded group. It suggests that cultural preferences are in part responsible for the way in which some groups take advantage of or reject policies and programs. It hints that the nonparticipation by some groups is the result of their own choice, that they "self-exclude."

Recent empirical work suggests that policy preferences may indeed vary by ethnic group but that variation may reflect an objective evaluation of what that policy means for the group. Based on an analysis of Afrobarometer data from 18 countries, Lieberman and McClendon (2012) conclude that the variation of preferences is not merely an expression of socioeconomic differences or group-level differences. Instead, they suggest that citizens use ethnicity as a "heuristic for judging their own life chances" and that "the overall well-being of the group affects an individual's own self-esteem" (p. 20). They find more persistent disagreement about public policies among people from different politically relevant ethnic groups and where group disparities of wealth are high. Excluded groups therefore may accurately perceive their disadvantage and, on the basis of knowing that they will receive lower returns to any human capital assets they accumulate, rationally choose to invest less in those assets for themselves and their children (World Bank 2006; Hickey and du Toit 2007).

Groups that may seem as if they are rejecting a policy or program by not participating fully may well be rejecting the terms on which they are being asked to participate. These adverse terms could be in the form of mistreatment by service providers, lack of attention to traditional knowledge systems, or the design of policy. Some studies have focused on rejection of health services by tribal groups in India (box 2.2) and the Pygmy and other indigenous groups in Africa (Ohenjo et al. 2006).

BOX 2.2

Indigenous Women Rejecting the Terms of Inclusion

Evidence on the use of health care by indigenous or tribal communities in different parts of the world shows that inclusion in services needs to go beyond the provision of facilities. Members of these communities need to feel that they are being treated with respect and dignity.

The Indian National Family Health Survey, for example, reports that less than 20 percent of Adivasi women gave birth in a health facility until 2005, compared with a national average of 40 percent. Between 1998 and 2005, the incidence of home births declined at a much slower pace for Adivasi women than it did for other women.

When asked why they did not use a health facility, the majority of Adivasi women said they did not consider it necessary to do so (World Bank 2011b). This response is readily interpreted by service providers as a sign of "low demand" and tends to be attributed to ignorance. But a number of studies suggest that other factors, such as discrimination against and mistreatment of tribal groups, may be at play.

One of the few studies from the early 1990s, for instance, documents the cultural chasm between Adivasi clients and non-Adivasi service providers in the Indian state of Maharashtra (Government of Maharashtra, UNICEF, and WHO 1991). It found that negative stereotypes of Adivasis as dirty pervaded the mindset of the *anganwadi* (child development center) workers who provide supplementary nutrition and early childhood support to preschool children and pregnant and lactating women. For their part, Adivasi women felt that they were treated without respect. A recent audit of maternal deaths in Madhya Pradesh reported serious problems of accountability to tribal women and multiple cases of botched childbirths in health centers (Subha, Sarojini, and Renu 2012).

Similarly, qualitative research conducted by the World Bank in the Sierra region of Peru shows that lack of respect for cultural practices and values is one of the most important deterrents preventing women from seeking an institutional birth (World Bank 2011a). Asked why they did not deliver their baby at a health facility, women provided the following responses:

- Attention is provided by unknown people, who do not speak indigenous languages.
- Traditional practices are discredited.

(*continued next page*)

BOX 2.2 (*continued*)

- Family members are not allowed to be present, and husbands are not allowed to help in the birth.
- Modesty does not allow them to fully disrobe, as required by health personnel.
- Vaginal examinations and other intrusive procedures are performed too frequently; combined with cold rooms, excessive light, and doors being opened, they may damage the baby.
- Women are given "improper" food that upsets the balance between "hot" and "cold" humors.
- There is no rope (*soga*) for vertical births, and head wrapping and traditional herbal remedies are not allowed.
- Placentas are not disposed of according to their practice, and women are not allowed to keep them.
- Time for after-birth rest is limited, and women and their babies must leave earlier than is thought safe.

Sources: Government of Maharashtra, UNICEF, and WHO 1991; World Bank 2011a, 2011b; Subha, Sarojini, and Renu 2012.

Concluding Reflections

This chapter focused on the importance of processes, practices, and identities. Although these are clear drivers of exclusion, they can also be influenced for positive change. For instance, focusing on positive images or even positive stereotypes can improve the achievements of excluded groups. Women who read scientific essays asserting that there are no gender differences in mathematical ability perform better in mathematical problems (Dar-Nimrod and Heine 2006). Furthermore, positive perceptions—feelings of participation, belonging, and being respected in society—promote self-esteem and a sense of security. These perceptions have significant impacts on the way people experience objective conditions, adapt to their circumstances, and achieve a sense of fulfillment and happiness (Frey and Stutzer 2010). Positive feelings have also been shown to stimulate other factors that are related to ability, including self-regulation, creativity, divergent thinking, multitasking, and perseverance (Hall n.d.).

References

Abrams, D., and M. A. Hogg. 1998. "Prospects for Research in Group Processes and Intergroup Relations." *Group Processes and Intergroup Relations* 1 (1): 7–20.

Africa Progress Panel. 2012. *Jobs, Justice and Equity: Seizing Opportunities in Times of Change*. Africa Progress Report, Geneva.

APA (American Psychological Association). 2012. "Ethnic and Racial Disparities in Education: Psychology's Contributions to Understanding and Reducing Disparities." Presidential Task Force on Educational Disparities. http://www.apa.org/ed/resources/racial-disparities.aspx (accessed April 5, 2013).

Banaji, M. R., and A. G. Greenwald. 2013. *Blindspot: Hidden Biases of Good People*. New York: Delacorte Press.

Barker, G., R. Verma, J. Crownover, M. Segundo, V. Fonseca, J. M. Contreras, B. Heilman, and P. Pawlak. 2012. "Boys and Education in the Global South: Emerging Vulnerabilities and New Opportunities for Promoting Changes in Gender Norms." *Thymos: Journal of Boyhood Studies* 6 (2): 137–50.

Bolivian National Institute of Statistics. 2001. Estadísticas Sociales (database). http://www.ine.gob.bo.

Bourdieu, P. 1989. "Social Space and Symbolic Power." *Sociological Theory* 7 (1): 14–25.

———. 1991. *Language and Symbolic Power*. Cambridge, MA: Harvard University Press.

Burnham, L., N. Theodore, and B. Ehrenreich. 2012. *Home Economics: The Invisible and Unregulated World of Domestic Work*. New York: National Domestic Workers Alliance.

Cornell, B., and I. Welch. 1996. "Culture, Information and Screening Discrimination." *Journal of Political Economy* 104 (3): 542–71.

Covert, B. 2013. "How to Include Domestic Workers in Immigration Reform." *Nation*, February 12. http://www.thenation.com/blog/172846/how-include-domestic-workers-immigration-reform (accessed May 21, 2013).

Dar-Nimrod, I., and S. J. Heine. 2006. "Exposure to Scientific Theories Affects Women's Math Performance." *Science* 314 (5798): 435–35.

Das, M. B. 2008. "Minority Status and Labor Market Outcomes: Does India Have Minority Enclaves?" Policy Research Working Paper 4653, World Bank, Washington, DC.

———. 2012. "Stubborn Inequalities, Subtle Processes: Exclusion and Discrimination in the Labor Market." Background paper for the *World Development Report 2013*, World Bank, Washington, DC.

de Laat, Joost. 2010. "Roma Inclusion: An Economic Opportunity for Bulgaria, Czech Republic, Romania and Serbia." Policy Note, World Bank, Human Development Sector Unit, Washington, DC.

Deshpande, A., and K. Newman. 2007. "Where the Path Leads: The Role of Caste in Post-University Employment Expectations." *Economic and Political Weekly* 42 (41): 4133–40.

DFID (Department for International Development). 2007. *Taking Action against HIV Stigma and Discrimination: Guidance Document and Supporting Resources*. London. http://www.icrw.org/publications/taking-action-against-hiv-stigma-and-discrimination (accessed October 7, 2013).

Ebenstein, A. 2010. "The 'Missing Girls' of China and the Unintended Consequences of the One Child Policy." *Journal of Human Resources* 45 (1): 87–115.

Elmslie, B., and S. Sedo. 1996. "Discrimination, Social Psychology, and Hysteresis in Labor Markets." *Journal of Economic Psychology* 17 (4): 465–78.

Fiske, S. T. 1998. "Stereotyping, Prejudice, and Discrimination." In *The Handbook of Social Psychology*, 4th ed., ed. D. T. Gilbert, S. T. Fiske, and G. Lindzey. New York: McGraw-Hill.

Frey, B. S., and A. Stutzer. 2010. *Happiness and Economics: How the Economy and Institutions Affect Human Well-Being*. Princeton, NJ: Princeton University Press.

Goldsmith, A. H., S. Sedo, W. A. Darity, Jr., and D. Hamilton. 2004. "The Labor Supply Consequences of Perceptions of Employer Discrimination during Search and On-the-Job: Integrating Neoclassical Theory and Cognitive Dissonance." *Journal of Economic Psychology* 25 (1): 15–39.

Government of Maharashtra, UNICEF (United Nations Children's Fund), and WHO (World Health Organization). 1991. "Women and Children in Dharni: A Case Study of Villages after Fifteen Years of ICDS." Western India Office, UNICEF, Mumbai.

Hall, C. n.d. "The Power of Affirmation. Applying Behavioural Science in Real World." CFED (Corporation for Enterprise Development). http://cfed.org/programs/innovation/mhernandez/can_combating_self-perceived_stereotypes_change_behavior/# (accessed May 20, 2013).

Hall, G., and H. A. Patrinos, eds. 2012. *Indigenous Peoples, Poverty, and Development*. Cambridge, U.K.: Cambridge University Press.

Hersch, Joni. 2008. "Profiling the New Immigrant Worker. The Effects of Skin Color and Height." *Journal of Labor Economics* 26 (2): 345–86.

Hickey, S., and A. du Toit. 2007. "Adverse Incorporation, Social Exclusion and Chronic Poverty." CPRC Working Paper 81, Chronic Poverty Research Centre, University of Manchester, Manchester.

Hoff, K., and P. Pandey. 2006. "Discrimination, Social Identity, and Durable Inequalities." *American Economic Review* 96 (2): 206–11.

Hoff, K., and J. E. Stiglitz. 2010. "Equilibrium Fictions: A Cognitive Approach to Societal Rigidity." NBER Working Paper 15776, National Bureau of Economic Research, Cambridge, MA.

IBGE (Instituto Brasileiro de Geografia e Estatística). 2012. 2010 Brazilian Census. http://www.sidra.ibge.gov.br/cd/cd2010rpu.asp?o=6&i.

Jha, S., and M. Adelman. 2009. "Looking for Love in All the White Places: A Study of Skin Color Preferences on Indian Matrimonial and Mate-Seeking Websites." *Studies in South Asian Film and Media* 1: 65–83.

La Cava, G., and S. Michael. 2006. *Youth in the Northern Caucasus: From Risk to Opportunity*. World Bank, Europe and Central Asia Region, Environmentally and Socially Sustainable Development, Washington, DC.

Leonhardt, D. 2013. "Better Colleges Failing to Lure Talented Poor." *New York Times*, March 17. http://www.nytimes.com/2013/03/17/education/scholarly-poor-often-overlook-better-colleges.html?pagewanted=all (accessed October 7, 2013).

Levenson, J. S., and A. L. Hern. 2007. "Sex Offender Residence Restrictions: Unintended Consequences and Community Reentry." *Justice Research and Policy* 9 (1): 59–74.

Lieberman, E. S., and G. H. McClendon. 2012. "The Ethnicity–Policy Preference Link in Sub-Saharan Africa." *Comparative Political Studies* 46 (5): 574–602.

Loury, G. 1999. "Social Exclusion and Ethnic Groups: The Challenge to Economics." Paper presented at the Annual World Bank Conference on Development Economics, Washington, DC, April 28–30.

Major, B., and C. P. Eccleston. 2005. "Stigma and Social Exclusion." In *The Social Psychology of Inclusion and Exclusion*, ed. D. Abrams, M. A. Hogg, and J. M. Marques, 63–88. New York: Psychology Press.

Major, B., and L. T. O'Brien. 2005. "The Social Psychology of Stigma." *Annual Review of Psychology* 56: 393–421.

Mamdani, M. 1996. *Citizen and Subject*. Princeton, NJ: Princeton University Press.

Minnesota Population Center. 2011. Integrated Public Use Microdata Series, International: Version 6.1 (machine-readable database). University of Minnesota, Minneapolis.

Ogden, J., and L. Nyblade. 2005. *Common at Its Core: HIV–Related Stigma across Contexts*. International Center for Research on Women, Washington, DC.

Ohenjo, N., R. Willis, D. Jackson, C. Nettleton, K. Good, and B. Mugarura. 2006. "Health of Indigenous People in Africa." *Lancet* 367 (9526): 1937–46.

OSCE (Office for Democratic Institutions and Human Rights). 2009. *Assessment of the Human Rights Situation of Roma and Sinti in Italy*. Report of a Fact-Finding Mission to Milan, Naples and Rome. High Commissioner on National Minorities, Warsaw and The Hague. http://www.osce.org/odihr/36374.

Parra, J. C., G. Joseph, and Q. Wodon. 2013. "The Effects of Religion on Social Cooperation: Results from a Field Experiment in Ghana." Working Paper, World Bank, Washington, DC.

Sen, A. 2008. "Violence, Identity and Poverty." *Journal of Peace Research* 45 (1): 5–15.

Silver, H. 2007. "Social Exclusion: Comparative Analysis of Europe and Middle East Youth." Middle East Youth Initiative Working Paper 1, Dubai School of Government.

Subha, S. B., N. Sarojini, and K. Renu. 2012. "An Investigation of Maternal Deaths Following Public Protests in a Tribal District of Madhya Pradesh, Central India." *Reproductive Health Matters* 20 (39): 11–20.

van de Walle, D. 2011. "Lasting Welfare Effects of Widowhood in a Poor Country." Policy Research Working Paper 5734, World Bank, Washington, DC.

Villarreal, M. A. 2010. "US–Mexico Economic Relations: Trends, Issues, and Implications." Library of Congress, Washington, DC.

WHO (World Health Organization) and World Bank. 2011. *World Report on Disability*. World Health Organization, Geneva.

Women's Refugee Commission. 2012. *In Search of Safety and Solutions: Somali Refugee Adolescent Girls at Sheder and Aw Barre Camps, Ethiopia*. New York.

World Bank. 2006. *World Development Report 2006: Equity and Development*. Washington, DC: World Bank.

———. 2011a. *Peru Recurso Programmatic AAA—Phase IV: Improving Health Outcomes by Strengthening Users' Entitlements and Reinforcing Public Sector Management*. Washington, DC: World Bank.

———. 2011b. *Poverty and Social Exclusion in India*. Washington, DC: World Bank.

———. 2013. *World Development Indicators*. Washington, DC: World Bank.

CHAPTER 3

Inclusion in What? Through What Channels?

Living in better housing has implications for jobs. People say that earlier their shoes would be all mucky, and they would leave the house stressed; now they appear for jobs looking more respectable. Also, in the previous barrio there were no addresses, now they can put down an address when searching for jobs.

—BARRIO RESIDENT, LOS ALAMOS, COLOMBIA,
MOVING OUT OF POVERTY STUDY (WORLD BANK)

What Do Individuals and Groups Take Part In?

This chapter lays out three interrelated domains—markets, services, and spaces—within which individuals and groups take part in society. These domains represent both barriers to and opportunities for social inclusion. Just as the different dimensions of an individual's life intersect, so do the three domains (figure 3.1). Intervening in one domain without consideration for the others is likely to be one of the most important reasons for the limited success of policies and programs in reducing social exclusion.

Markets

In their day-to-day interactions, individuals and groups engage in society through four major markets—land, housing, labor, and credit. The four markets intersect at the individual and the household level.

Figure 3.1 Domains of Social Inclusion

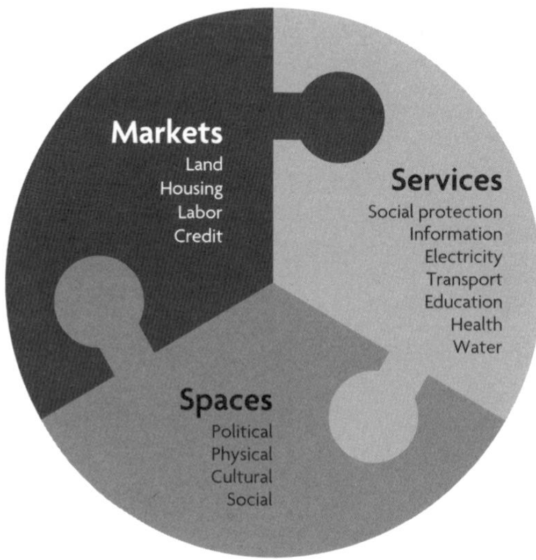

Land and housing markets. Land has been a historical driver of exclusion. The roots of exclusion of indigenous populations globally for instance, lie in significant part in the appropriation of their lands by their colonizers or other nonindigenous groups. Major social upheavals have been caused by unequal agrarian relations, which at once straddle land and labor markets.

In many parts of the world, women's historical lack of de facto access to land has underpinned their lack of enforceable property and other rights. Today, as large tracts of land are being acquired for commercial purposes, issues of land use and ownership—with their potential for exclusion of local smallholders—have again come to occupy the global stage (Deininger 2011).

Social exclusion through access to land is not just a rural phenomenon. Urban land markets are notoriously skewed in favor of the rich and powerful. Of late, laws that govern their use and sale have been the subject of considerable debate. One of the manifestations of exclusion from urban land markets is unequal access to housing, which creates negative externalities in other areas, such as sanitation.

On the side of inclusion, land ownership can confer status and security (see Deininger and Feder 1998; Carter 2000), especially for women, who are often denied equal shares of parental and other property. Panda and Agarwal (2005), for instance, find that ownership of land (but not any other asset) protects women from domestic violence. Realizing the importance of land in social and economic relations, Binswanger-Mkhize, Bourguignon, and van den Brink (2009) make a persuasive case for land redistribution for greater inclusion in countries that have had a history of inequalities based on land.

Labor markets. Like land markets, labor markets are crucial sites for the play of social relations. They reflect the existing and historical inequalities in a society and are tied up with social stratification (see Polanyi 1944). For instance, slavery was at its core an involuntary system of division of labor in which slaves worked on farms and plantations. Caste, similarly, is a system of occupational segregation that became a form of social stratification that systematically excluded certain groups.

Disparity in labor market outcomes is most visibly demonstrated by the gap in earnings between preferred and excluded groups. In their study of 18 Latin American countries, Ñopo, Atal, and Winder (2010) find sizable gender and ethnic wage gaps between indigenous and nonindigenous populations, partly as a result of disparities in education and other characteristics. However, there is an important net gender wage gap that cannot be explained by differences in measured human capital and other characteristics. It is likely driven by discrimination in both employment type and wages. The *World Development Report 2012: Gender Equality and Development* (World Bank 2012b) also finds unexplained gender wage gaps in all regions of the world, despite progress in overall gender wage gap reduction. The *World Development Report 2013: Jobs* (World Bank 2013) stresses the social value of jobs and makes a case for leveling the playing field in order to achieve higher-order goals.

Credit markets. Land and labor markets are intricately linked to credit markets, especially in developing societies. The most extreme form of coalescence between the three types of markets is forced labor, which still persists in many countries. In Nepal, for instance, as part of the Kamaiya and Haruwa/Charuwa systems, indebted families, often from the most disadvantaged castes, pledge themselves or their children to work because they cannot pay their debts to moneylenders, who are often also landowners. Under these labor arrangements, agricultural workers agree to bondage in return for advance payments of salary from landlords at rates far below minimum wages or in lieu of loans at very high interest rates. Workers attached to the labor market through bonded labor mechanisms are rarely able to accumulate sufficient savings to repay the bond and are thus effectively in serfdom for the remainder of their lives. The transition from bonded labor to greater labor freedom is fraught with risk, because freedom severs connections with former "employers," who provided housing and employment. Generating alternative means of livelihoods can leave former bonded laborers without shelter, income, or access to services (World Bank 2011).

The global push toward "financial inclusion" may be overtly about the penetration of financial instruments into untapped markets, but it is equally about social inclusion. In the current milieu, where social assistance and wages, even for unskilled workers, are increasingly being channeled through banks and other formal payment mechanisms, lack of access to financial systems is an important axis of exclusion. Financial services are, moreover, increasingly tied up with access to digital technology, such as smart cards and automatic teller machines, which may add an additional layer of exclusion to individuals and groups that are either uneducated or otherwise already disadvantaged.

In fragile and conflict-affected states, only 15 percent of adults have bank accounts (Demirgüç-Kunt, Klapper, and Randall 2013). Poor access to credit and shocks can affect minorities disproportionately in more developed financial markets, too, as evident in the mortgage crisis in the United States. Most of these foreclosures were on owner-occupied properties with mortgages that were originated between 2005 and 2008. The majority (an estimated 56 percent) of families who lost homes were non-Hispanic and white, but this is partly explained by the fact that more white families took loans. African Americans and Latinos were disproportionately affected relative to their share of mortgage originations. For example, although African Americans and Latinos received 26 percent of all loans to low-income borrowers, they accounted for about 33 percent of foreclosures in this income category. This pattern held for all income categories, mostly because borrowers of color were more likely to have received higher-rate subprime loans (Bocian, Li, and Ernst 2010).

Services

Access to services is essential to improving the terms on which individuals and groups take part in society. Health and education services enhance human capital. Social protection services cushion vulnerable groups against the effects of shocks and promote their well-being. Transport services enhance mobility, promote access to other services, and connect people to opportunities. Water and sanitation are essential for good health, and access to energy is important for maintaining one's livelihoods and building human capital. Information services enhance connectedness and allow individuals to take part in the "new economy."

The literature on ethnic diversity and provision of public services is divided on whether greater diversity improves access and quality or reduces it for members of a minority or subordinate group. Some experts argue that when the subordinate group is more numerous, it has a better chance of holding providers accountable and therefore gets better services (Guha 2007). Another strand of the literature claims that greater diversity in a service area improves access and quality for all. Whether service improves or not is to a great extent influenced by contextual factors, such as earnings at the local level, the extent of animosity among ethnic groups, and the institutional capacity to deliver services (see, for instance, Alesina, Baqir, and Easterly 1999).

Overall, subordinate groups tend to have lower access to and receive poorer quality of basic services. In rural areas of the Lao People's Democratic Republic, for example, estimates suggest that a higher proportion of women from the excluded community (non-Lao-Tai) never attended school (34 percent compared with 6 percent of Lao-Tai women). Men from the excluded group fare better than women, but still worse than the majority group: 17 percent of non-Lao-Tai men never attended school, compared with only 4 percent of Lao-Tai men. Disparities are also visible in access to health services. In Vietnam, where poverty reduction has been impressive, indigenous peoples are less likely to be covered by health programs or receive vital vaccinations, despite impressive improvements in overall access to health (Hall and Patrinos 2006, 2012). In South Africa, antenatal care has been free for almost two decades, but nonwhite women and those living in rural areas are less likely than white women to receive antenatal care or to have a skilled attendant present at the time of delivery (Burgard 2004; Say and Raine 2007; Silal et al. 2012). Data from African countries show that groups that speak minority languages as their mother tongue typically have lower access to services such as water and electricity. In Uganda, for instance, where electricity coverage is low in general, almost half the Muganda respondents in the 2010 Uganda Demographic and Health Survey reported having electricity, but less than 5 percent of the Lugbara and Ngakaramajong

Figure 3.2 Access to Electricity Varies by Ethnicity in Uganda, 2010

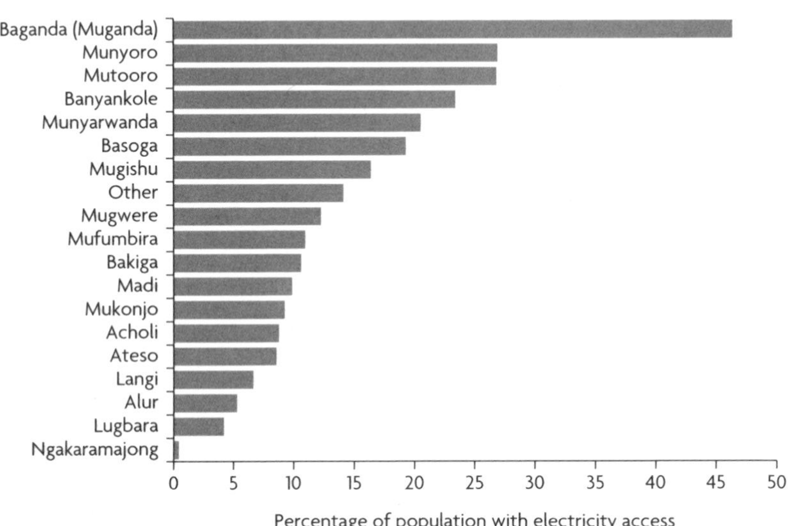

Source: World Bank, based on data from the Demographic and Health Survey 2011.
Note: Names of ethnic groups appear as they are in the survey.

did (figure 3.2). Similar results show up in self-reported water insecurity from the Afrobarometer: the Langi, the Ateso, and the Alur report the highest incidence of having experienced water insecurity "many times or always," whereas the Mutooro, Mukiga, and Munyankole are most likely to report never having experienced such insecurity (figure 3.3).

Because excluded or subordinate groups start from a low base, trends in improvements in access to services for them can be better than those for nonexcluded groups. Moreover, because they are often targeted for social assistance and other social protection programs, they are also over-represented among these programs' beneficiaries. In Vietnam, for example, indigenous people tend to receive a higher proportion of preferential credit; free health care; tuition exemption and reduction; and support for agriculture, forestry, and aquaculture. In India, indigenous people (especially the poorest 20 percent) are more likely to benefit from the Integrated Child Development Services program, and they appear well represented as beneficiaries of the National Rural Employment Guarantee program (Das et al. 2012). South Africa deliberately sought to equalize the coverage of its social assistance programs that had predominantly whites among the beneficiaries by targeting blacks (see chapter 7).

Figure 3.3 Water Insecurity Varies by Ethnicity in Uganda, 2009

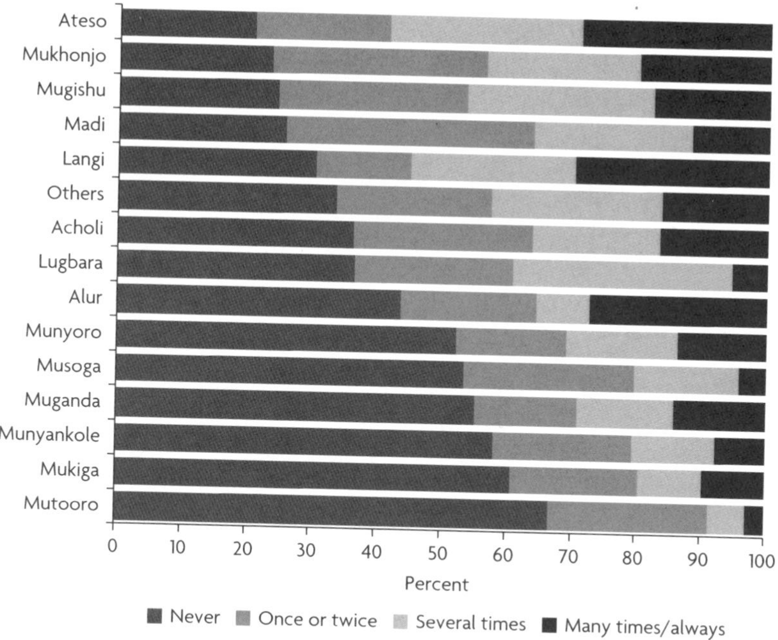

Source: World Bank, based on data from Afrobarometer 2008/09.
Note: Self-reported water insecurity for year preceding the survey. Names of ethnic groups appear as they are in the survey.

Spaces

A final domain of inclusion is space. At one level, the notion is esoteric and fluid. At another, it has been prolifically used in the sociology, political science, philosophy, and psychology literature. Both philosopher Michel Foucault and sociologist Pierre Bourdieu focused on the relationship between power, knowledge, and space. In fact, many of Foucault's ideas about space have been taken up by creative architects, who have sought to create urban spaces that seek to include rather than exclude.

Physical spaces have a social, political, and cultural character that solidifies systems and processes of exclusion. The most overt example of exclusion occurs when physical spaces are reserved for dominant groups, such as whites-only clubs during apartheid in South Africa or during slavery in the United States. Even today, literature in the United States suggests a subculture created by dominant groups to implicitly exclude minorities, even when they can afford to buy homes in their neighborhoods. Neighborhoods thus become white or black; the term "white flight" is used to document the departure of white families when black people start to move to their neighborhoods.

In his classic work on segregation, Schelling (1978) shows that aggregate segregation of neighborhoods can occur just from the desire of each individual not to belong to an extreme minority in his or her neighborhood. Each time a member of a minority moves out of an area, it becomes more likely that others will do so, which leads to extreme segregation in the aggregate. Black neighborhoods are considered poor or "bad" or unsafe, reflecting at once a judgment of the social and economic character of the neighborhood. Similarly, there is evidence to suggest that Dalits in India and Nepal are still sometimes barred from entering temples and other physical spaces considered "pure." Physical space has also been a focus of analysis in feminist geography (Women and Geography Study Group 1984; Rose 1993), with women often relegated to "interiors."

Excluded groups can react to their disadvantage by claiming certain spaces, but doing so can have mixed effects. Clustering in certain geographical areas can serve as opportunity enclaves for the excluded, who, when excluded from the primary market, concentrate in secondary markets, which they use for social and economic mobility (Wilson and Portes 1980; Portes and Jensen 1989). This phenomenon has been documented for Cubans in Miami and other immigrants who skirt discrimination by consolidating their positions in secondary markets. Not all strategies of clustering necessarily lead to social mobility, as illustrated in differential child mortality patterns in Ghana, where the Ga have higher mortality rates than other ethnic groups. Weeks et al. (2006) find a close association between ethnic differences in child mortality and residential clustering in Accra. The Ga live in one-room dwellings with poor amenities, exposing women and children to health risks. If the Ga woman is unmarried or is non-Christian, the risk of losing a child during birth increases further, regardless of where the woman lives.

Economic and social spaces are often linked to political space—an idea that simultaneously subsumes notions of voice, agency, and participation. Because at its core social inclusion is also about accountability of the state to its citizens, it is as much about political space as it is about having an equitable share in markets and services. It is not just poor people or traditionally excluded groups that demand greater voice and space: in the Arab Spring, a group of educated young people felt excluded from (mainly) political spaces. Contemporary movements for voice, accountability, and transparency underscore people's need for claiming space as citizens.

Poverty and minority status often compound the lack of access to political space. Many countries have seen a rolling back of state power since the 1980s, accompanied by a widening of economic opportunities. Yet state power continues to underpin many processes of exclusion and inclusion, and rent seeking becomes an important process of exclusion. For instance, the power to award mining leases or to sit in positions that can influence public sector hiring offers ample scope for kickbacks. Although politicians do not necessarily or exclusively favor their own ethnic or cultural group, groups with little or no political representation risk having their interests excluded from consideration (Marcus et al. 2013).

Being able to claim space is intrinsic to inclusion, because it facilitates freedom to think, act, aspire, and take up opportunities. Social psychologists have written prolifically about the impact of harassment, bullying, and similar acts of violence on individuals' ability to take part in society. In the 2011 National School Climate Survey of 8,584 American self-identified lesbian, gay, bisexual, and transgender (LGBT) students between the ages of 13 and 20, 82 percent reported having been verbally harassed (for example, called names or threatened) at school because of their sexual orientation, and 64 percent reported having been harassed because of their gender expression the previous year. Almost two-fifths of respondents reported experiencing physical harassment (for example, being pushed or shoved) at school in the past year because of their sexual orientation, and 55 percent reported cyberbullying (being harassed or threatened via electronic media) by their peers. Such psychological violence affects access to services, such as education, as well as the sense of self. For example, students who experienced higher levels of victimization because of their sexual orientation or gender identity were two to three times more likely than students who experienced lower levels of victimization to have missed school the previous month. They were also more than twice as likely to report that they did not plan to pursue postsecondary education (for example, college or trade school) and to suffer from depression and low self-esteem (Kosciw et al. 2012). Although LGBT students were harassed because of other characteristics as well, their religious or ethnic identities were not nearly as important as their sexual identities (figure 3.4).

Figure 3.4 LGBT Students in the United States Feel Unsafe for Many Reasons

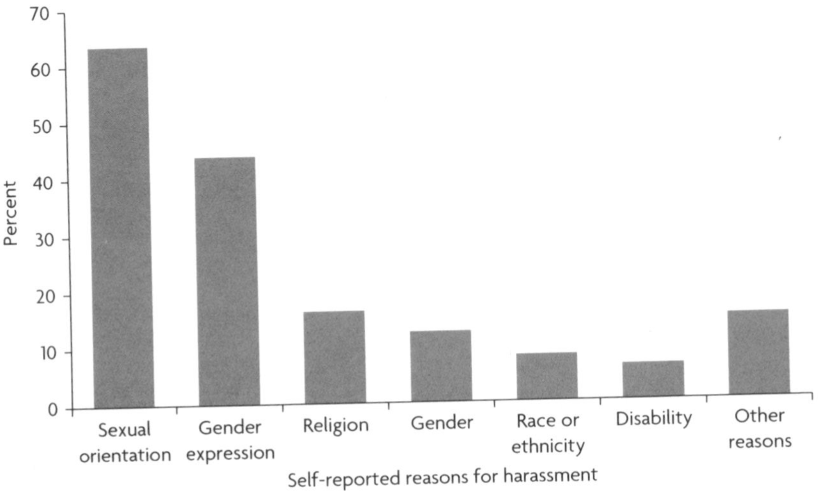

Source: Kosciw et al. 2012.
Note: Self-reported reasons for harassment. The nationally representative sample consisted of 8,584 lesbian, gay, bisexual, and transgender (LGBT) students between the ages of 13 and 20 from 3,224 school districts.

What Influences the Terms on Which Individuals and Groups Take Part in Society?

This report considers three related channels through which inclusion can be enhanced: ability, opportunity, and dignity (figure 3.5). All three channels act in tandem to produce the conditions on the basis of which people can take part in society. All three are also dependent on the background and social standing of the individual or group. In fact, it is sometimes difficult to tell whether a poor outcome reflects poor ability or poor opportunity, the roots of which go back to a previous generation.

Ability

Ability is innate to individuals. However, ability, when measured through achievement tests, may not be randomly distributed. Instead, it can be a function of family background and intergenerational endowments.

The literature on early childhood education indicates that the brain starts to develop in utero. Although brains are elastic enough to compensate for maternal or other in utero deprivations, they may not be able to fully do so. In addition, depriving children of stimulation and nutrition

Figure 3.5 What Affects the Terms on Which People Take Part in Society?

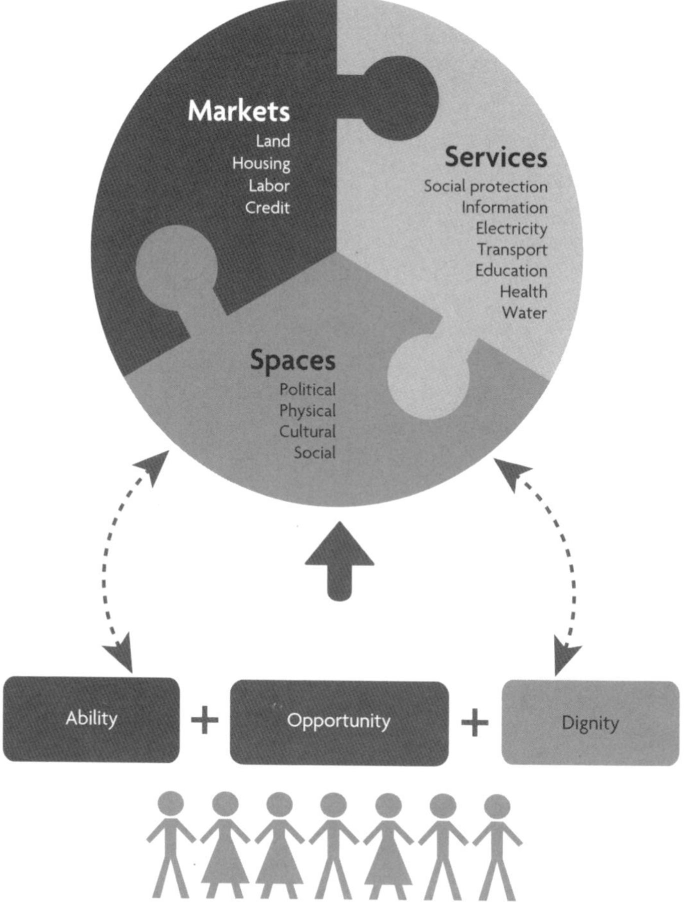

in their early months and years permanently affects their development. Children born with low birthweight to very young mothers, for instance, start life with poor initial conditions. The empirical literature documents the adverse effects of hunger and malnutrition on the performance of children.

A child's development, however, is not a matter of genes alone. Both neuroscience and social science research shows that the social environment, particularly of the family, affects a child's development. Taking a cue from these facts, James Heckman (2012) makes a strong case for "predistribution," arguing that investment in very young children could compensate for the exclusion their parents may have faced. Such early investment could help arrest to some extent the intergenerational transmission of the outcomes of exclusion. Using U.S. data, Heckman shows that cognitive and noncognitive skills (such as motivation, ability to work on long-term plans, and the social skills needed to work with others) are equally predictive of many social outcomes: a 1 percent increase in either type of ability has a roughly equal effect, for instance, on reducing undesirable outcomes such as teenage pregnancy. Individuals with high levels of cognitive and noncognitive skills are also less likely to be incarcerated. In fact, for the lowest deciles, the drop in incarceration is greater for noncognitive than cognitive ability (Heckman 2012).

The average endowments of their ethnic group can also have an impact on individuals' abilities. Borjas (1992) outlines the notion of "ethnic capital" to show that individuals who are members of high-performing groups tend to perform better than individuals from other groups. Earlier chapters discussed the depressing effect of exclusion on the performance of disadvantaged groups and the fact that when identity is made salient these groups perform worse than their potential would have predicted (Hoff and Pandey 2004). This report argues elsewhere that reference groups and role models are important in the "capacity to aspire," to use the coinage of anthropologist Arjun Appadurai. When disadvantaged groups see others around them performing at a low level, they set a much lower bar than they would have if they belonged to high-performing groups.

Some of the research on female employment finds that even after controlling for a range of household and demographic characteristics, women's employment outcomes are significantly correlated with the extent of gender inequality at the cluster or village level (Das and Desai 2003). Ability and achievement can therefore be said to be socially mediated.

Opportunity

Inequality of opportunity is one of the major constraints to the realization of human potential. Recent work on the Human Opportunities Index (HOI) underscores this fact and focuses policy attention on investments that equalize opportunities at the beginning of the life cycle. The HOI measures advances in the supply of basic opportunities (health, safe water, education) to children, with a goal of universal coverage. It aims to level the playing field in the provision of these services in order to equalize opportunity

(Molinas et al. 2012). The underlying assumption is that equalizing the supply of these services gives all individuals an equal chance of translating their capabilities into enhanced well-being. The HOI places emphasis on children, given evidence that interventions to equalize opportunity early in life are most efficient.

This report takes the idea of equality of opportunity further. It argues that identity can constrain both the supply of and the demand for opportunity.

Providing full opportunity is not only an institutional challenge in many countries; the process of expanding opportunities can itself be exclusionary. Take the case of health facilities in remote areas where the indigenous women described in box 2.2 in chapter 2 live. These women live in such remote areas that getting services to them that are of the same quality and quantity as those provided to their urban counterparts is fiscally and institutionally challenging. The placement of health centers often depends on the voice of the residents. Some of the most remote residents also have the weakest voice. Even if health centers are available, quality can be uneven, because medical staff is often absent. Moreover, there is also "low demand" for facilities, or of opportunity, for a number of reasons. The indignity and humiliation they experience at the hands of service providers deter women from wanting to go to the facility. Demand for the opportunity to give birth in a health facility could also be physically constrained by threats and violence, as dominant groups in some areas prevent subordinate groups from accessing markets, services, and spaces.

Opportunity is also mediated by the special needs of some groups. Because of initial conditions, including innate characteristics (such as disability status) or life experiences, some people may require remedial efforts in order to access the same degree of opportunity. An estimated 12–16 percent of all children in the United States come into the school system with a disability that hampers their ability to learn (AAP 2001). Children with disabilities who receive targeted support in addition to schooling are more likely to graduate, find employment, and live independently (Shonkoff and Meisels 2000). Yet remedial services are seriously deficient, mirroring the wider social, economic, and political exclusion of persons with disabilities worldwide (Yeo and Moore 2003).

As another example, an estimated 3 million children work in the sex trade around the world. Even if they are removed from these circumstances, catching up with their peers who are already in regular school settings will require additional help, in the form of medical care, economic

BOX 3.1

Internalizing Exclusion, and Dropping out of School

Low-income students have always trailed their richer peers in school performance, but these gaps have been widening in recent years. In the United States, class has overtaken race as a predictor of academic success (DeParle 2012). Economic inequality drives these growing gaps.

The rich have gotten richer, and wealthy parents are outspending their lower-income counterparts on their children's education. They pay for enrichment activities such as sports, music lessons, and summer camps. They hire coaches to support their children academically. Poorer children not only compete against peers whose parents have more money to spend. They also suffer from perceptions—from family, friends, society, and not least themselves—that can become major obstacles in their uphill struggle.

Angelica Gonzalez, a young woman from a struggling, low-income family in Galveston, Texas, seemed to have beaten the odds: despite attending a high school in Galveston, Texas, deemed "academically unacceptable," she still managed to do extraordinarily well, ranking at the 84th percentile nationwide for the math and reading portions of the Standardized Aptitude Test (SAT). Her dream was to get into college and to do better than her mother and grandmother, who worked at Walmart, always struggling to make ends meet.

But when Angelica makes it into Emory University—a top-ranked institution in Atlanta, Georgia—her family mocks her, saying "Now you go to some big fancy school!" Her boyfriend does not see the point of her getting a degree either. He wants her to work in her dad's local furniture store instead.

College does not start well for Angelica. She fails to access the extensive financial support Emory would have granted her. Emory costs nearly $50,000 a year, but it is one of the few top schools that promises to meet the financial needs of any student good enough to be admitted. But Angelica fails to fill in the financial aid forms correctly, partly because she does not know how to get hold of her father, from whom she needs financial details. As a result, Emory keeps underestimating her needs. Angelica senses that something has gone wrong, but she doesn't complain. Her reaction is not uncommon: poor students and their parents are much less likely to challenge institutions than their middle-income peers. They are not used to institutions responding to them. Angelica gets a private loan instead. To protect her mother from worries, she has

(box continues next page)

BOX 3.1 *(continued)*

her boyfriend co-sign her bank loan. In return, her boyfriend asks her to get engaged—binding her future to him and the furniture store.

On campus, Angelica often feels alienated from her richer peers. She sometimes feels as if she is the only one on campus without a credit card. Her roommate moves out without explanation. A professor suggests she consider cheaper schools, so she does not need to spend so much time working after school to pay her bills. That's the beginning of the end. "It was pretty clear if I couldn't afford to be there, I shouldn't waste her time." Depressed, Angelica fails the professor's course, starts skipping more classes and working longer hours. She finally drops out without a degree.

Three and a half years after enrolling at Emory, she is back in Galveston. She works as a clerk in her boyfriend's furniture store, earning $8.50 an hour, struggling to pay back the loan that never got her a degree.

Source: DeParle 2012.

support, and remedial therapy and counseling, before they can successfully take up educational opportunities (Kristof and WuDunn 2010).

Finally, opportunity is dynamic over the life cycle and over life events. Equalizing opportunities at the beginning of the life cycle does not ensure the capacity for equal outcomes over time. There are critical junctures in the life cycle, including first entry into the job market and job searches for career advancement, when both demand and supply factors play an important role in reallocating opportunity. There are also catastrophic and unforeseen events, such as economic crises and natural disasters, which reallocate opportunity, with unequal impacts on population subgroups. In the recent financial crisis in the United States, for instance, African Americans were twice as likely as whites to lose their jobs, and it took them much longer to regain employment (Lynch 2012).

Dignity

In an article in *Foreign Policy*, historian Leon Aron (2011) lays out the implications of dignity, which often have nothing to do with poverty but with feeling alienated and unrespected:

> From the Founding Fathers to the Jacobins and Bolsheviks, revolutionaries have fought under essentially the same banner: advancement of

> human dignity.... "Dignity before bread!" was the slogan of the Tunisian revolution. The Tunisian economy had grown between 2 and 8 percent a year in the two decades preceding the revolt. With high oil prices, Libya on the brink of uprising also enjoyed an economic boom of sorts. Both are reminders that in the modern world, economic progress is not a substitute for the pride and self-respect of citizenship.

The idea that dignity matters for individuals and groups is not new for development theory and practice. The word *dignity* is mentioned in several human rights covenants and charters. It appears in the Preamble of the Charter of the United Nations, is referred to in Article 1 of the Universal Declaration of Human Rights, and appears in Article 10 of the International Covenant on Civil and Political Rights, which states that "all persons deprived of their liberty shall be treated with humanity and with respect for the inherent dignity of the human person." Amartya Sen's idea of capabilities (Sen 1999) encompasses the notion of human dignity, as does Nussbaum's list of 10 "central human capabilities" (Nussbaum 2000).

Although rooted in philosophy and human rights activism, the idea of dignity is increasingly gaining currency in mainstream economic, social, and political thought. In his analysis of protest movements across the world, journalist Thomas Friedman (2012) speaks of the "politics of dignity." The application of the idea of "social recognition" is becoming increasingly common in companies, whose human resource departments seek to recognize diversity and pluralism in the organization as a way to promote productivity and belongingness to the organization.

Dignity as it relates to social inclusion is intrinsically linked to respect and recognition. When, through their institutions and norms, dominant cultures and processes actively disrespect individuals and groups who are considered subordinate, those individuals or groups can either opt out, as argued earlier, submit, or protest (box 3.2). As Appiah (2006) writes:

> Since ... old restrictions suggested substantially negative norms of identification, constructing a life with dignity entails developing positive norms of identification instead.... But if one is to be out of the closet in a society that deprives homosexuals of equal dignity and respect, then one must constantly deal with assaults on one's dignity. Thus, the right to live as an "open" homosexual is not enough. It is not even enough to be treated with equal dignity *despite* being homosexual, for that would mean accepting that being homosexual counts to some degree against one's dignity. Instead, one must ask to be respected *as* gay. [Author's emphasis.]

BOX 3.2

Self-Exclusion or Self-Defense? Quilombos, the "Runaway" Slave Communities in Brazil

Africans who came to Latin America as slaves and their descendants were integrated into the local social and economic structures under unmentionable conditions. Not surprisingly, many slaves escaped ("marooned") and settled in remote areas. Although the majority of settlements disbanded after the abolition of slavery, some have persisted until today. Current residents of these semi-autonomous communities are known by various names, including *quilombola, mocambo, palenquero*, and the more general *cimarrón*.

For more than a century, these enclaves were ignored by the state and largely isolated from the rest of society. Isolation enabled these people to preserve their unique cultures, but it prevented them from benefiting from advances in living standards.

In Brazil, the First National Meeting of Quilombola Communities took place in 1995. It produced an official document that called for land registration and social policies for these communities. In 2003, only 724 *quilombola* communities were recognized as such. With the incorporation of the Brazil Quilombola Program into the national plan, the government granted rights, including land ownership rights, to 3,524 self-identified *quilombola* communities and promoted their social and economic inclusion.

Piggybacking on an immunization campaign, a government-sponsored study on *quilombolas* conducted in 2006 quantifies the conditions of these communities. Their settlements are relatively small; about half have fewer than 300 people, and three-quarters have fewer than 200 houses, though *quilombola* families tend to be multigenerational. A majority of *quilombola* enclaves have electricity, but only a quarter have trash collection or are connected to a public sewerage system. Only half of household heads have more than four years of schooling.

The heightened attention to *quilombolas* has translated into concerted efforts by the Brazilian government and civil society for social inclusion on *quilombola* terms. Policies, particularly in education and health, are tailored to *quilombola* heritage and way of life.

A World Bank and Japanese Trust Fund project targeting more than 15,000 *quilombola* families in three Brazilian states used a consultative process to identify

(box continues next page)

BOX 3.2 *(continued)*

community needs and appropriate forms of integration. Since its launch in 2009, the initiative has helped found more than 50 community associations and provided funding and technical assistance for agriculture and local crafts. The project is also bringing telephone and Internet connections to the *quilombolas*, integrating these long-isolated communities into the national and global network on their own terms.

Sources: Kent 1965; Price 1996; MDS 2008; Girard 2011; World Bank 2012a.

Feelings of being treated with dignity and respect can promote trust and social harmony. Lister (2004, 2008) looks at recognition as it relates to political participation, arguing that it is emblematic of the notion of social inclusion. Drawing from projects such as the All Together in Dignity Fourth World movement, she finds that recognition is highly relevant to inclusion through the avenues of participation and voice. For example, she discusses how participants of various projects find "the experience of being listened to and taken seriously unusual," because they were often treated with disrespect. They complained that people with political and social power did not think of them as "human beings with the rights and capacities to participate in public debate" (Holman 1998, 16, quoted in Lister 2004).

Recognition, which is a core aspect of dignity, can be literal and symbolic. Lack of recognition renders some individuals and groups invisible. They are often not counted in official statistics, for a variety of reasons. For instance, in many cultures, a disabled member of the household is not reported in the household roster when survey personnel come to conduct interviews. In other cases, groups such as refugees who cross borders without documents are also not counted. Other undocumented people include stateless people and legal citizens who lack documents to prove their residency or eligibility for various benefits.

Like many of the processes and practices discussed earlier, ideas of dignity—of according dignity or being treated without dignity—are measurable. The empirical literature on dignity has been led by medical ethicists and advocates of respectful treatment of patients, especially the terminally ill, the elderly, and people with significant physical and cognitive impairments, at the hands of medical providers. Using data from the Commonwealth Fund 2001 Health Care Quality Survey of 6,722 adults in the United States, Beach et al. (2005) analyze the association between two measures of respect (involvement in decisions and treatment with dignity) and patient outcomes (satisfaction, adherence, and receipt of optimal preventive care). After controlling for respondents' demographic characteristics, they show that the probability of reporting a high level of satisfaction is higher for people treated with dignity. Being involved in decisions was significantly associated with adherence to treatment for whites, whereas being treated with dignity was significantly associated with adherence for racial or ethnic minorities. Because measures of dignity are still being developed, the terms *dignity, respect,* and *recognition* are often used interchangeably.

Surveys reveal negative attitudes toward traditionally excluded groups, even in countries where formal institutions embody principles of equality, recognition, and respect. For example, the Life in Transition Survey—conducted jointly by the European Bank for Reconstruction and Development and the World Bank in 29 transition economies and 5 Western European countries in 2010—reveals that large percentages of the population are unwilling to live in the same neighborhood with homosexuals (55 percent of respondents), Roma (49 percent), and people living with HIV/AIDS (43 percent). Many other groups—immigrants, people with a different religion or race, and cohabitating unmarried couples—also shared the experience of being unwanted (table 3.1).

A 2011 survey in China of 128,000 migrants in urban areas asked respondents whether they thought migrants were "always looked down on" in the cities in which they lived. Between one-third and one-fourth of urban migrants thought they were always looked down on by locals, a finding that varied little with age or education (figure 3.6). Feelings of being looked down on increased with the length of stay in the city, suggesting that migrants encountered unpleasant behavior if they stayed long enough and interacted with more people. The survey also asked migrants about their feelings of happiness. It found that happiness is positively correlated with feelings of being integrated and of liking their city. But across the board, and at the multivariate level, people with higher levels of education were significantly unhappier than their less educated counterparts—despite the fact that education is negatively correlated with feelings of being looked down on. This finding implies that happiness and dignity are not the same and that educated migrants, especially younger people, may have higher aspirations and unmet needs (Shi 2012).

Table 3.1 Unwanted Neighbors across Europe and Central Asia

Group	Percentage of respondents not wanting group as neighbor
Drug addicts	83
Pedophiles	81
Heavy drinkers	69
Homosexuals	55
Roma	49
People who have HIV/AIDS	43
Immigrants or foreign workers	16
People of a different race	14
Jewish people	11
People of a different religion	10
Unmarried couples living together	9
People who speak a different language	7
Poor people	6
Elderly people	4
Families with children	4

Source: Lakhani, Sacks, and Heltberg 2012, based on results of Life in Transition Survey.

Concluding Reflections

This report defines social inclusion in two ways. The first is a broad sweep that defines it as "the process of improving the terms for individuals and groups to take part in society." A second, sharper definition takes into account how the terms can be improved and for whom. It articulates social inclusion as "the process of improving the ability, opportunity and dignity of people, disadvantaged on the basis of their identity, to take part in society."

Part I of this report discussed the fact that social inclusion is both a process and an outcome. It spans different levels of people (individuals, groups, and entire societies) who take part in markets, services, and spaces. In addition, markets, services, and spaces are interrelated categories, and intervention in one domain can have effects on another. Although identities affect the manner and extent of inclusion, no one is fully excluded from or fully included in his or her social universe. It is the intersection of identities that confers advantage or disadvantage. The process of making sure that individuals and groups can take part on terms that are acceptable to them is

Figure 3.6 Migrants in Urban China Speak of "Being Looked Down on" by Locals, 2011

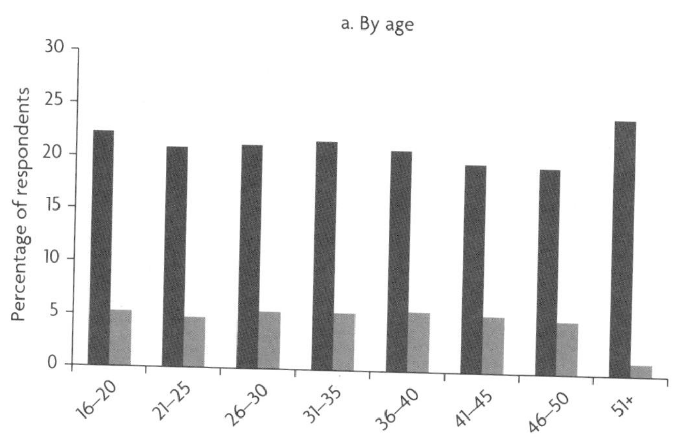

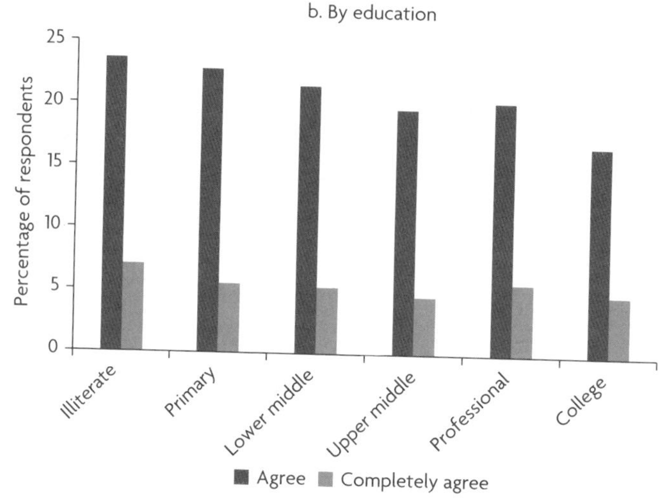

Source: Shi 2012.

Note: Based on responses to the question, "Do you agree with the view that migrants are always looked down on by locals?" in the 2011 Migrant Survey conducted by the National Health and Family Planning Commission of the People's Republic of China.

the essence of social inclusion. It can be achieved by enhancing the abilities, opportunities, and dignity of individuals and groups. These three channels are also interrelated and overlapping. Chapters 4–8 discuss why the imperative for social inclusion is so urgent and how change can be influenced.

References

AAP (American Academy of Pediatrics). 2001. "The Continued Importance of Supplemental Security Income (SSI) for Children and Adolescents with Disabilities." *Pediatrics* 107 (4): 790–93.

Alesina, A., R. Baqir, and W. Easterly. 1999. "Public Goods and Ethnic Divisions." *Quarterly Journal of Economics* 114 (4): 1243–84.

Appiah, K. A. 2006. "The Politics of Identity." *Daedalus* 135 (4): 15–22. http://www.scribd.com/doc/163184582/The-Politics-of-Identity-Appiah.

Aron, L. 2011. "Everything You Think You Know about the Collapse of the Soviet Union Is Wrong." *Foreign Policy*, July/August. http://www.foreignpolicy.com/node/848301 (accessed April 5, 2013).

Beach, M. C., J. Sugarman, R. L. Johnson, J. J. Arbelaez, P. S. Duggan, and L. A. Cooper. 2005. "Do Patients Treated with Dignity Report Higher Satisfaction, Adherence, and Receipt of Preventive Care?" *Annals of Family Medicine* 3 (4): 331–38.

Binswanger-Mkhize, H. P., C. Bourguignon, and R. van den Brink, eds. 2009. *Agricultural Land Redistribution: Towards Greater Consensus*, Washington, DC: World Bank.

Bocian, D. G., W. Li, and K. S. Ernst. 2010. *Foreclosures by Race and Ethnicity: The Demographics of a Crisis*. CRL Research Report, Centre for Responsible Lending, Durham, NC. http://www.responsiblelending.org/mortgage-lending/research-analysis/foreclosures-by-race-and-ethnicity.pdf.

Borjas, G. J. 1992. "Ethnic Capital and Intergenerational Mobility." *Quarterly Journal of Economics* 107 (1): 123–50.

Burgard, S. 2004. "Race and Pregnancy-related Care in Brazil and South Africa." *Social Science and Medicine* 59 (6): 1127–46.

Carter, M. R. 2000. "Land Ownership Inequality and the Income Distribution Consequences of Economic Growth." Working Paper, World Institute for Development Economics Research, Helsinki. http://www.wider.unu.edu/publications/working-papers/previous/en_GB/wp-201/_files/82530864866142466/default/wp201.pdf.

Das, M. B., and S. Desai. 2003. *Why Are Educated Women Less Likely to Be Employed in India? Testing Competing Hypotheses*. Social Protection Paper, World Bank, Washington, DC.

Das, M. B., G. Hall, S. Kapoor, and D. Nikitin. 2012. "India: The Scheduled Tribes." In *Indigenous Peoples, Poverty, and Development*, ed. G. Hall and H. A. Patrinos, 205–49. Cambridge, U.K.: Cambridge University Press.

Deininger, K. 2011. "Challenges Posed by the New Wave of Farmland Investment." *Journal of Peasant Studies* 38 (2): 217–47.

Deininger, K., and G. Feder. 1998. "Land Institutions and Land Markets." Policy Research Working Paper 2014, World Bank, Washington, DC. http://go.worldbank.org/BEIQ75PPY0.

Demirgüç-Kunt, A., L. Klapper, and D. Randall. 2013. "The Global Findex Database. Financial Inclusion in Fragile and Conflict-Affected States." Findex Notes, World Bank, Washington, DC. http://inec.usip.org/resource/global-findex-database-financial-inclusion-fragile-and-conflict-affected-states.

DeParle, J. 2012. "For Poor, Leap to College Often Ends in a Hard Fall." *New York Times*, December 22. http://www.nytimes.com/2012/12/23/education/poor-students-struggle-as-class-plays-a-greater-role-in-success.html?pagewanted=all (accessed October 7, 2013).

Friedman, T. L. 2012. "The Politics of Dignity." *New York Times*, January 31. http://www.nytimes.com/2012/02/01/opinion/friedman-the-politics-of-dignity.html (accessed January 14, 2013).

Girard, P. R. 2011. *The Slaves Who Defeated Napoleon: Toussant Louverture and the Haitian War of Independence, 1801–1804*. Tuscaloosa, AL: University of Alabama Press.

Guha, R. 2007. "Adivasis, Naxalites and Indian Democracy." *Economic and Political Weekly* 42 (32): 3305–12.

Hall, G. H., and H. A. Patrinos, eds. 2006. *Indigenous Peoples, Poverty, and Human Development in Latin America*. New York: Palgrave Macmillan.

———. 2012. *Indigenous Peoples, Poverty, and Development*. Cambridge, U.K.: Cambridge University Press.

Heckman, J. 2012. "Promoting Social Mobility." *Boston Review*, September/October. http://www.bostonreview.net/forum/promoting-social-mobility-james-heckman (accessed October 7, 2012).

Hoff, K., and P. Pandey. 2004. "Belief Systems and Durable Inequalities: An Experimental Investigation of Indian Caste." Policy Research Working Paper 3351, World Bank, Washington, DC.

Holman, B. 1998. *Faith in the Poor*. Oxford, U.K.: Lion.

Kent, R. K. 1965. "Palmares: An African State in Brazil." *Journal of African History* 6 (2): 161–75.

Kosciw, J. G., E. A. Greytak, M. J. Bartkiewicz, M. J. Boesen, and N. A. Palmer. 2012. *The 2011 National School Climate Survey: The Experiences of Lesbian, Gay, Bisexual and Transgender Youth in Our Nation's Schools*. New York: GLSEN (Gay, Lesbian & Straight Education Network). http://glsen.org/download/file/MzIxOQ==.

Kristof, N. D., and S. Wudunn. 2010. *Half the Sky: How to Change the World.* London: Virago.

Lakhani, S., A. Sacks, and R. Heltberg. 2012. "Unwelcome Neighbors: Understanding Social Exclusion." Background paper draft, World Bank, Washington, DC.

Lister, R. 2004. "A Politics of Recognition and Respect: Involving People with Experience of Poverty in Decision-Making That Affects Their Lives." In *The Politics of Inclusion and Empowerment: Gender, Class and Citizenship*, ed. J. Andersen and B. Siim, 116–39. London: Palgrave.

———. 2008. "Recognition and Voice: the Challenge for Social Justice." In *Social Justice and Public Policy: Seeking Fairness in Diverse Societies*, ed. G. Craig, D. Gordon, and T. Burchardt, 105–22. Bristol, U.K.: Policy Press at the University of Bristol.

Lynch, D. 2012. "First Black President Can't Help Blacks Stem Wealth Drop." *Bloomberg News,* September 5.

Marcus, R., S. Espinoza, L. Schmidt, and S. Sultan. 2013. "Social Exclusion in Africa: Towards More Inclusive Approaches." Background paper draft, World Bank, Washington, DC.

MDS (Ministério do Desenvolvimento Social e Combate à Fome). 2008. "Políticas sociais e chamada nutricional Quilombola: estudos sobre condições de vida nas comunidades e situação nutricional das crianças (Social Policies and Nutrition Call Quilombola: Studies on Living Conditions in Communities and Nutritional Status of Children)." *Cadernos de Estudos Desenvolvimento Social em Debate* 9, Brasília.

Molinas, V., J. R., R. Paes de Barros, C. J. Saavedra, M. Giugale, L. J. Cord, C. Pessino, and A. Hasan. 2012. *Do Our Children Have a Chance? A Human Opportunity Report for Latin America and the Caribbean.* Washington, DC: World Bank.

Ñopo, H., J. P. Atal, and N. Winder. 2010. "New Century, Old Disparities: Gender and Ethnic Wage Gaps in Latin America." IZA Discussion Paper 5085, Institute for the Study of Labor, Bonn.

Nussbaum, M. C. 2000. *Women and Human Development: The Capabilities Approach.* Cambridge: Cambridge University Press.

Panda, P., and B. Agarwal. 2005. "Marital Violence, Human Development and Women's Property Status in India." *World Development* 33 (5): 823–50.

Polanyi, Karl. 1944. *The Great Transformation.* Boston: Beacon Hill.

Portes, A., and L. Jensen. 1989. "The Enclave and the Entrants: Patterns of Ethnic Enterprise in Miami before and after Mariel." *American Sociological Review* 54: 929–49.

Price, R., ed. 1996. *Maroon Societies: Rebel Slave Communities in the Americas.* Baltimore, MD: Johns Hopkins University Press.

Rose, G. 1993. *Feminism and Geography.* Cambridge, U.K.: Polity Press.

Say, L., and R. Raine. 2007. "A Systematic Review of Inequalities in the Use of Maternal Health Care in Developing Countries: Examining the Scale of the Problem and the Importance of Context." *Bulletin of the World Health Organization* 85 (10): 812–19.

Schelling, T. C. 1978. *Micromotives and Macrobehavior*. New York: Norton.

Sen, A. 1999. "The Possibility of Social Choice." *American Economic Review* 89 (3): 349–78.

Shi, L. 2012. "Migration and Social Inclusion: Analysis of the Well Being of Rural Migrants in China." Background paper draft, World Bank, Washington, DC.

Shonkoff, J. P., and S. J. Meisels. 2000. *Handbook of Early Childhood Intervention*, vol. 2. Cambridge, U.K.: Cambridge University Press.

Silal, S., L. Penn-Kekana, H. Bronwyn, S. Birch, and D. McIntyre. 2012. "Exploring Inequalities in Access to and Use of Maternal Health Services in South Africa." *BMC Health Services Research* 12 (1): 120.

Weeks, J. R., A. G. Hill, A. Getis, and D. Stow. 2006. "Ethnic Residential Patterns as Predictors of Intra-Urban Child Mortality Inequality in Accra, Ghana." *Urban Geography* 27 (6): 526–48.

Wilson, K. L., and A. Portes. 1980. "Immigrant Enclaves: An Analysis of the Labor Market Experiences of Cubans in Miami." *American Journal of Sociology* 86 (2): 295–319.

Women and Geography Study Group. 1984. "Special Women and Geography Group Circular." Women and Geography Study Group, Institute of British Geographers/Royal Geographical Society, Collections of the Royal Geographical Society (with IBG), London.

World Bank. 2011. "Social Safety Nets in Nepal." Draft report, Washington, DC.

———. 2012a. "In Brazil, Descendants of Escaped Slaves Seek to Overcome Isolation and Poverty." World Bank, Washington, DC. http://www.worldbank.org/en/news/feature/2012/10/24/Brazil-descendants-slaves-quilombolas-poverty (accessed February 14, 2013).

———. 2012b. *World Development Report 2012: Gender Equality and Development*. Washington, DC: World Bank.

———. 2013. *World Development Report 2013: Jobs*. Washington, DC: World Bank.

Yeo, R., and K. Moore. 2003. "Including Disabled People in Poverty Reduction Work: Nothing about Us, without Us." *World Development* 31 (3): 571–90.

PART II

TRANSITIONS, TRANSFORMATIONS, AND PERCEPTIONS

CHAPTER 4

Transitions, Transformations, and the Changing Context of Inclusion

For the loser now
Will be later to win
For the times they are a-changin'.

—BOB DYLAN, "THE TIMES THEY ARE A-CHANGIN'" (1964)

It seems as though many more people are talking about social inclusion. The social movements that followed the food, fuel, and financial crises of the early years of the millennium, and the ongoing financial crises, have shaken the complacency of the high growth years of the late 20th century. Home foreclosures in the United States poignantly brought home the catastrophe that strikes families who lose their homes. The Occupy Wall Street movement trained its eyes on the top 1 percent of the wealthiest Americans and spearheaded mirror "occupy" movements elsewhere in the world. The Middle East was shaken in 2011, not by war but by a surge of protest against the social order. Other emerging markets, including Brazil and Turkey, are reverberating with the protest of rich and poor alike. Microblogs in China reflect deepening demand for citizens' voice. In Africa, farmers are protesting against the acquisition of their lands for commercial purposes. Natural disasters have become common, and climate change is affecting the lives of citizens across welfare groups. The global play for natural resources is leading to significant tensions in many parts of the world. These events have complex implications for social inclusion. They are underpinned by larger transitions and transformations.

Much of the political upheaval witnessed today can be linked to demographic, spatial, and economic transitions and changes in knowledge and information that are transforming societies. The cumulative impact of the transitions witnessed in the past several decades has changed the profile of the global community and reshaped some of the social inclusion issues that will be faced in the future. The new global population is increasingly older, but it also has large youth cohorts; it lives in urban areas and under new types of living arrangements; it is less poor, better educated, and more interconnected but also in many ways more unequal than before. In addition, migration is becoming one of the most potent forces of social churning, creating new challenges for citizens, policy makers, and politicians alike. These and other transitions present opportunities for greater inclusion, but they also create new types of exclusion and exacerbate the exclusion of already disadvantaged groups.

This chapter looks at major transitions and transformations of the past several decades as a frame of reference to prognosticate on the drivers of exclusion and the potential for inclusion in the coming years. It focuses on transitions in four areas: demographic, spatial, economic, and knowledge. It argues that the cumulative impact of these large-scale transitions has changed the context for inclusion, either by creating new groups that deserve attention or by changing the forms of, and opportunities for, both inclusion and exclusion. The chapter also highlights the fact that there are significant differences across countries and regions, some of which are being excluded from the fruits of progress more than others or are likely to face particular issues of inclusion. Chapter 5 then considers attitudes and perceptions in response to some of these transitions, giving credence to the idea that large-scale transitions have also affected how people react to their social reality, which in turn affects the opportunities and challenges for social inclusion.

Complex Demographic Transitions

Fertility and Mortality: Changing Families and Age Structure

Demographic transitions observed today are far more complex than earlier transitions and affect multiple groups in myriad ways. High fertility and mortality rates, for example, have implications beyond population growth. At the household level, high fertility is associated with low access to education and health, with all its implications for future life choices. For women living in countries with high fertility rates, lack of control over their own fertility is a key axis of their exclusion from the rest of the world. There are also significant impacts at the country level, with high-fertility countries being left out of positive global trends and having poor human development outcomes. More generally, the combination of low fertility and mortality with other complex demographic transitions, as manifested in major transformations in age and family structures, living arrangements, and diversity of populations, has significant social inclusion implications (table 4.1).

Table 4.1 Demographic Transitions: Illustrative Implications for Social Inclusion

	What will social inclusion entail?		
Affected group	Markets	Services	Spaces
Elderly people	• Enabling older workers to remain productive • Ensuring that social security and pension systems allow for aging with dignity	• Enabling better coverage and quality of formal and informal care arrangements; social security; new forms of health services, assistive technology, and transport services	• Making public spaces accessible for elderly (for example, wheelchair access)
Youth	• Enhancing youth employment	• Supporting the development of marketable skills and noncognitive skills	• Acknowledging aspirations • Enhancing voice and participation in decision making
Single parents, split families, homosexual couples, widows, orphans	• Equalizing access to jobs, credit, and housing for groups that are traditionally excluded • Creating flexible work arrangements, so that more groups can participate in the labor market	• Providing child care services • Providing social protection services for the vulnerable among the traditionally excluded	• Acknowledging and fulfilling demands for recognition, political representation, and legal standing
Certain groups of women	• Ensuring access to land, housing and property, and credit markets • Ensuring access to the labor market and better terms of employment	• Supporting the development of marketable skills and noncognitive skills • Putting in place mechanisms to prevent violence and services for survivors of violence • Providing child care services • Providing legal services	• Making public places safe and secure • Ensuring better representation in positions of authority • Enforcing laws that equalize opportunity

Fertility has declined all over the world since 1970, but the decline has been uneven. As of 2013, 88 out of 198 countries had fertility rates that were below the replacement level of 2.1.[1] Yet some countries, many of which are in conflict or fragile situations, continue to have very high fertility rates (box 4.1). Niger, for example, has a total fertility rate (TFR) of more than 7.0 births per woman, with very small declines since 1975–80. Afghanistan, Chad, the Democratic Republic of Congo, Mali, Somalia, Uganda, and Zambia all have TFRs of more than 6.0. At the other end of the spectrum, fertility rates below replacement level mean that the populations of some economies are expected to decrease by at least 10 percent by 2050. These economies include Belarus, Bosnia-Herzegovina, Bulgaria, Croatia, Cuba, Georgia, Japan, Latvia, Lithuania, Moldova, Portugal, Romania, the Russian Federation, Serbia, and Ukraine. Many Asian countries are also experiencing a "retreat from childbearing" by women of reproductive age (see, for instance, Lesthaeghe 2010). These countries are either importing labor or will need to do so in the near future, which has implications for migration, the number of foreign workers, and their families.

Age structures of populations have been altered; many developing countries will grapple simultaneously with bulging youth cohorts and rapidly aging populations in the years ahead (box 4.2). Today's unprecedented youth cohort in many developing countries has generated new interest in the "demographic dividend," but not all countries have the vision or the capacity to put in place policies that can reap it (box 4.3). Reaping a demographic dividend requires concerted action on poverty, employment, and human development, as well as skillful management of the political economy. China, among a few other countries, has famously made good use of its large young labor force (World Bank and DRC 2013).

If unmanaged, large youth cohorts can come with significant economic, social, and political cost. In conflict countries, where the demographic window has opened or is about to open, these issues can become even more acute, as young people are vulnerable to being recruited for armed conflict. Youth are also more likely to be unemployed than adults in countries where their numbers are large (figure 4.1); many countries will struggle to absorb the new labor force entrants.

Although jobs are an important piece of the youth puzzle, employment is not the only important issue for youth. In fact, as the *World Development Report 2013* notes, jobs have benefits that go beyond incomes to social

BOX 4.1

World Population, 1950–2100

The population of Sub-Saharan Africa is expected to double in size and to account for more than 20 percent of the world population by 2050. The world will soon overwhelmingly comprise people born in developing regions, particularly Africa and fragile countries. This trend has implications for international migration, urban growth, and competition for investment in new and untapped markets. In turn, it will mark a continuing shift in the global relations of power. Unless the countries that will have the largest populations and the largest markets also have the strongest voices in local and global decision making, it can have negative political consequences as well.

Figure B4.1.1 World Population, by Region, 1950–2100

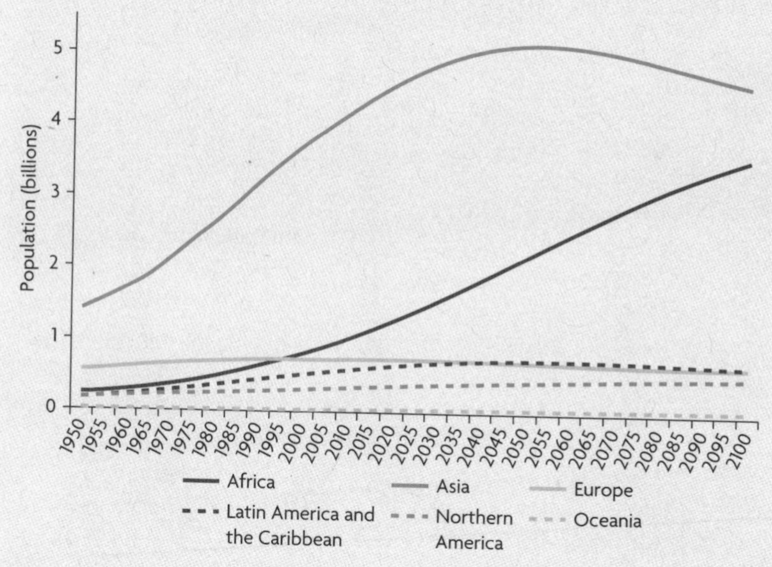

Source: UN 2011b.
Note: Medium-variant estimates.

BOX 4.2

Population Pyramids Are History

Transitions in fertility and mortality and uneven migration patterns will make population pyramids extinct by 2050, in all except the very high fertility countries. Figure B4.2.1 shows age structures of three very different contexts: Uganda, where the fertility transition has been slow and late; Poland, which has very low fertility and low mortality; and the Arab Republic of Egypt, which falls in between these two scenarios. The figures show that by 2050, half of Uganda's population will be below 20 years of age; Egypt's population, which is young now, will be older and replaced by a much smaller cohort of young people; and Poland will have a full-fledged aging crisis. Each of these three scenarios underscores the need for planning and vision.

Figure B4.2.1 Population Pyramids in Uganda, Poland, and the Arab Republic of Egypt, 1950, 2010, and 2050

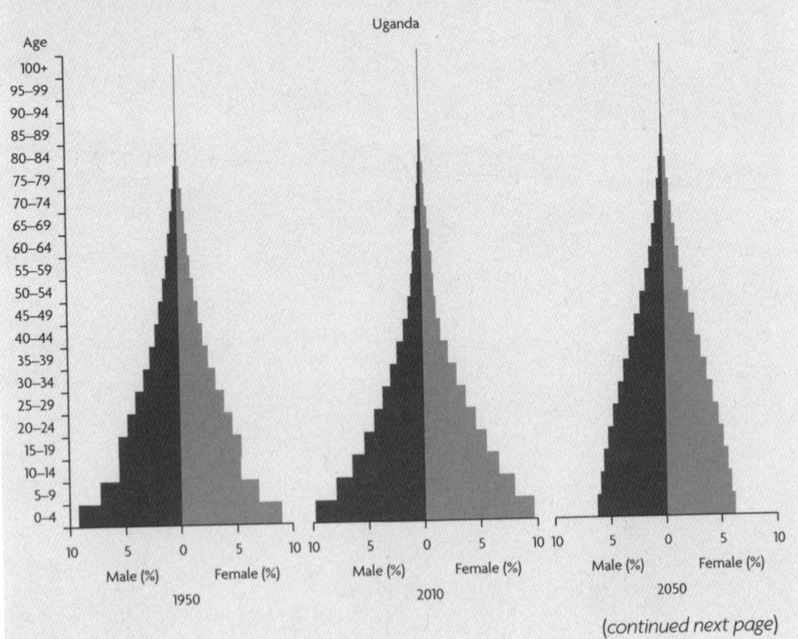

(continued next page)

BOX 4.2 *(continued)*

Figure B4.2.1 Population Pyramids in Uganda, Poland, and the Arab Republic of Egypt, 1950, 2010, and 2050 *(continued)*

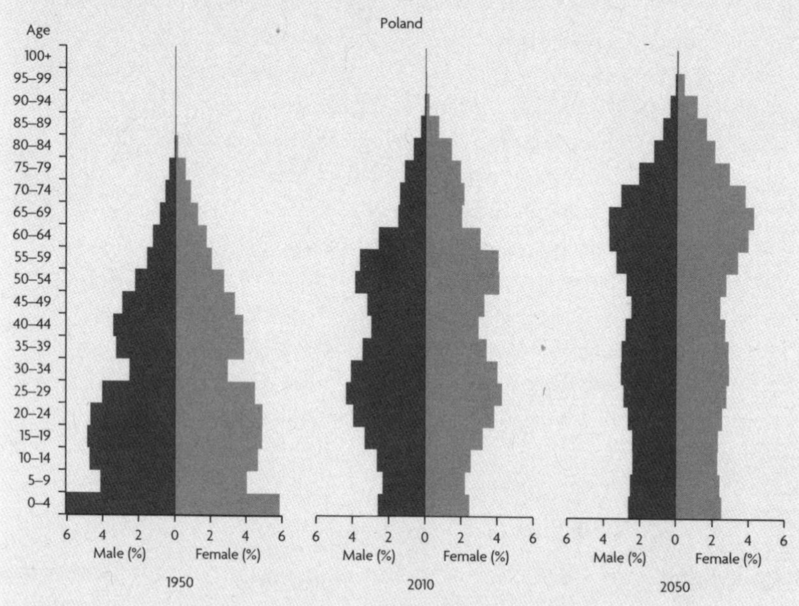

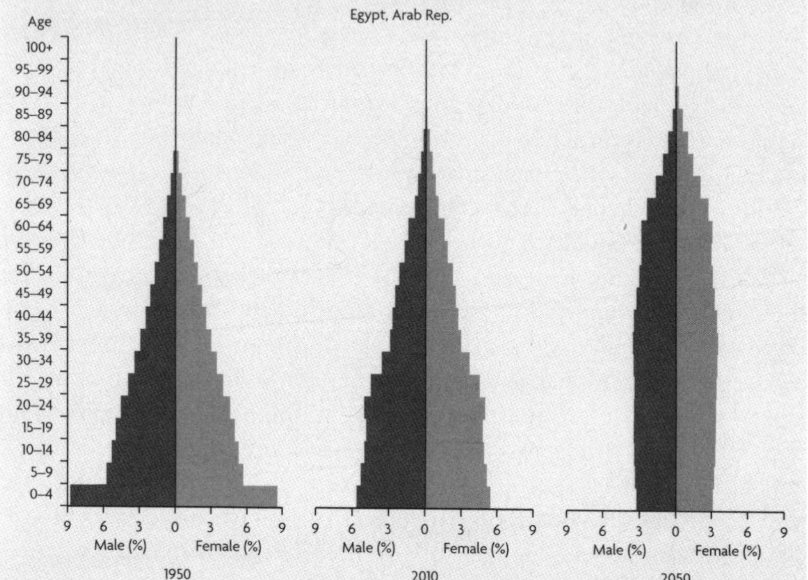

Source: World Bank, based on data from UN 2011b.

BOX 4.3

Young People in Morocco: Cost or Dividend?

Thirty percent of Morocco's population is between the ages of 15 and 29. Half of these people are neither in school nor working. Most active labor market programs in Morocco target a small section of youth who have tertiary training. But most youth have less than secondary education or no education and end up in informal private sector jobs that come without security or benefits. Better jobs call for competency in French, a skill that most youth leaving public schools lack.

In addition to economic costs, there are social costs to youth being excluded from the labor market. Employment is integral to dignity, in particular for young men in Morocco, who are culturally expected to start a family once they finish education. Failure to secure employment undermines self-esteem and social standing and can lead to depression and frustration. In a recent World Bank study, young men openly described their vulnerability to crime and drugs and women described their vulnerability to prostitution. One in three young people reported wanting to seek better prospects abroad.

Source: World Bank 2012a.

cohesion and personal well-being, which is just as, if not more, important (World Bank 2013).

Large numbers of the elderly are likely to generate new pressures for social inclusion. By 2050, one person in five in less developed countries and nearly one in three in developed countries is expected to be over 60, with some variation across countries. An increasing number of older adults are living alone, rather than in joint family situations as in previous generations. This change is particularly important for developing countries, where extended families have been the norm until very recently.

Apart from the fiscal and institutional challenges of providing for the elderly (through pensions, social security, and public health care), there may well have to be a major restructuring in work arrangements across the population. Such restructuring could include increasing the age of retirement, shifting employment of the elderly from jobs that require physical strength to ones that require knowledge and experience, and increasing part-time employment. Here, too, the intergenerational aspects will need to be carefully managed, as increasing retirement ages could have an adverse impact on youth employment. Finally, societies

Figure 4.1 In Countries Where Their Numbers Are Large, Youth Are More Likely Than Adults to Be Unemployed

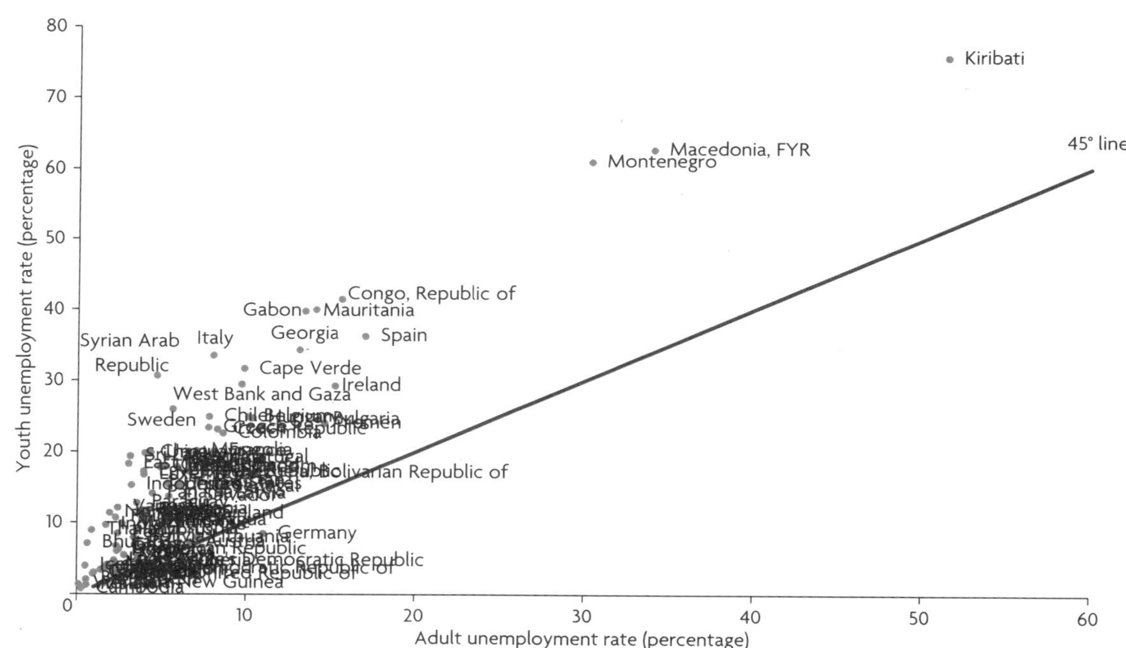

Source: Lee et al. 2012; ASPIRE (Atlas of Social Protection—Indicators of Resilience and Equity), International Income Distribution Database (I2D2).
Note: Values are included for all countries for which data for both variables were available in the period 2005–2011. Latest data available are used.

and families will have to be more cognizant of the needs of the elderly if they are to provide better care arrangements and facilitate more dignified aging.

Despite the worldwide decline in mortality, some populations have been excluded, both within and across countries or regions. Exclusion is reflected most starkly in skewed sex ratios. Women have a biological propensity to live longer and have higher survival chances at birth, so more men than women in a population suggests discrimination against females, which takes place at different stages in their lives. Women in many countries die needlessly in childbirth, and girls die needlessly through neglect. Most of the preventable maternal and child deaths take place among the poor and among racial and ethnic minorities. The pattern of excess boys that has been written about most prolifically in the context of India and China is actually more widespread. It is true that the two most populous countries account for the largest number of excess female deaths, but similar trends are observed in Albania, Armenia, Azerbaijan, Georgia, Kosovo, the former Yugoslav Republic of Macedonia, Montenegro, Pakistan, and the Republic of Korea. In Vietnam, sex ratio at birth has increased continually over the past three decades (Guilmoto 2011). Technological advances have made it possible to detect the sex of a child early in a pregnancy and to terminate a pregnancy more easily. Although some countries, such as India and China, have laws that prohibit doctors from revealing the sex of the child to parents, the laws are not enforced.

Apart from the fact that they reflect serious bias against women and girls, skewed sex ratios have implications for marriage markets and migration patterns. In China, for example, the share of unmarried men above the age of 30 is predicted to increase dramatically in the next few decades (Eberstadt 2011). Anecdotal accounts of Indian brides from other states in the female-deficit state of Haryana indicate that women enter the marriage market in unknown territories, usually from a position of weakness, going through significant physical and mental stress in the process of their adaptation, often without support.

Although the HIV/AIDS epidemic seems on the decline, there are still a number of countries that have high levels of the disease. In Southern Africa, the region with the highest prevalence of the disease, life expectancy fell from 61 years in 1990–95 to 51 years in 2005–10. Although it has recently started to increase, life expectancy in the region is not expected to recover to the level in the early 1990s before 2035. As a consequence, the growth rate of the population in the region has declined (UN 2011a). People with HIV/AIDS face higher risk of death and are stigmatized and excluded from a number of domains. Their children are at greater risk of orphanhood, and the impacts of the disease permeate their families, as discussed in chapter 5.

Developing countries and populations are not the only ones excluded from the huge progress in mortality decline. Eastern Europe has experienced reductions in life expectancy since the late 1980s. Despite having recorded some recovery since the late 1990s, Moldova, the Russian Federation, and Ukraine currently have the lowest life expectancies among developed countries (below 70 years), driven mainly by very high rates of male mortality. Brainerd and Cutler (2005) mark out a "mortality belt" in Eastern Europe, where men die much earlier than women and their male counterparts in other Organisation for Economic Co-operation and Development (OECD) countries. They attribute this pattern to two main factors: alcohol use, especially as it relates to external causes of death (homicide, suicide, and accidents), and stress associated with a poor outlook for the future.

In addition to fertility patterns, far-reaching demographic changes have led to new family formations and living arrangements. For instance, delayed marriage and childbearing have played a role in the fertility transition. Women are also increasingly having children outside of wedlock, and couples are cohabiting rather than marrying more than before, leading to a decline in marriage. The norm of a two-parent heterosexual family is under question, especially in some OECD countries and parts of Latin America.

In developing countries, urbanization, modern social mores, and migration have meant that extended families are increasingly moving to a nuclear model. Table 4.2 shows the recent decline in the proportion of extended and joint families (accompanied by an increase in single, semi-single, and nuclear families) in Bangladesh, often considered a "traditional" country. These new family formations have important social consequences at the individual, household, community, and national levels.

Split families in China are aberrant enough to warrant serious policy concern. Nuclear families allow women greater freedom and control over their own lives, but they also impose a greater burden of caregiving on them, especially in countries where informal arrangements dominate the provision of care. Outward migration is also known to have profound effects on family life. A thread of the literature from Kerala, India, and Sri Lanka focuses on the impact on the mental health of both men

Table 4.2 Bangladesh's Family Structure Has Changed over Time
(percentage of all households)

Household type	2000	2005	2010
Single	1.6	2.1	2.4
Nuclear	55.1	57.9	57.0
Semi-single	8.3	8.4	9.7
Extended	21.7	19.1	19.2
Joint	13.4	12.6	11.7

Source: World Bank, based on data from Bangladesh Household Income and Expenditure Surveys for 2000, 2005, and 2010.
Note: Households are classified as follows (following Amin 1998): a single household includes just one member; a nuclear household includes a married couple and unmarried children; a semi-single household includes a single parent and children or a household head and relatives but no married couple; an extended household includes one married couple and children, relatives, or both. A joint household is an extended household with multiple couples.

and women who return from work overseas. Some of the literature on households headed by women whose husbands migrate shows that wives who stay behind tend to have greater freedom of choice and control over resources (see, for instance, Yabiku, Agadjanian, and Sevoyan 2010 for Mozambique).

Migration: Toward More Diverse Populations

Migration is likely to become a more dramatic and volatile demographic process than fertility or mortality, leading to more diverse societies and challenges to family structures. In Germany, for example, foreigners will make up 30 percent of the total population by 2030 and more than half of the population of major cities such as Frankfurt and Berlin (Ulrich and Muenz 1995).The United States has had a relatively liberal immigration policy compared with many other countries in the OECD. Foreign-born residents represent nearly 13 percent of its population, up from 6 percent in 1980 (MacDonald and Sampson 2012).

The prolonged recession and unemployment in the United States and Europe and a simultaneous boom in many developing countries have had an effect on migration patterns. Anecdotal accounts indicate that skilled job seekers from southern Europe are moving to take advantage of opportunities in economically stronger countries, such as Germany and the countries of Scandinavia (Demling 2012). There are similar accounts of Portuguese workers migrating to Brazil and Mozambique, given the high levels of unemployment in Portugal and better opportunities for high-skilled workers in the new receiving areas.

In each of these cases, workers hit or at risk of being hit by the recession are now finding new avenues for inclusion. However, they are likely to face new challenges in their new countries. There is little historical evidence to understand what happens when workers from previously colonizing countries migrate to their erstwhile colonies because of vulnerability, not colonization.

Migration within countries is also becoming larger in size and significance. In Latin America, for instance, much internal migration is between cities. Like international migration, internal migration is non-linear, complex, and country specific. The ongoing internal migration in China, for example, is the greatest and fastest movement of humans in history. In 2010, 19.5 percent of the people in China were migrants, more than 15 percent of whom moved from one city to another (World Bank and DRC 2013). The existence of the registration system, the *hukou*, which does not allow families of migrants the same access to markets, services, and spaces in the host area as the families of natives, has come under increasing scrutiny. The inclusion of urban migrants in Chinese cities is now a top priority of the government, which recognizes the far-reaching impacts that the unique nature of Chinese migration has had on urban and rural social structures.

People who migrate under the most extreme forms of duress, such as war, natural disaster, or extreme poverty, end up being some of the most excluded groups in their host countries or regions. About 15.4 million of the global migrant populations are refugees who fled armed conflict. The number of forcibly displaced people within borders is even larger, with 27.5 million of the 44 million people who are involuntarily or forcibly displaced across the world classified as internally displaced (UNFPA n.d.).[2]

In addition to forced migration as a result of conflict, human trafficking is pervasive and has many faces, including forced or bonded labor; domestic servitude and forced marriage; organ removal; and the exploitation of children in begging, the sex trade, and warfare. Probably as a result of statistical bias and national legislation, sexual exploitation is the most commonly identified form of human trafficking (79 percent), followed by forced labor (18 percent). Women are disproportionately involved in human trafficking as victims (two-thirds of the reported victims worldwide), whereas the majority of traffickers are male (UNODC n.d.).

Spatial Transitions

Urbanization

> Borborema [a city in the state of São Paulo] without open sewers just wouldn't be Borborema. One day a company called me for a job, but when they realized I lived in Bode [a *favela*] they changed their minds, thinking that I was one of those marginais they couldn't trust.
>
> —Resident of a *favela* in Brazil,
> Voices of the Poor study (World Bank)

Urbanization was one of the most dramatic transitions of the previous century. It will continue to unfold in this century. In the mid-20th century, less than a third of the world population, and about half of the population in developed countries, lived in urban areas.[3] The steady increase in urban populations since then has resulted in nearly half of the world population living in urban areas at the turn of the 21st century. Urban population has continued to increase in the 2000s, not just as a result of migration from rural to urban areas (which is estimated to account for 40 percent of urbanization) but also as a result of high fertility in urban areas (Montgomery 2009).

The importance of urbanization for social inclusion lies in both the prospects and the barriers it presents. For instance, urban space offers anonymity that allows some groups to meld in. In the 1960s, noted Indian sociologist M. N. Srinivas put forward a theory that caste hierarchies and the norms that discriminated against groups that had been historically disadvantaged, would be diluted as urbanization proceeded. This is indeed what happened: although caste is far from eradicated, even in urban areas, its sting has definitely dulled. At the individual and household level, urbanization offers the possibility for social mobility through a range of new opportunities. Migrants from rural areas move to cities and towns seeking new jobs, business opportunities, and education. Cities and towns also offer a different social milieu than do villages. Old norms and values give way to new and more diverse ones. The village society tends to rely on proximity between kin and clan groups, which is less pronounced in urban areas. But, as pointed out earlier, in urban areas, too, ethnic groups and migrants from the same sending area often live in close proximity and draw on networks from their places of origin. New social networks and social capital are also built, and professional and neighborhood groups become new sources of social support.

Not all social processes in urban areas are necessarily positive for excluded groups; new axes of exclusion are also created (table 4.3). Mental health issues, substance abuse, and poor security all affect

Table 4.3 Spatial Transitions: Illustrative Implications for Social Inclusion

	What will social inclusion entail?		
Affected group	Markets	Services	Spaces
Slum residents	• Reforming housing markets and urban zoning laws to ensure equitable access • Addressing discrimination in employment	• Extending basic services across the board	• Acknowledging and fulfilling demands for recognition, political representation, and legal standing
Poor migrant workers, internally displaced people, refugees, people affected by conflict, families of migrants left behind in sending areas	• Ensuring equitable access to labor market, fair wages, and worker protection • Intervening in markets to ensure employment for displaced people, movement of goods and services during times of stress	• Extending basic services across the board • Tailoring services for migrants to adjust to their new milieu • Ensuring food security	• Acknowledging and fulfilling demands for recognition, political representation, and legal standing • Protecting women and children from the risk of trafficking and violence during times of war and physical displacement
Residents of low-lying and coastal areas		• Providing disaster risk-reduction services	
Indigenous populations in remote areas, citizens whose lands are acquired for large infrastructure and urban development	• Ensuring that people are fairly compensated for land acquisition by the state and private entities • Protecting traditional land rights of indigenous people	• Providing culturally appropriate services	• Ensuring that communities are consulted before major decisions affecting them are made; meeting the demand for information • According respect and regard to traditional systems of knowledge

individuals more in urban areas than in rural areas. Poorer or otherwise excluded groups live in areas that expose them to these factors more intensely. There are also challenges for city and municipal authorities. Urban growth is often unplanned in developing countries, creating serious problems of service delivery and housing. Access to basic services and assets becomes the fulcrum around which social exclusion pivots, often intensifying preexisting disadvantages. Even households that are not poor may end up living in substandard, crowded housing, with poor access to basic services. Kibera, in greater Nairobi, is the largest urban slum in Africa, housing about 250,000 people (Marras 2012). It is contaminated with animal and human feces as a result of an open sewage system.

Residents of slums also tend to experience extreme weather events more intensely as a result of their living conditions. The study of Mombasa by Moser et al. (2010) shows the cumulative impact of physical, social, and legal vulnerabilities related to poverty, physical location, and exclusion from most basic services. For instance, the lack of formal land tenure rights makes the poor more vulnerable to severe weather. They squat on the most fragile land, and, because they do not have tenure rights, they are less likely to receive municipal services. Because they lack tenure, households are also reluctant to invest resources in adaptation measures to build resilience in their plots.

Although there has reportedly been a decline in the share of people living in slums—from 46 percent of the world's urban population in 1990 to 33 percent in 2010 (UNFPA 2011)—there are still more than 800 million slum residents across the developing world. Of these, only a quarter gained access to improved water, sanitation, or durable and less crowded housing over the past decade (UNFPA 2011).

Cities are polarized between those that have access to basic services and those that do not. The *favelas* in Brazil are a case in point. The Brazilian mantra is to move from "divided cities" to "integrated cities," recognizing that *favelas* are a visual testimony to the country's inequality.

Polarization within cities is also one of the root causes of the crime that has beset many cities in Latin America and the Caribbean and Africa. Over time, violence can become institutionalized, making it difficult to dismantle. Governance challenges in urban areas contribute to some groups feeling left out and having few opportunities for voice and redress. Land mafia, drug lords, and other extortionists then step into the role of what should have been core state functions.

Finally, at the national level, social exclusion is often characterized by an urban-rural dichotomy. As discussed in chapter 2, there is often an intersection of spatial and social exclusion, with excluded groups inhabiting poorer or more fragile areas. Increasingly, with urban areas driving prosperity and progress, rural areas are being left behind. A case in point is China, where patterns of growth and migration have rendered entire villages bereft of human and social capital. Overall, income inequality in China is on the rise, characterized by inequality between urban and rural areas. The pattern of China's urbanization process has created new challenges for both urban and rural areas. In particular, there is increasing policy interest in the well-being of people "left behind" by migrant family members. These "left-behind" individuals and groups experience a range of vulnerabilities, including poor access to services and significant psychological and social isolation (Jingzhong and Murray 2010).

Climate Change, Disasters, and Excluded Groups

One of the most profound spatial transitions of this century is occurring as a result of climate change. Although there is contestation over the pace of climate change, there seems to be no doubt of its existence,

> With rain one was at ease, one was full of the seed and oil. Now nothing, it is the drought. Now if one doesn't buy milk one doesn't drink it, because Lakssiba (the livestock) have left. Lakssiba too want to live, they want grass, straw. There is no meat, there is no harvest, there is no grass.
>
> —Focus group participant, Ait Yahia, Morocco,
> Moving Out of Poverty study (World Bank)

> During El Niño I could hardly catch any fish. The rains were so heavy that nobody was able to distinguish between lake and land. Fishing is not as promising as it was in the past. The water level has decreased and the mature fish hide very far away.
>
> —Life history participant, Kagera, Tanzania,
> Moving out of Poverty study (World Bank)

with rapid and catastrophic consequences for livelihoods, crops, and ecosystems. A recent report portends a scenario of a world that will be 4°C warmer in 2100 than in preindustrial times, leading to catastrophic heat waves, droughts, and floods in many regions (World Bank 2012b). The regions most vulnerable to climate change are in the tropics and subtropics and toward the poles, where multiple impacts are likely to come together. For example, small island states and the least developed countries have identified a global warming threshold of 1.5°C above which there would be serious threats to their survival. Ironically, many of these countries and regions are the least responsible for greenhouse gas emissions and have the least economic, institutional, and technical capacity to cope and adapt.

Periods of climate-related stress, such as a drought, reduce food availability, with people in conflict-affected areas hit hardest. Sen (2001) argues that food insecurity during periods of climatic stresses is higher in countries affected by conflict, because they end up spending more on the military than on social programs and have poorly functioning markets and services. Conflict also affects agricultural production by blocking the ability to import (UN 1993) and by removing men from farming. These fragile populations often take refuge in countries with greater food security. A 2012 primer from the World Food Programme draws attention to the food crisis in Mali, where an estimated 1.7 million people are at risk of hunger since the coup (WFP 2012). About a third of them have moved to Burkina Faso, causing stress on resources there. More than 1.5 million people in Haiti are estimated to be at risk of malnutrition because of a heavy storm season that damaged as much as 90 percent of the country's harvest in 2012 (Huffington Post 2013). Within these situations, children, the elderly, women, and people with disabilities are at greatest risk.

Excluded groups are more vulnerable to extreme events. Many people with challenges to their mobility face compounded constraints when severe weather events occur. Qualitative fieldwork in a community in North Mombasa, for instance, shows how flooding and rains disproportionately affected the mobility of people with disabilities (Moser et al. 2010). Gender is also an important dimension of climate change. It is estimated, for instance, that more women than men die in natural disasters, mostly because they stay at home (Neumayer and Plümper 2007). Take also the case of indigenous people who inhabit ecologically fragile areas and are more dependent for their livelihood on natural resources. They are therefore disproportionately affected by changes in environmental conditions. Despite sharing a close relationship with environmental resources, these groups are not equitably represented in environmental governance processes, although decisions made by them have significant implications for carbon emissions.

Arnold (2011) argues that natural catastrophes, although devastating, can provide a blank slate not just for reconstruction but for transformation of societies. Steps to improve gender equality, for instance, can easily be integrated into the recovery process by issuing joint titles (in the name of both man and woman) for newly constructed houses, distributing relief through women, and funding women's groups to monitor the recovery process.

Indigenous knowledge and community action can help in disaster management. The 2004 tsunami made the global community recognize the importance of indigenous knowledge in disaster preparedness. Journalistic accounts showed how the Moken indigenous people (or sea gypsies) in Thailand and the native inhabitants of the Andaman and Nicobar Islands in India were able to escape to safety. In Indonesia, Acehnese houses made of local materials survived without damage, even as modern houses made of cement and brick came down. In Guatemala, many Mayan communities were able to escape unhurt during Hurricane Stan in 2005. They attributed their preparedness to Kumatzin, a board game with Mayan illustrations that is used to inculcate from childhood the ability to prepare for and survive natural disasters. Where entire villages are affected by a natural event, drawing on community resources can also aid government action. The communities that live on the *char* lands in Bangladesh, for instance, have to move constantly to avoid being flooded by the course changes of the rivers. Bangladesh has shown that concerted policy action and strong social capital can prevent fatalities from the regular floods and cyclones that affect its low-lying areas.

Green policies can contribute to economic growth, but they may not be win-win, especially in the short term and for the poor. In a micro characterization of the link between poverty and green growth, Dercon (2012) argues that not all measures that maximize green growth will maximize poverty reduction or promote development. Take the case of low-carbon energy production. It is more labor intensive and hence likely to benefit the poor, but the size of the subsidy or public investment required may crowd out aggregate pro-poor impacts. Similarly, environmental pricing and regulation affect the poor as producers, because they may not have sufficient access to human capital to substitute for more expensive energy or other natural resources in their production. The tradeoff can be starker if adaptation and other resilience-enhancing investments induce the poor to adhere to lower-return/lower-risk livelihoods with little chance of escaping poverty. Because excluded groups are often, though not always, overrepresented among the poor, it is important to analyze the distributional impacts of a policy change by excluded group.

The implications for "inclusion" in the face of climate change depend on environmental factors but depend equally on social and economic ones. The pressures of climate and environmental change will likely have the greatest impact on the growth prospects of poorer countries. The *World Development Report 2010: Development and Climate Change* (World Bank 2009) calls for an equitable and effective global agreement for dealing with climate change that would recognize the needs and constraints of developing countries, assist them with the finance and technology to meet the increased challenges to development, ensure they are not locked into a small share of the global commons, and establish mechanisms that decouple where mitigation happens from who pays for it.

Economic Transitions

Poverty Reduction and the Rise of the Middle Class

In tandem with and underlying other transitions over the last few decades are deep economic transitions. Globalization and regional integration, coupled with substantial reforms at the national level, have led to impressive growth and poverty reduction across the globe. Based on the $1.25-a-day threshold, the poverty headcount was halved in the past two decades, falling from 43 percent to 22 percent of the world population between 1990 and the onset of the financial crisis in 2008. In South Asia, the region that shares the largest number of poor people with Sub-Saharan Africa, an average annual growth rate of 6 percent between 1990 and 2010 was matched by an 11-point decline in the percentage of people living below the $1.25-a-day poverty threshold. The rate of poverty reduction was even higher in East Asia and the Pacific.

At the $2.50-a-day poverty threshold, however, only East Asian countries show progress; Africa and South Asia actually show an increase in the share of people living below this threshold (figure 4.2). Furthermore, global

Figure 4.2 Fewer People Live on Less Than $1.25 a Day, but There Is Mixed Progress for People Living on Less Than $2.50 a Day

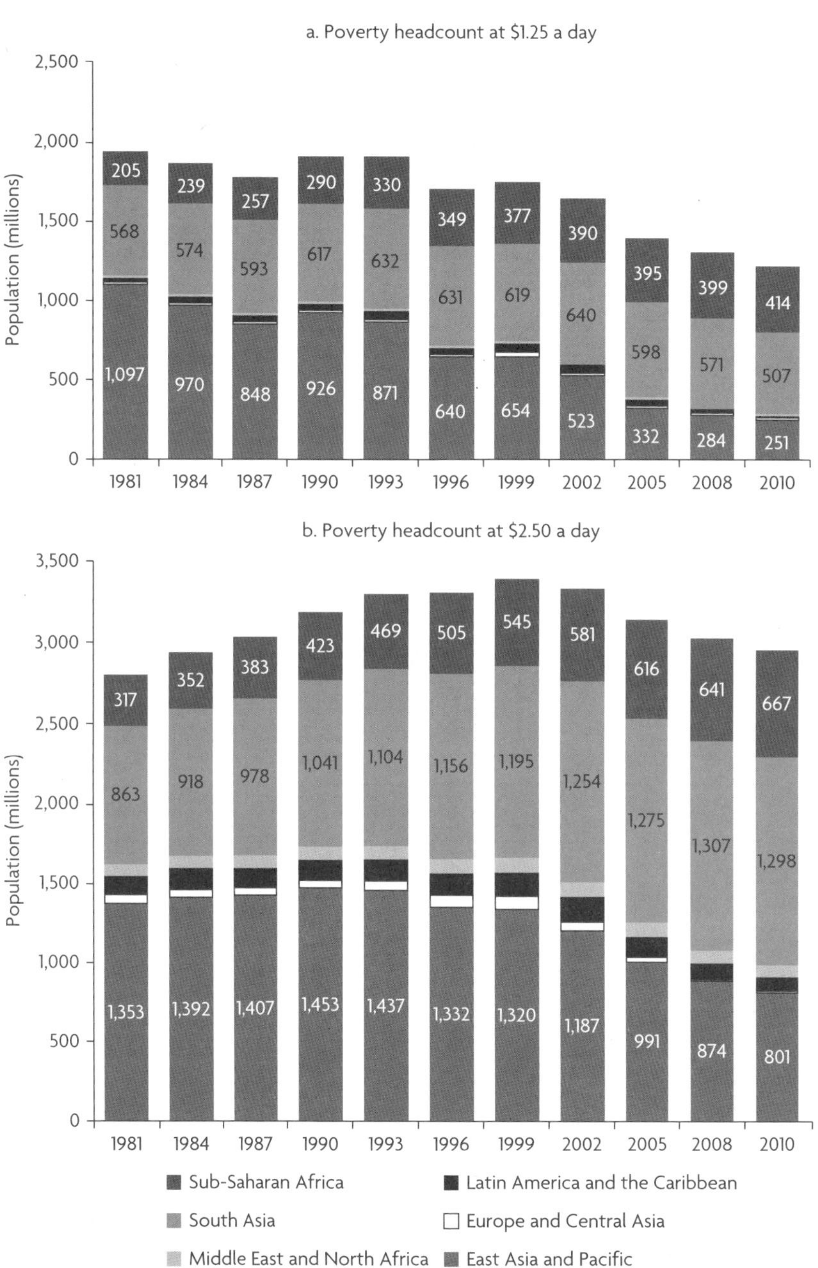

Source: PovcalNet (World Bank).

poverty is increasingly concentrated in fragile states, where the rate of poverty decline has been slower. These countries are projected to account for half of the world's poorest people by 2015, compared with one-third in 2010 (Chandy and Gertz 2011)—despite the fact that nearly half of fragile states are now classified as middle-income countries (OECD 2013).

Within countries, it appears that poverty reduction has been uneven for different groups as well. For example, across the Asian and Latin American countries that have managed to reduce poverty in the last few decades, poverty reduction rates were lower for indigenous than nonindigenous populations, except in China (figure 4.3). Not everyone benefited equally from growth and poverty reduction.

The decline in poverty has meant an increase in the number of people who can be considered middle class, with important social and political implications (table 4.4).[4] Globally, for the first time in history, by 2030, more than half the world's population is expected to become "middle class" (Kharas and Gertz 2011). Ferreira et al. (2013) show that the middle class and the poor now account for roughly the same share of Latin America's population; only a decade ago, the share of the poor was about 2.5 times

Figure 4.3 Poverty Reduction Has Been Slower among Indigenous People Than among Nonindigenous People

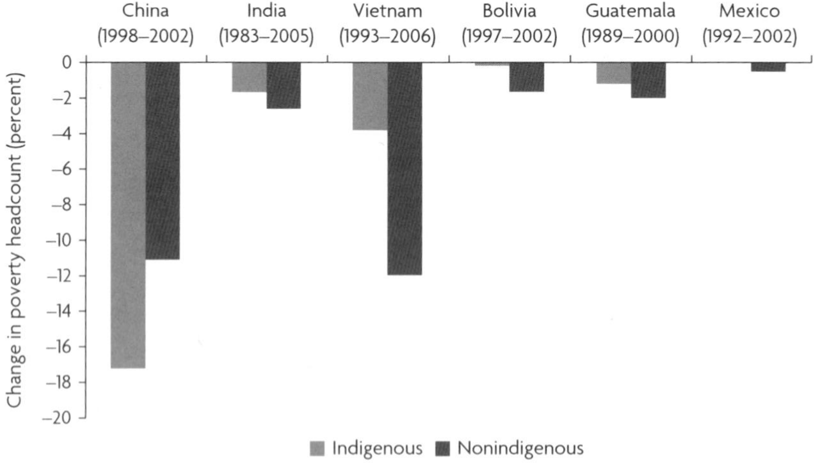

Source: Hall and Patrinos 2012.
Note: Average yearly changes in the poverty headcount (FGT0)—the fraction of the population that lives below a defined poverty line—are based on compounding growth rates.

Table 4.4 Economic Transitions: Illustrative Implications for Social Inclusion

	What will social inclusion entail?		
Affected group	Markets	Services	Markets
Larger middle class	• Ensuring better jobs, housing, and access to credit markets	• Providing better quality of services and infrastructure	• Ensuring greater participation in decision making and greater transparency and accountability from the state and service providers
Poor and food-insecure people Groups affected by crises and left out from growth	• Ensuring equitable access to labor markets, fair wages, and worker protection • Ensuring adequate food availability • Intervening in markets to ensure employment for displaced persons, movement of goods and services during times of stress • Providing adequate social housing	• Providing social protection services, especially effective social safety nets, for the vulnerable among the traditionally excluded	• Managing social tensions arising from inequality and deprivation, through better access and voice

that of the middle class. This new group of people is significantly reordering the social contract in several Latin American countries. Indeed, when combined with education, information, and higher disposable income, the new class of upwardly mobile people around the world has a greater "capacity to aspire" and wants to participate on different terms in society.

The relationship of the middle class to the state is quite different from that of the poor to the state. The middle class demands voice and accountability as a right; the poor can often be reduced to being supplicants by a strong state. Protests against corruption in India, through street demonstrations, political action, and information and communication technology (ICT) on websites like ipaidabribe.com, succeeded in shaming the state, ostensibly by members of its own elite.

In many countries, the middle class has a vested interest in continuing the benefits that have historically accrued to them, for instance, through subsidies; it therefore reacts adversely to reforms. Take the case of subsidy cuts in education, transportation, and energy, which have ignited the anger of middle-class and poor people alike in countries as diverse as Brazil, Bulgaria, Chile, Hungary, Nigeria, and several others. Essentially, the relations between the state and society are undergoing a change, with rising numbers of the middle class demanding a different kind of accountability but also wanting to preserve their benefits in the face of a rising lower-middle class. Empirical evidence on what this means is relatively thin, but the trends appear to be clear.

The middle class and the elite are also an important agent for change, as chapter 6 shows. Recent evidence from the United States suggests that policies favored by affluent Americans (the top income decile) have a one in two chance of being adopted; in contrast, the support of the poor has virtually no impact on the prospects of a policy being adopted (Gilens 2012). This is not to say that elites necessarily opt for antipoor or exclusionary policies—most affluent Americans would support broadening access to higher education, for example (Gilens 2012). Moreover, when elites have a stake in public systems, the systems tend to perform better. In Sweden, for example, everyone was required to attend state schools until the early 1990s. In 1992, the country introduced an innovative school voucher system, offering students the freedom to choose any school they wanted. The municipality would pay the school an amount equivalent to the average cost incurred by the child in a state school. Private schools could participate as long as they did not charge an additional fee. In this manner, private schooling became affordable to everyone, and schooling outcomes improved (Baker 2004; *The Economist* 2007; Böhlmark and Lindahl 2012). It helped that affluent Swedes did not mind paying higher taxes under Sweden's progressive tax policy.

Economic Crises and Food Insecurity

In contrast to the dramatic growth that characterized the last years of the previous millennium, growth rates in most countries have slowed, as a result of crises in recent years. With the onset of the financial crisis in 2008, the global economy shrank for the first time since World War II, with social and economic impacts reverberating around the globe. The crisis overlapped with an earlier food and energy crisis, which in 2006–08 pushed the prices of staple items beyond the reach of millions of people.

Economic and other crises tend to affect already disadvantaged groups more than they do others. The effects of a global crisis can be transmitted through various channels (such as trade, public budgets, credit, investment, aid, and remittances). The nature and magnitude of each of these impacts usually differ by gender, increasing the economic insecurity and burden of unpaid work among women (Floro, Tornqvist, and Taş 2010). The overlapping crises since 2008 have had a disproportionate impact on the most vulnerable groups, which rely solely on informal coping mechanisms, with significant long-term consequences on their well-being (Heltberg, Hossain, and Reva 2012). Moreover, these groups usually take longer to recover from the effects of such shocks.

Despite reductions in poverty across the board, hunger has remained a stark axis of exclusion; it affects certain groups and areas disproportionately. Food price volatility has exacerbated the problem, and countries that are in conflict are disproportionately affected. According to the Global Hunger Index (GHI), which ranks countries' hunger situation as "alarming" or "extremely alarming," the proportion of people who are food insecure remains high, despite considerable progress in reducing hunger since 1990 (figure 4.4). Angola, Bangladesh, Ethiopia, Mozambique, Nicaragua, Niger, and Vietnam—all of which started from a low base—saw the largest improvements. Twenty-six countries have "extremely alarming" or "alarming" levels of hunger. The countries with "extremely alarming" GHI scores in 2011 are Burundi, Chad, the Democratic Republic of Congo, and Eritrea; most of the countries with "alarming" scores are in Sub-Saharan Africa and South Asia. Improvements in South Asia have been very slow, especially since 1996. Within countries, food insecurity is often correlated with ethnicity and region, with the most excluded groups and people living in remote areas at greatest risk. In Nepal, historically disadvantaged castes and residents of the mountainous western regions have the highest incidence of self-reported food insecurity (World Bank 2011). Issues of hunger and food insecurity have always been very political; they have become rallying cries for movements that are contesting the claim that growth has led to shared prosperity.

Concerns around Inequality

Incomes of the poorest have risen, but so have the incomes of the richest, although inequality trends are highly heterogeneous across countries. Milanovic (2012) outlines three types of inequality: across countries, across countries (weighted by population), and across the world's individuals. He shows that although inequality across countries (measured by Gini coefficients) increased between 1950 and 2010, inequality across countries (weighted by population) fell, as a result of the role of fast-growing populous countries, such as India and China. Inequality across individuals,

Figure 4.4 Hunger Is Widespread, with Slow Declines between 1990 and 2011 in Regions That Need the Greatest Progress

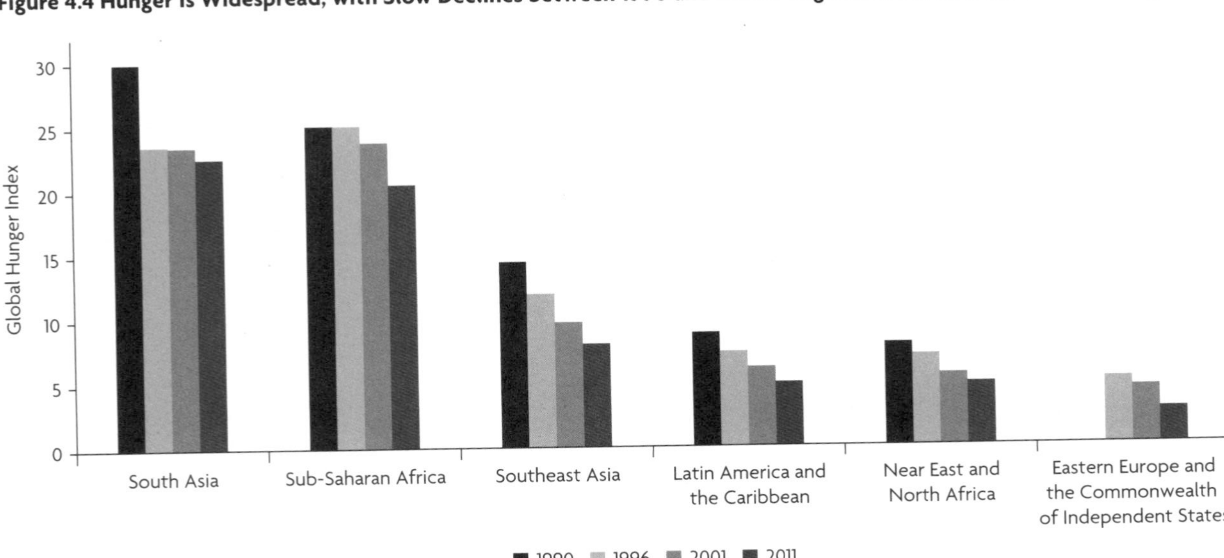

Source: Von Grebmer et al. 2012.
Note: The Global Hunger Index combines three equally weighted indicators: the proportion of people who are undernourished, the prevalence of underweight in children under the age of five, and the mortality rate of children under age five. It ranks countries on a 100-point scale, with 0 the best score (no hunger) and 100 the worst.

in contrast, seems to be higher, but it has been on a downward path since 2000 (figure 4.5). However, people tend to react to inequality as it affects them, usually in the countries or regions where they live. Within countries, both the United States and China are in the throes of rising inequality, which remains high in South Africa and is increasing in India as well. In contrast, inequality across Latin America, which had been very high in the 1990s, has shown a considerable decline. Overall, it is estimated that 71 percent of the world's population lives in countries where income inequality has been increasing since the 1990s, including China, India, Russia, and the United States. Another 7 percent lives in countries where inequality has stayed the same for at least two decades (Conference Board of Canada 2011).

Inequality reduces the opportunity for social mobility. Brunori, Ferreira, and Peragine (2013) find that inequalities in opportunities are positively correlated with overall income inequality and negatively correlated with measures of intergenerational mobility, both in incomes and in years of schooling. To put it simply, children born to poor parents in

Figure 4.5 Inequality across Countries (Weighted by Population) Fell between 1950 and 2010, but Inequality across the World's Individuals Is Relatively Higher

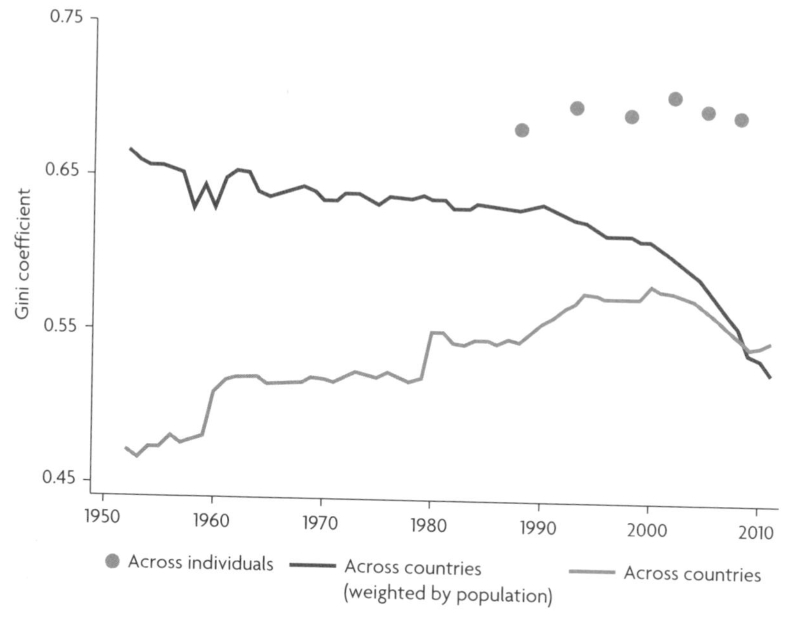

Source: Milanovic 2012.

unequal societies are much less likely to have the opportunity to move out of poverty, leading to the persistence of intergenerational poverty. In turn, thwarted avenues for social mobility lead to frustrated aspirations and can increase the likelihood of political unrest. In fact, such thwarted aspirations often lead to exaggerated perceptions of economic inequality, as chapter 5 discusses.

Not Just Transitions but Revolutions in Knowledge, Information, and Citizen Action

Education and Information Technology

Education is the unparalleled agent of social change. It has expanded across the board, even in the poorest countries.

The world currently has the largest cohort of young people in history. This cohort has attainments, aspirations, and hopes that are quite different from those of its parents' generation. When combined with the fact that its members are also better educated than their parents were, have greater access to information, and have better connectedness, the world could well be poised for the greatest movement toward social inclusion. In Sub-Saharan Africa, for instance, there was a fivefold increase in the gross secondary school enrollment rate, from 7 percent to 36 percent, between 1970 and 2009. At the global level, the corresponding figure nearly doubled, from 36 percent to 68 percent (World Development Indicators database).

Education affects social inclusion in many other ways. It often changes relationships of power within society and within households. Groups that were considered subordinate acquire voice and confidence when educated. They tend to be more assertive in holding the state and service providers accountable and in demanding dignity and respect from groups that were considered dominant. At the household level, educated young women have greater say in decision making and are able to access opportunities outside their homes in ways their mothers never did.

These changes affect intrafamily power relations. A large body of literature focuses on the enormous impact education can have on women's inclusion into markets, services, and spaces. When young women in Bangladesh were asked during focus group discussions how education had changed their lives, they described "being able to speak" as the most important gain (World Bank 2008). Despite these dramatic developments, educational expansion is far from a completed agenda. School dropout rates are still high among the most excluded groups, and educational quality remains a challenge even in countries that have taken strides in expanding quantity. Finally, as noted elsewhere in this report, educational institutions become sites where exclusion plays out (see, for instance, box 3.1 in chapter 3).

When combined with the global revolution in information technology, advances in education have enormous implications for social inclusion. It means not only that people in developing countries are rapidly catching up with their developed peers but also that there are greater channels through which social inclusion can take place, even for poorer countries and households.

In both India and China, three-fourths of the population is estimated to have access to mobile phones. In much of Central America and some Latin American countries, including Brazil, as well as in developing countries with large youth cohorts, such as Indonesia and the Islamic Republic of Iran, the number of cell phones and mobile phone subscriptions exceeds the number of people. Owning a mobile phone can alter the quality of life of individuals, through greater connectedness to markets, services, and spaces. For instance, farmers in remote areas are often at the mercy of middlemen, who pay a lower price than the farmers would get in the market. A number of initiatives are using mobile technology to inform farmers of market prices through their mobile phones. A study of farmers in the Philippines finds that owning a mobile phone had positive impacts on the household-level growth rate of per capita consumption (Labonne and Chase 2009).

The role of information technology in collective action is also being widely recognized by citizens who claim their political and social space through online engagement. Virtual groups are able to mobilize individuals for a number of causes and to voice discontent against perceived wrongs.

Although education and information technology have created new opportunities for social inclusion, they also are conduits for continuing and new forms of exclusion. Individuals and households left out of the expansion in education are usually from groups that face cumulative disadvantage. They are overrepresented among the uneducated and underrepresented among the highly educated. Part I of this report discusses the fact that group identity has a bearing on individual outcomes in a variety of ways. Box 3.1 in chapter 3, for instance, tells the story of a young woman who had to drop out of college because it was a site for the play of social exclusion. Family background, networks, social skills, and ability to navigate the social space become as salient as academic performance.

The delivery of education—in terms of the curriculum, the manner in which teachers treat students, and the quality of education—affects the performance of excluded groups. With overall progress, and improvement in the educational attainment of the average population, there is a risk that the divide between excluded and nonexcluded groups will grow.

As in education, the divide between people who have access to information technology and people who do not is evident. Access to the Internet is still very expensive in many countries, and richer people, people who live in urban areas, and people who belong to certain demographic groups and speak English have a clear advantage. Table 4.5 shows that in Lagos and Rio de Janeiro, the cost of going online for the average person actually increased over time. An hour of Internet access in a cybercafé can cost the resident of a developing city twice as much of his or her daily income as such access can cost the resident of a developed city.

There is an age and a gender dimension to the digital divide as well, and people with disabilities face particular challenges. The deeper the impact of the Internet and of information flowing electronically, the more excluded, groups that remain unconnected will be. For instance, many job applications or applications for admissions to educational institutions are increasingly being accepted only electronically. In several countries, government services such as making an appointment to renew a driver's license, identification card, or voter registration can be accessed only online.

Citizens' Responses to Transitions and Transformations

The historic developments of the last 40 years have redefined the context for the 21st century. Individuals and groups feel the impacts of these transitions cumulatively and through multiple channels. The reactions are unprecedented as well and are reflected through a new political and social activism. The massive sit-ins of the Occupy Wall Street movement have found echoes in other parts of the world and in other forms of dissent. The nature of these new movements—dynamic, evolving, and often played out in virtual space—does not lend itself to easy analysis.

Contemporary protest movements have much in common with the past, but they also seem to have a distinctive character. Current movements embody protest as a process of mass networked, connected, collaborative, and ongoing action common across countries (Castells 2011). Participants come from mixed demographic and socioeconomic backgrounds and choose to protest in ways that are closer to their lifestyle and mindset. A host of innovative protests have utilized art, dance, and drama to speak

Table 4.5 Internet Access Is Still Very Expensive in Many Large Cities

2000		2005	
City	Percentage of income	City	Percentage of income
Delhi	83	Lagos	75
Calcutta	79	Cairo	23
Karachi	77	Dhaka	15
Moscow	73	Rio de Janeiro	15
Mumbai	62	São Paulo	14
Dhaka	62	Buenos Aires	13
Tehran	47	Beijing	12
Beijing	39	Karachi	10
Lagos	35	Mexico City	10
Buenos Aires	34	Tokyo	9
London	31	Calcutta	9
Jakarta	28	Istanbul	9
Cairo	26	Jakarta	8
Manila	21	Los Angeles	7
Tokyo	14	Osaka	7
Rio de Janeiro	14	Mumbai	7
Osaka	14	Tehran	7
Shanghai	13	London	6
Seoul	13	Moscow	6
Mexico City	13	New York	6
Los Angeles	11	Delhi	6
New York	10	Shanghai	6
		Manila	5
		Seoul	5
Developing country average	40	Developing country average	14
Developed country average	26	Developed country average	7

Source: World Information Access 2007.

out against what is perceived as being unfair to groups that feel left out of mainstream economic and social processes.

Many developing countries are articulating these demands in terms of rights. In India, for instance, since 2005, rights-based movements and judicial activism have led to the passage of laws for the right to information, employment, and education. Another law seeks to protect the rights of Adivasis (tribal groups who claim to be India's original inhabitants) over their lands and forests, and a right to food movement is currently very strong. These movements have led in turn to greater citizen oversight of the design and implementation of many social programs. Across Africa and Asia, citizens are protesting against the manner in which land is being acquired for infrastructure and commercial farming and intensifying action against the way in which minerals are being extracted from their countries.

Another important development in the past few years has been the revival of feminist protests and changes in the gender aspects of protest movements. Three trends stand out. First, there is a strong strand of protest against curbs on women's sexual and reproductive rights, ranging from abortion rights in the United States to the Billion Rising Campaign against gender-based violence. Second, men are increasingly joining the protests against the violation of women's rights. Third, women are increasingly joining social protest movements. In the Arab Republic of Egypt, female political activists and reporters continued to contribute to the revolution even after they were sexually harassed in Tahrir Square (Project Syndicate n.d.).

Just as citizens' movements to assert demands and be a part of the transformations have intensified, so too have state responses to these movements changed. New forms of protest, which involve the resurgence of actors such as students and new actors such as the middle class, place new pressures on states that are unused to such movements. The fear of contagion from the Arab Spring led many states to crack down on actual or anticipated protest. Although the number of social protests in China is under serious contestation, the government has sought to control microblogs from time to time. The mass protests against the rape of a young woman in Delhi in 2012 were controlled using force. Controls by the state in the Middle East are also well known. Yet states also realize that they will need to put in place reforms that address the new demands and the fact that, at their core, many of the new protests are demands for social inclusion.

Concluding Reflections

Global and national transitions have significant implications for social inclusion; the pace and complexity of the transitions underscore the need for attention to social inclusion. These transitions highlight the importance of looking at macro-level trends to plan for a socially inclusive future.

From an economic perspective, future policy will need to provide rapid and effective responses to expanding numbers of youth and the elderly while providing the basic needs of an increasingly urbanized and unequal population, without leaving a large carbon footprint for the generations to come. From a political perspective, it will be essential to understand the changing attitudes, behaviors, and demands of youth and the middle class and to create new opportunities and mechanisms for greater participation by them in decision making. At the same time, responsive governance and careful targeting of public services to a new profile of global citizens will be essential. From a social perspective, future policies and institutions will need to promote the affiliation of different social groups with the evolving social, political, and economic reality of increasingly diverse societies.

Notes

1. Figures are based on latest data available (usually 2011 but 2010 for some countries and 2007 for one country). The medium-variant estimates of the United Nations Population Division for 2005–10 indicate that 76 countries are below replacement level.
2. These figures do not include the 5 million people displaced by the Syrian conflict between 2011 and 2012, 1 million of whom are registered as refugees in neighboring countries.
3. Urbanization estimates by the United Nations have been criticized for overestimating the world's urban population because they estimate the growth rates for urban-rural populations, a conflation of natural increase in population, migration, and reclassification of settlements. Some argue that this practice inhibits the ability of demography to contribute to an understanding of the implications of urbanization (see B. Cohen 2006; J. Cohen 2010).
4. Although there is no standard definition of the "middle class," from a material perspective, it means meeting basic needs and having extra disposable income. It can be defined in absolute terms (exceeding a certain level of income) or relative terms (the middle segment of an income distribution). Banerjee and Duflo (2008) define people earning between $2 and $10 a day (in 2005 purchasing parity terms) in developing countries as middle class. Ravallion (2010) extends the upper bound to $13 a day (derived from the U.S. poverty line in 2005). Birdsall (2010) classifies all people earning more than $10 a day (except for the top 5 percent of the income distribution) as middle class.

References

Amin, S. 1998. "Family Structure and Change in Rural Bangladesh." *Population Studies* 52 (2): 201–13.

Arnold, M. 2011. "Looking through the Window of Opportunity and Seeing Gender Equality." *Development in a Changing Climate*, (blog), November 28. World Bank, Washington, DC. http://blogs.worldbank.org/climatechange/climate-change-may-be-big-window-opportunity (accessed May 5, 2013).

ASPIRE (Atlas of Social Protection—Indicators of Resilience and Equity). World Bank, Washington, DC. http://datatopics.worldbank.org/aspire.

Baker, M. 2004. "Swedish Parents Enjoy School Choice. *BBC News*, October 5. http://news.bbc.co.uk/2/hi/uk_news/education/3717744.stm (accessed August 10, 2013).

Banerjee, A. V., and E. Duflo. 2008. "What Is Middle Class about the Middle Classes around the World?" *Journal of Economic Perspectives* 22 (2): 3–28.

Birdsall, N. 2010. "The (Indispensable) Middle Class in Developing Countries; or, the Rich and the Rest, not the Poor and the Rest." In *Equity in a Globalizing World*, ed. R. Kanbur and M. Spence, 157–89. Washington, DC: World Bank.

Böhlmark, A., and M. Lindahl. 2012. "Independent Schools and Long-Run Educational Outcomes: Evidence from Sweden's Large Scale Voucher Reform." Working Paper 19, Institute for Evaluation of Labour Market and Education Policy, Uppsala, Sweden.

Brainerd, E., and D. M. Cutler. 2005. "Autopsy on an Empire: Understanding Mortality in Russia and the Former Soviet Union." *Journal of Economic Perspectives* 19 (1): 107–30. http://people.brandeis.edu/~ebrainer/jep05.pdf.

Brunori, P., F. H. G. Ferreira, and V. Peragine. 2013. "Inequality of Opportunity, Income Inequality and Economic Mobility: Some International Comparisons." Policy Research Working Paper 6304, World Bank, Washington, DC.

Castells, M. 2011. "Social Movements in the Age of the Internet" (lecture). London School of Economics, London, England. http://www.lse.ac.uk/publicEvents/events/2011/20111124t1830vSZT.aspx (accessed October 7, 2013).

Chandy, L., and G. Gertz. 2011. "Poverty in Numbers: The Changing State of Global Poverty from 2005 to 2015." *Global Views Policy Brief* 1, Brookings Institution, Washington, DC.

Cohen, B. 2006. "Urbanization in Developing Countries: Current Trends, Future Projections, and Key Challenges for Sustainability." *Technology in Society* 28 (1): 63–80.

Cohen, J. 2010. "Beyond Population: Everyone Counts in Development." Working Paper 220, Center for Global Development, Washington, DC.

Conference Board of Canada. 2011. "World Income Inequality: Is the World Becoming More Unequal?" http://www.conferenceboard.ca/hcp/hot-topics/worldinequality.aspx (accessed April 8, 2013).

Demling, A. 2012. "Germany or Bust: Southern European Jobseekers Head North in Droves." Spiegel Online International, November 16.

Dercon, S. 2012. "Is Green Growth Good for the Poor?" Policy Research Working Paper 6231, World Bank, Washington, DC.

Eberstadt, N. 2011. "World Population Prospects and the Global Economic Outlook: The Shape of Things to Come." Working Paper Series on Development Policy 5, American Enterprise Institute, Washington, DC.

Economist, The. 2007. "Free to Choose, and Learn." May 3. http://www.economist.com/node/9119786 (accessed August 10, 2013).

Ferreira, F. H. G., J. Messina, J. Rigolini, L.-F. Lopez-Calva, M. A. Lugo, and R. Vakis. 2013. *Economic Mobility and the Rise of the Latin American Middle Class* (in Spanish). Washington, DC: World Bank.

Floro, M., A. Tornqvist, and E. O. Taş. 2010. "The Impact of the Economic Crisis on Women's Economic Empowerment." Working Paper 26, American University, Washington, DC.

Gilens, M. 2012. *Affluence and Influence: Economic Inequality and Political Power in America*. Princeton, NJ: Princeton University Press.

Guilmoto, C. Z. 2011. "Sex Ratio at Birth in Viet Nam: New Evidence on Patterns, Trends and Differentials." Monograph 8, Vietnam Population and Housing Census, Ministry of Planning and Investment, General Statistics Office, Hanoi.

Hall, G., and H. A. Patrinos, ed. 2012. *Indigenous Peoples, Poverty, and Development*. Cambridge, U.K.: Cambridge University Press.

Heltberg, R., N. Hossain, and A. Reva. 2012. *Living through Crises: How the Food, Fuel, and Financial Shocks Affect the Poor*. Washington, DC: World Bank.

Huffington Post. 2013. "Haitians Aren't Getting Enough Food, UN Says." April 2. http://www.huffingtonpost.com/2013/04/03/haiti-food-un_n_3005688.html.

International Income Distribution Database (I2D2). World Bank, Washington, DC.

Jingzhong, Y., and J. Murray. 2010. *Left Behind Children in Rural China*. Social Sciences Academic Press (Beijing, China) and Paths International (Reading, U.K.).

Kharas, H., and G. Gertz. 2011. *The New Global Middle Class: A Cross-Over from West to East*. Wolfensohn Center for Development, Brookings Institution, Washington, DC. http://www.brookings.edu/~/media/research/files/papers/2010/3/china%20middle%20class%20kharas/03_china_middle_class_kharas.pdf (accessed October 7, 2013).

Labonne, J., and R. S. Chase. 2009. "The Power of Information: The Impact of Mobile Phones on Farmers' Welfare in the Philippines." Policy Research Working Paper 4996, World Bank, Washington, DC. http://www-wds.worldbank.org/servlet/WDSContentServer/WDSP/IB/2009/07/16/000158349_20090716115612/Rendered/PDF/WPS4996.pdf.

Lee, J., M. Lundberg, D. Margolis, D. Newhouse, D. Robalino, F. Rother, and A. Tasneem. 2012. "Youth Employment: A Human Development Agenda for the Next Decade." World Bank, Washington, DC.

Lesthaeghe, R. 2010. "The Unfolding Story of the Second Demographic Transition." *Population and Development Review* 36: 211–51.

MacDonald, J., and R. J. Sampson. 2012. "The World in a City: Immigration and America's Changing Social Fabric." *Annals of the American Academy of Political and Social Science* 641 (1): 6–15.

Marras, S. 2012. "GIS, Web, and 3D. Tools for Holistic and Shareable Knowledge. The Experience of the Map Kibera Project." *Territorio* 61: 110–14.

Milanovic, B. 2012. "Global Income Inequality by the Numbers: In History and Now." Policy Research Working Paper 6259, World Bank, Washington, DC. http://documents.worldbank.org/curated/en/2012/11/16920534/global-income-inequality-numbers-history-now---an-overview--.

Montgomery, M. R. 2009. "Urban Poverty and Health in Developing Countries." *Population Bulletin* 64 (2): 2–15.

Moser, C., S. Georgieva, A. Norton, and A. Stein. 2010. *Pro-Poor Adaptation to Climate Change in Urban Centers: Case Studies of Vulnerability and Resilience in Kenya and Nicaragua*. Report 54947-GLB, World Bank, Washington, DC.

Neumayer, E., and T. Plümper, 2007. "The Gendered Nature of Natural Disasters: The Impact of Catastrophic Events on the Gender Gap in Life Expectancy, 1981–2002." *Annals of the Association of American Geographers* 97 (3): 551–66.

OECD (Organisation for Economic Co-operation and Development). 2013. *Fragile States 2013: Resource Flows and Trends in a Shifting World*. Paris: OECD.

PovcalNet: An Online Poverty Analysis Tool. World Bank, Washington, DC. http://iresearch.worldbank.org/PovcalNet/index.htm.

Project Syndicate. n.d. "Ending the War against Women." http://www.projectsyndicate.org/commentary/eliminating-global-gender-violence-and-inequality-by-george-a--papandreou-and-ouafa-hajji (accessed April 19, 2013).

Ravallion, M. 2010. "The Developing World's Bulging (But Vulnerable) Middle Class." *World Development* 38 (4): 445–54.

Sen, A. 2001. *Development as Freedom*. Oxford: Oxford University Press.

Ulrich, R., and R. Muenz. 1995. "Immigration and Population Change in Germany." *Migration News* 2 (1).

UN (United Nations). 1993. *World Economic Survey 1993*. New York: United Nations.

———. 2011a. *World Mortality Report 2009*. Department of Economic and Social Affairs, Population Division, New York.

———. 2011b. *World Population Prospects: The 2010 Revision*. United Nations Secretariat, Department of Economic and Social Affairs, Population Division, New York. http://esa.un.org/wpp.

UNFPA (United Nations Population Fund). n.d. "Migration: A World on the Move." UNFPA, New York. http://www.unfpa.org/pds/migration.html.

———. 2011. *State of the World Population 2011: People and Opportunities in a Population of Seven Billion*. New York: UNFPA.

UNODC (United Nations on Drugs and Crime). n.d. "Factsheet on Human Trafficking." http://www.unodc.org/documents/human-trafficking/UNVTF_fs_HT_EN.pdf.

von Grebmer, K., C. Ringler, M. W. Rosegrant, T. Olofinbiyi, D. Wiesmann, H. Fritschel, O. Badiane, M. Torero, Y. Yohannes, and J. Thompson. 2012. *2012 Global Hunger Index: The Challenge of Hunger: Ensuring Sustainable Food Security under Land, Water, and Energy Stresses*. Washington, DC: International Food Policy Research Institute (IFPRI). http://www.ifpri.org/sites/default/files/publications/ghi12.pdf.

WFP (World Food Programme). 2012. "Sahel Crisis: Country by Country." August 8. http://www.wfp.org/stories/sahel-crisis-by-country (accessed March 19, 2013).

World Bank. Moving Out of Poverty [research initiative]. World Bank, Washington, DC. http://www.worldbank.org/en/topic/poverty.

———. Voices of the Poor (research initiative). World Bank, Washington, DC. http://go.worldbank.org/H1N8746X10.

———. 2008. *Whispers to Voices: Gender and Social Transformation in Bangladesh*. Bangladesh Development Series 22. Dhaka: World Bank.

———. 2009. *World Development Report 2010: Development and Climate Change*. Washington, DC: World Bank.

———. 2011. "Social Safety Nets in Nepal." Draft report, World Bank, Washington, DC.

———. 2012a. *Kingdom of Morocco: Promoting Youth Opportunities and Participation*. Washington, DC: World Bank.

———. 2012b. *Turn Down the Heat: Why a 4°C Warmer World Must Be Avoided*. Report for the World Bank by the Potsdam Institute for Climate Impact Research and Climate Analytics. Washington, DC: World Bank.

———. 2013. *World Development Report: Jobs*. Washington, DC: World Bank.

World Bank and DRC (Development Research Center of the State Council, People's Republic of China). 2013. *China 2030: Building a Modern, Harmonious, and Creative Society*. Washington, DC: World Bank.

World Development Indicators (database). World Bank, Washington, DC. http://data.worldbank.org/data-catalog/world-development-indicators.

World Information Access. 2007. "The Urban Digital Divide II: Rich v. Poor Cities." August 1. http://www.wiaproject.org/index.php/51/the-urban-digital-divide-i-global-cities-v-regional-centers.

Yabiku, S. T., V. Agadjanian, and A. Sevoyan. 2010. "Husbands' Labour Migration and Wives' Autonomy, Mozambique 2000–2006." *Population Studies* 64 (3): 293–306.

CHAPTER 5

Attitudes and Perceptions of Inclusion

Men are disturbed not by things, but by the view which they take of them.

—EPICTETUS

Of late, there has been a plethora of reports, discussions, and debates on attitudes and perceptions of people about the world around them and about social, economic, and political issues. What was considered the domain of psychologists, psephologists, and market researchers appears to be surely and steadily entering the domain of core development practice (Norris 2009). The dramatic transformations reported in chapter 4 seem to have blurred the boundaries between positivism and subjectivism, as policy makers and researchers alike seek answers to complex questions.

Several countries in the Organisation for Economic Co-operation and Development (OECD) now conduct regular surveys that measure attitudes and life satisfaction. Many multilateral agencies, including several agencies of the United Nations, the International Organization for Migration (IOM), and others rely on perception surveys for their programming.[1] The World Values Surveys, the Life in Transition Surveys conducted by the European Bank for Reconstruction and Development and the World Bank, and the Latino Barometer and Afrobarometer are examples of surveys that capture cross-country attitudes and are increasingly being used for formulating policies and programs. Economists, who have long focused on gross domestic product (GDP) as the gold standard of progress, are veering toward subjective reports of well-being.[2]

Although attitudes and perceptions are sometimes mentioned in the same breath, there is a distinction between them. One formulation of an attitude is a "mindset or a tendency to act in a particular way as a result of both an individual's experience and temperament." A perception is the interpretation of a situation or stimuli. "The person interprets the stimuli into something meaningful to him or her, based on prior experiences. However, what an individual interprets or perceives may be substantially different from reality" (Pickens 2005, 52). There is now a strong body of literature on the measurement of attitudes; the measurement of perceptions is also becoming more refined. What is less well known is how attitudes and perceptions change. This chapter is devoted to some empirical findings of attitudes and perceptions as they relate to social inclusion.

Why do attitudes and perceptions matter for social inclusion? Attitudes matter most of all because they are a barometer of people's potential behavior. Human beings act on the basis of how they feel. Their feelings of being included and respected are central to the opportunities they access and the way in which they take part in society. Conversely, which groups get included and excluded, and on what terms, is shaped by people's attitudes about each other and about themselves. The importance of attitudes and perceptions also spills over to levels above the individual. A large body of literature shows that prejudices, stereotypes, and misperceptions affect the way policy is implemented and even designed. This chapter shows that attitudes play a key role in the treatment of individuals and groups, both by other members of the society and by the state.

Perceptions also mediate social inclusion and shine a light on the processes through which exclusion takes place. Perceptions of unfairness and injustice, and frustration with social and political institutions or society at large, often reflect individuals' feelings of powerlessness. In highly stratified societies, particularly where political power is concentrated in the hands of a few, perceptions can be a significant measure of social inclusion. Feelings of fairness, justice, and "being part of society" can be manifestations of how much the society recognizes, respects, and listens to its members.

Over time, there has been greater acceptance of the fact that some practices can be judged on the basis of feelings and that these feelings can influence policy. Take sexual harassment, once considered normative, with victims of harassment having little recourse. Even after passage of the Civil Rights Act of 1964, federal courts in the United States refused to view sexual harassment as a form of employment discrimination. Basu (2003) describes how the definition of sexual harassment moved from overt threats to innuendo and now to feelings of being harassed. Moreover, the definition, which used to cover only men's harassment of women, has been expanded to include women's harassment of men and same-sex harassment. In essence, sexual harassment is widely recognized as a practice that can be vindicated on the basis of the feelings of the person harassed, even if the harasser does not regard the act to be harassment. Underlying the practice are power relations that play out and place certain groups and individuals at risk. Intended to intimidate those considered weaker, these relations in effect succeed in excluding weaker groups from a range of activities.

This chapter uses some recent surveys to highlight why paying attention to attitudes and perceptions is important for social inclusion. Based primarily on the World Values Surveys, the chapter tries to unpack some of the channels and underlying perceptions through which attitudes can influence social inclusion. It also discusses perceptions of citizens about their relations with formal institutions in their country, including the state. Most important, the chapter makes the case that attitudes and perceptions are not intractable, that they change over time. It concludes by arguing that efforts to increase social inclusion will have a better chance of succeeding if the role of attitudes and perceptions is taken into account.

Subjective Assessments of Individuals and Groups

The literature on happiness and subjective well-being makes the strong case that, although objective indicators are important, people's subjective reports can often be at variance with their objective condition. This dichotomy between objective and subjective reports of well-being presents a conundrum for policy makers, who are often puzzled over why people who seem to have everything report being less happy than people who have little. In Africa, for instance, poor people report being more hopeful than the rich, and in poorer countries in Latin America, the poor assess their health as better than the poor in richer countries (Graham 2011). Diener and Biswas-Diener (2005) show that life satisfaction scores among the *Forbes* group of richest Americans are similar to the scores of groups that are considerably worse off in objective terms (table 5.1). Clearly, something other than their objective conditions is driving their happiness and sense of well-being.

The drivers of subjective well-being may have a lot to do with what people value. Two groups that are very poor may have very different reported levels of happiness. The Maasai in Kenya, for instance, lack access to basic

Table 5.1 Life Satisfaction Is Not Tied to Absolute Wealth

Group	Score
Forbes' richest Americans	5.8
Maasai (Kenya)	5.4
Amish (Pennsylvania)	5.1
Inughuit (Northern Greenland)	5.1
Cloistered nuns (United States)	4.8
Illinois nurses	4.8
Illinois college students	4.7
Calcutta slum dwellers	4.4
Neutral	4.0
Calcutta sex workers	3.6
Uganda college students	3.2
Calcutta homeless	3.2
California homeless	2.8
New prisoners (Illinois)	2.4
Mental inpatients	2.4
Detroit sex workers	2.1

Source: Diener and Biswas-Diener 2005.
Note: Response scale: 7 = extremely satisfied, 4 = neutral, 1 = extremely dissatisfied.

infrastructure yet show a remarkably high life satisfaction score that is almost on par with that of the richest Americans. In contrast, the homeless in California, despite their average incomes being higher than the incomes of the Maasai, show low satisfaction. These scores could well reflect the importance of social relationships, an aspect of life in which the Maasai are better off than the homeless in a rich state in the United States. Hence, "people's expectations and the respect they receive from society seem to moderate the effects of income on life satisfaction" (Diener and Biswas-Diener 2005, 13).

Subjective reports of how people regard their own situation and that of others could also have to do with whom they compare themselves with and what they aspire to. Their aspirations are related to whom they want to be like—in short, whom they regard as their reference group. Policy makers may think the person who has risen out of poverty should be satisfied with her life, but how she feels depends on her reference group, which could include her neighbor, her relative, or even herself at another point in time.[3]

Stouffer et al. (1949) report that African American soldiers stationed in the South during World War II were more satisfied with their lives than African American soldiers stationed in the North, despite the fact that living standards in the South were much lower. The reason was that the soldiers in the South compared themselves with the local African American population—who faced racial discrimination and lived in acute poverty—rather than with other soldiers across the country (see Walker and Smith 2002). A similar phenomenon has been observed in the labor market, where women facing worse labor market outcomes than men reported feeling less deprived, because they compared themselves not with men but with other women (see, for instance, Serajuddin and Verme 2012).

Sometimes there is a strong correlation between objective and subjective reports of happiness, satisfaction, and well-being. The World Bank's Moving Out of Poverty study (Narayan, Pritchett, and Kapoor 2009) finds that happiness increases as people move out of poverty: only about 19 percent of people who moved out of poverty between 1995 and 2005 put themselves in the bottom three happiness categories (on a 10-point scale), compared with more than half of the chronic poor. Similarly, the literature on subjective well-being and happiness indicates that once basic objective needs (such as food, education, health) are met, self-reported well-being becomes more sensitive to factors such as rising aspirations, relative income differences, and the security of gains (Graham 2011). In a study on the relationship between subjective well-being and income mobility in Peru and the Russian Federation, Graham and Pettinato (2002) find that people with the greatest absolute gains in income have the most pessimistic subjective assessment of their well-being. They attribute this finding to global integration and unemployment in these countries, which shifted people's reference groups and made them increasingly wary of losing their position on the mobility ladder relative to a "global community." Referencing growth prospects for one's own country against the prospects of a region may similarly influence anticipation about the future. The second round of the Life in Transition Survey, for example, found Poles to be largely optimistic about their future. This finding was in sharp contrast to perceptions of people in other countries in the region (Romania, Hungary), very few of whom expressed optimism and satisfaction with their life (LiTS 2010). The finding could well reflect the fact that between 1990 and 2010, Poland's economy grew in real terms by 81 percent, with a significant decline in poverty (the proportion of people living under $5 a day came down from 25 percent to 12 percent between 2000 and 2010).

Poland was also the only country in the European Union to have avoided recession in 2009 (Plonka 2013).

Attitudes toward Excluded Groups

Attitudes toward excluded groups are important because they can determine how society treats these groups, how these groups engage with society, and how the policies that aim to improve their status are implemented. Excluded groups vary across contexts. Four main groups are discussed here: foreigners (usually migrants), homosexuals, people with HIV/AIDS, and women. Although women are a more heterogeneous and cross-cutting category than the other groups, their status in the labor market, education, and political leadership has traditionally been lower than that of men in almost every society and therefore deserves special attention.

Data from the World Values Surveys show changes in the attitudes toward these groups. Five waves of representative national surveys were conducted between 1981 and 2008; a sixth wave was being finalized in 2013. The surveys cover nearly 100 societies, with random samples of adult populations averaging about 1,400 respondents per country.[4] Limited access was available to the 2010–12 survey data in Foa (2012). Other data sources are used to juxtapose attitudes against objective indicators.

Attitudes and perceptions mediate social inclusion through various channels. The measured attitude, for instance, may be the rejection of a certain category as neighbor (a question asked in the World Values Surveys), but these attitudes are often manifestations of negative perceptions about those groups. Attitudes toward foreigners, for example, often have their roots in feelings of economic or cultural insecurity. They can be based on the perception that migrants take jobs away from natives, that they are perpetrators of crime and violence, or that they are a burden on the welfare system. There is also a view that links migrants to terrorism. Finally, a cultural argument is often made in "us" versus "them" terms. Migrants bring their own values and norms, which are distinct from those in their receiving areas. Although these differences can have salutary consequences for diversity and pluralism, integration of migrants can also be a contentious process.

A recent empirical analysis that explores the determinants of negative attitudes toward certain groups (response to the unwanted neighbors question) in the Life in Transition Survey (LiTS 2006, 2010) for Europe shows that controlling for a range of variables, country-specific factors are far more important than individual socioeconomic and demographic characteristics in explaining patterns of negative attitudes.[5] By the same token, stigmatization of homosexuality and HIV/AIDS status are usually based on religious and moral beliefs, and gender attitudes are shaped by norms of power and masculinity, although they may be justified as religious mores. The end result of these attitudes is exclusion of certain groups from markets, services, and spaces, as laid out in table 5.2.

Attitudes toward Foreigners and Migrants

As discussed in chapter 4, migration will be one of the most volatile global transitions in the near future. Its impacts on attitudes toward foreigners are already coming to the surface.

Table 5.2 What Is Driving Negative Attitudes toward Other Social Groups?

Group	Question in World Values Surveys	Likely perception about the group that underlies the negative attitude	Domain of exclusion
Foreigners and migrants	Would you have them as neighbors?	• Take away jobs from natives “Contaminate” the culture • Are ungrateful to host country and loyal to another country • Commit illegal acts • Do not assimilate, learn language, adhere to rules • May become a majority or politically powerful • Represent religious “other” • Could affect election outcomes • Represent drain on the welfare system	Markets Spaces
Homosexuals	Would you have them as neighbors?	• Are immoral and unnatural; behave in way that violates religious tenets	Spaces
HIV/AIDS affected	Would you have them as neighbors?	• Are immoral; many people conflate HIV/AIDS with homosexuality • Are infectious	Spaces Services
Women	Is university education more important for a boy than for a girl? Do men have more right to jobs when jobs are scarce? Do men make better political leaders than women do?	• Are subordinate to, weaker than, and less capable than men • Should be restricted to the home and to private spaces • Are incapable of functioning as well as men • Man's role is to be breadwinner, so he should have better opportunities • Men have “natural” leadership qualities	Services Markets Spaces

Source: World Bank, based on data from the World Values Surveys.

Animosity toward migrants is common across many societies. It usually arises from the perception that they are taking jobs away from natives, a view that colors day-to-day interactions between migrants and the host populations as well as restricting migrants' access to markets. Such conflict is likely to be more intense when the receiving area is ethnically homogeneous (so that migrants and native populations are easily identifiable), when migrants dominate certain economic activities, or when migrants fare better than natives. There is also apprehension about an influx of less skilled workers, which natives fear will reduce already low wages.[6] Migrants, particularly asylum seekers, are also seen as imposing a fiscal burden as a result of the popular perception that they use more services and pay less in taxes than nonmigrants. This belief has already triggered a set of policy responses in countries undergoing fiscal austerity. For example, the end of restrictions on the free mobility of Bulgarian and Romanian workers within the European Union has led to fears that unemployed people, often depicted by the media as "indigent gypsies," will flood welfare-generous European states (Guild 2013).[7]

Survey data lend credence to the popular perception that animosity against immigrants is widespread and that it changes over time. The World Values Surveys ask respondents which groups they would not like to have as neighbors (figure 5.1). The responses indicate that people who come from different linguistic, racial, and religious backgrounds are viewed negatively in many societies. For example, the latest publicly available round of the survey, conducted between 2005 and 2008, shows that in Hong Kong SAR, China; the Islamic Republic of Iran; Jordan; and Malaysia, immigrants and foreigners were viewed unfavorably by 57–79 percent of respondents. People in India also appeared to have negative attitudes toward different religious and linguistic groups, but Foa (2012) shows that these attitudes improved significantly in the most recent surveys, conducted between 2010 and 2012. Among the 21 countries for which comparable data are available from 1981 to 2012, 10 show strongly positive changes and 11 show strongly negative changes. No obvious pattern distinguishes societies with sizable declines from those with sizable gains, and some changes are within the margin of error (Foa 2012).

Changes in attitudes toward migrants reflect the changing terms of political life and public policy.[8] In OECD countries, for example, the number of people rejecting migrants as neighbors rose from 1 in 12 respondents in 1980 to about 1 in 8 respondents in 2010. This 34 percent increase is considerable and coincides with the growth of conservative political parties that advocate for limiting the inflow of migrants (Norris 2005, cited in Foa 2012).

The changes in anti-migrant sentiment also correlate with the stock of the migrant population in each region. Foa (2012) uses the most recent round of the World Values Surveys data to look at the relationship between increases in the migrant population and the change in the ratio of people accepting versus rejecting migrants. Such a comparison is useful if one believes that each region has a natural baseline against which changes should be measured. Foa finds that the proportion of migrants in the general population has fallen in some regions, such as Sub-Saharan Africa and Latin America. In these regions, anti-migrant sentiment has also declined. The exception remains Europe and Central Asia, where the size of the foreign-born population fell sharply following the collapse of the Soviet Union and Yugoslavia but unleashed processes of nationalism have served both to increase anti-migrant sentiment and, in a number of cases, to drive out resident minorities (Campos and Kuzeyev 2007, cited in Foa 2012). The World Values Surveys for 2005–08 show a weakly positive relationship between the share of a country's population that rejects migrants or foreign workers as neighbors and the proportion of migrants in that country's population in 2005 (figure 5.2). Jordan and Hong Kong SAR, China, stand out in terms of the relatively large size of their migrant population and the high levels of anti-foreigner attitudes. In contrast, Australia, Canada, and Switzerland are outliers with relatively large foreign populations, but less than 10 percent of respondents in these countries hold negative views of foreigners or migrants.

Factors other than migration could also have influenced the acceptance or rejection of foreigners across countries. First, it is possible that migration is seen as a threat under some conditions but not others. It is also possible that the nature of migrant flows has changed. Today, international migrants may seem more "culturally distant" in the countries where they settle, compared to earlier migration flows (Baker et al. 2009). Moreover, migration has occurred against a backdrop of rising tensions over religious issues, in both Western societies and a number of developing countries, notably in East and South Asia. Second, national discourses around ethnicity or citizenship can influence attitudes toward foreigners. For example, in high-income countries witnessing recent waves of immigration, foreigner rejection is higher in countries with strongly ethnic or cultural conceptions of citizenship (such as France or Italy) than in countries with "thinner"

Figure 5.1 Whom Would You Not Like as a Neighbor?

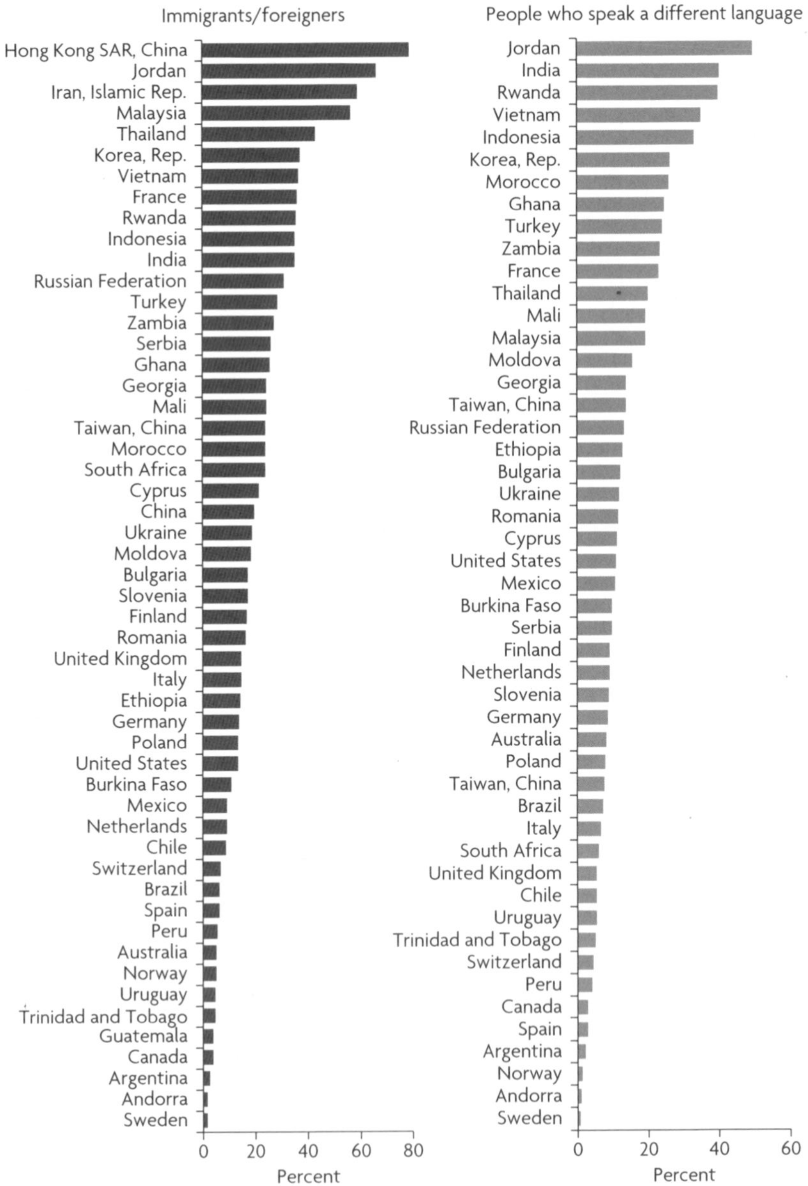

(figure continues on next page)

Figure 5.1 Whom Would You Not Like as a Neighbor? *(continued)*

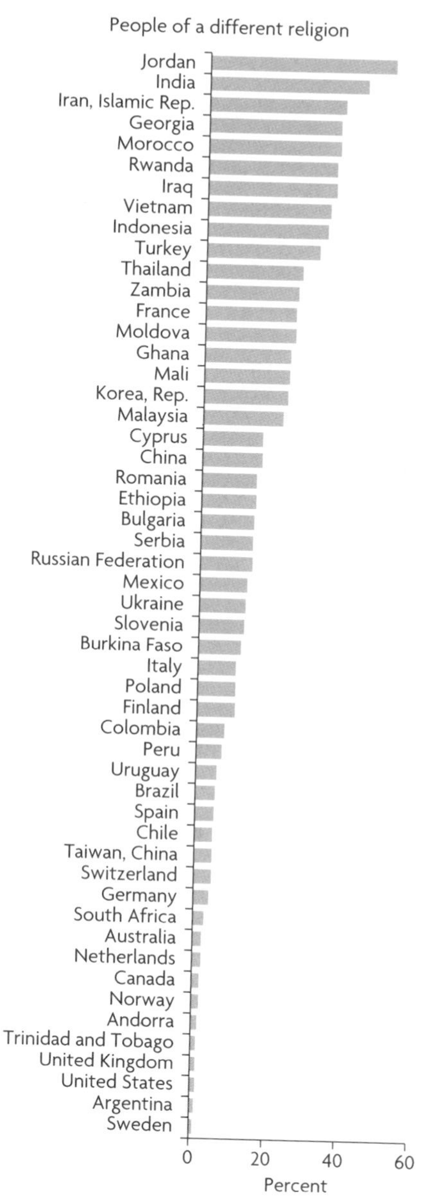

Source: World Bank, based on data from the World Values Surveys 2005–08.
Note: Data were collected at different times between 2005 and 2008 in each country or area.

Figure 5.2 Antipathy toward Foreigners Is Correlated with the Proportion of Migrants in the Population

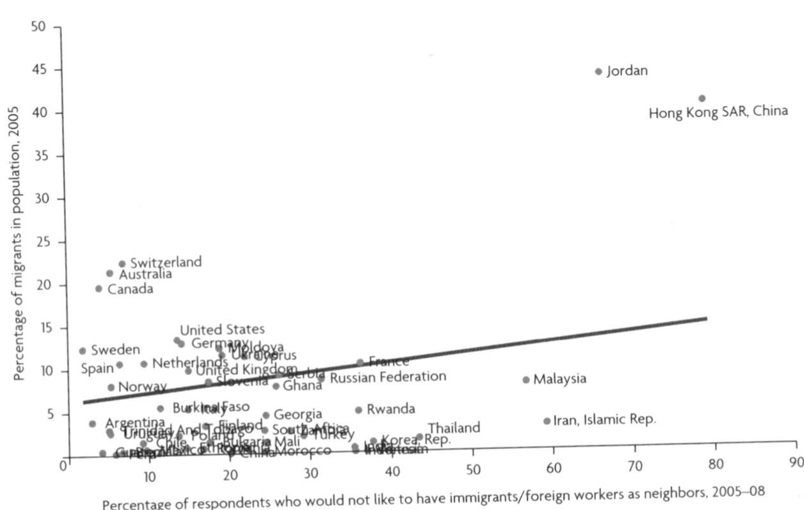

Source: World Bank, based on data from the World Values Surveys 2005–08 and World Development Indicators 2005.
Note: Attitudes data were collected between 2005 and 2008. Data on the migrant population are from 2005 (data are measured in five-year intervals in the WDI).

conceptions of civic identity (such as Canada, the United Kingdom, or the United States) (Foa 2012). Third, Kleemans and Klugman (2009) argue that acceptability of immigration is likely to be higher if jobs are available. This finding suggests that reforms that link future liberalization to the demand for labor, so that inflows of migrants will respond to vacancy levels, could attract public support and alleviate the concern that migrants will substitute for or undercut local workers. Fourth, perceptions toward foreigners and migrants may also be a reflection of contemporaneous issues affecting a country. Consider Bulgaria, Romania, and Slovenia, three post-transition states that joined the European Union. These countries have witnessed increased foreigner acceptance over the past few decades, perhaps because foreign contacts are increasingly associated with tourism, investment, and student exchange rather than with a history of foreign domination, the threat of terrorism, or competition in the labor market. Finally, other factors that may explain negative sentiments could include unemployment or high crime rates, the nature of immigration policies, and media coverage of the issues related to migration.

Attitudes toward People with HIV/AIDS and Homosexuals

Two groups of people, homosexuals and people with HIV/AIDS, have been singled out for discrimination and exclusion in the last few decades. The HIV/AIDS epidemic in Africa, combined with overall antipathy toward lesbian, gay, bisexual, and transgender (LGBT) populations in most parts of the continent, have fueled attacks against them. Homosexuality is illegal in many countries, although it is common for homosexuals to face social exclusion even where homosexuality is not illegal. Discrimination against these two groups is also related because both are perceived to be "immoral" based on religious or cultural ideologies. More than 90 percent of World Values Surveys (2005–08) respondents in Jordan, the Islamic Republic of Iran, and Georgia, and more than 80 percent in Turkey, the Republic of Korea, Ethiopia, and Burkina Faso reported negative attitudes toward homosexuals (figure 5.3). Negative attitudes toward homosexuals were closely linked with negative attitudes toward people with HIV/AIDS. The top five countries where attitudes toward homosexuals were negative (Jordan, the Islamic Republic of Iran, Georgia, Turkey, and the Republic of Korea) were also the top five countries in which people with HIV/AIDS were viewed unfavorably. There is almost a one-to-one relationship between negative attitudes toward homosexuals and people with HIV/AIDS (figure 5.4).

Discrimination against and stigmatization of people with HIV/AIDS has been categorized by UNAIDS as a primary obstacle in the fight against the disease. Stigmatization of people with HIV/AIDS prevents individuals from seeking information, adopting preventive behavior, getting tested, disclosing their sero-status, and accessing treatment even where services are available. People with or associated with HIV/AIDS are at risk of losing their employment, property, livelihoods, and social status. They may lose their children, families, and social networks and may be refused care at health facilities. These effects are more prominent among already disadvantaged groups. Women and children are more prone than men to property grabbing, abandonment, and violence as a result of their HIV status or association with the disease. Similarly, men who have sex with men (MSM), injecting drug users, sex workers, and prisoners often face greater discrimination when diagnosed with HIV. These groups experience multilayered stigma and discrimination, making them likely to be refused services (DFID 2007). In a survey of people receiving antiretroviral therapy in Botswana, 37 percent of respondents said it was more difficult to cope with the social consequences of their HIV status than the medical ones, and 14 percent said they were equally difficult to handle (DFID 2007).

Figure 5.3 Antipathy toward Homosexuals and People with HIV/AIDS as Neighbors Is Very High in Some Countries and Areas

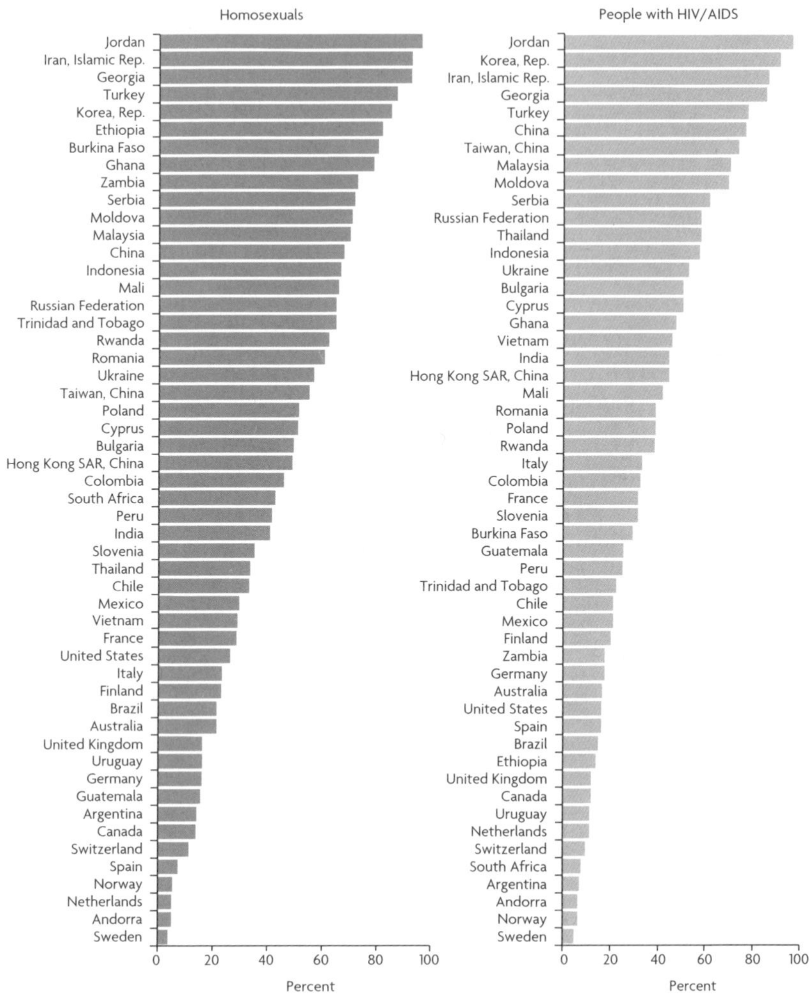

Source: World Bank, based on data from World Values Surveys 2005–08.
Note: Data were collected at different times between 2005 and 2008 in each country or area.

It is well known that people with HIV/AIDS and LGBT groups face discrimination; it is less well known that attitudes toward them are becoming more liberal and accepting. Foa (2012) shows that change in attitudes toward people with HIV/AIDS has been positive, with India seeing the greatest change between 1981 and 2012. In the first survey conducted in

Figure 5.4 Attitudes toward Having Homosexuals and People with HIV/AIDS as Neighbors Are Correlated

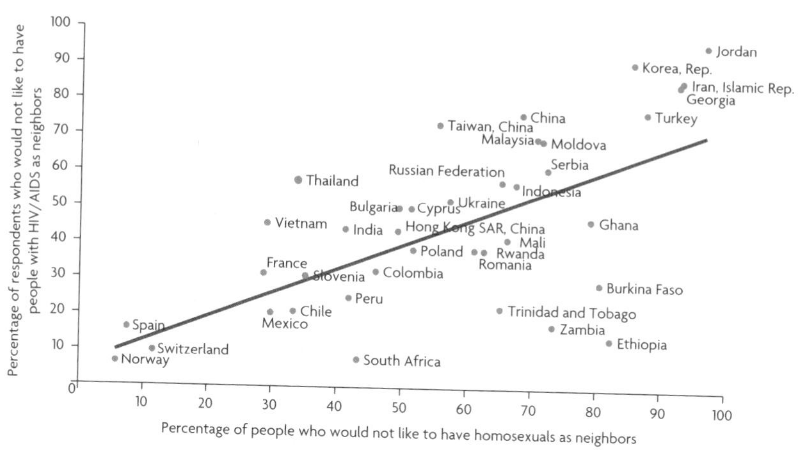

Source: World Bank, based on data from the World Values Surveys 2005–08.
Note: Data were collected at different times between 2005 and 2008 in each country or area.

India, in 1990, there was almost universal rejection of minorities of several kinds. In more recent surveys, the level of rejection is still high by international standards, but it is no longer universal, as reflected in a large positive shift. Zimbabwe and Nigeria also saw greater acceptance of people with HIV/AIDS.[9] In many countries, change can be attributed to the plateauing of the epidemic combined with an intensive public education campaign (see box 5.1).

As in the case of acceptance of people with HIV/AIDS, there is growing acceptance of homosexuals as neighbors. This positive change is particularly strong in India, where rejection of homosexuality was nearly universal in 1990, and Mexico. Public education campaigns have been instrumental in increasing the acceptance of homosexuality, which was decriminalized in 2003 in Mexico and in 2009 in India. Attitudes in Europe and Latin America and the Caribbean have also become more liberal, but these regions already had a high base, so the change is in the direction of considering homosexuality more normal (and in recognizing LGBT rights such as same-sex marriage) rather than merely tolerating or accepting it.

Attitudes toward Gender Equality and Women

The gaps between the attainment of males and females in a range of outcomes are well documented. Attitudes about women are usually a reflection

BOX 5.1

Mobilizing Civil Society to Increase Access to HIV/AIDS Prevention in South Africa

An estimated 5.6 million people in South Africa are living with HIV/AIDS (Robins and von Lieres 2004; UNAIDS 2012), with infection rates for young women about four times those of young men (UNAIDS 2012). The skepticism in the 1990s of key members of the South African government, such as then president Thabo Mbeki and health minister *Manto Tshabalala-Msimang*, delayed the introduction of a public antiretroviral (ARV) program; until the mid-2000s, ARVs were the preserve of people who could afford to pay for them privately (Robins 2006).

The Treatment Action Campaign (TAC) has mobilized a cross-section of South African society, from working-class black urban communities unable to afford ARVs and facing stigma and discrimination to trade unions, black and white middle-class business professionals, health professionals, scientists, the media, and ordinary South African citizens. It now has more than 16,000 members (TAC n.d.). TAC allied itself with the South African government against the high prices of ARVs set by the international pharmaceutical industry, leading major pharmaceutical companies to reduce ARV prices, which in turn has enabled the large-scale provision of ARVs through state clinics.

TAC has also fought high-profile battles in the South African courts. For example, in a 2001 High Court case, it established that the state's constitutional obligation to provide health care extended to HIV/AIDS treatment. This ruling led to the establishment of the national ARV program in 2003. TAC also took the government to court for refusing to provide prevention of mother-to-child transmission treatment (PMTCT), playing an important role in the establishment of South Africa's PMTCT program.

Testimonies from people taking ARVs in South Africa (Robins 2006) and Zimbabwe (Campbell et al. 2011) suggest that with declines in their health arrested or their health significantly improved, people taking ARVs are able to continue working and engage in social activities—that is, ARV treatment can help prevent people with HIV/AIDS from becoming socially and economically excluded, though the stigma associated with HIV/AIDS persists. At both the grassroots level and in the national media, TAC also campaigns against discrimination against people with HIV/AIDS in communities, schools, hospitals, and workplaces. It has organized highly visible media activity and public demonstrations.

Source: Marcus et al. 2013.

of social norms and can be correlated with the way institutions treat women. For example, low female labor force participation in the Middle East and North Africa could be partly attributed to attitudes about the roles and responsibilities of men and women inside and outside the household. The World Values Surveys data show that this region has the most gender-related discriminatory attitudes, with nearly half of respondents believing that education is more important for boys than girls and that men make better political leaders than women. In contrast, less than 15 percent of respondents in countries in the OECD, East Asia and Pacific, and Latin America and the Caribbean express such attitudes (figure 5.5).

Despite continuing gender inequality in many domains, there has been progress in women's rights and opportunities in the past few decades. Muñoz Boudet et al. (2013) document how women are gaining increased control over economic decisions and other strategic life choices as the social norms limiting women's work to domestic confines get relaxed. The main drivers of change are education, urbanization, and the expansion of female labor force participation, provided that the institutional context is favorable toward gender equality. Relative

Figure 5.5 Attitudes toward Gender Equality Are Most Conservative in the Middle East and North Africa

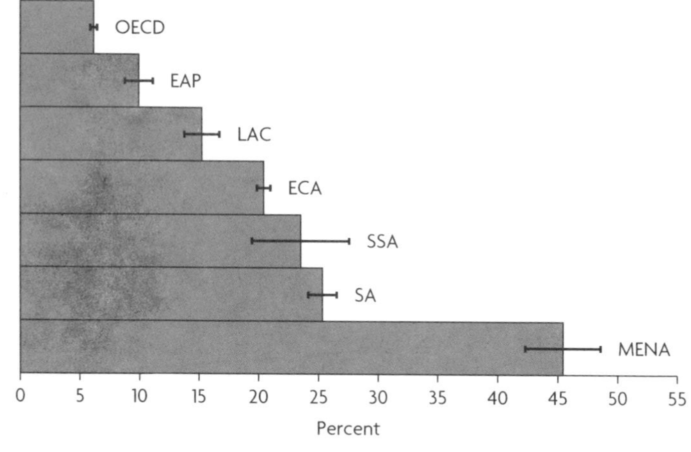

Source: Foa 2012, based on data from the World Values Surveys 2010.
Note: Every country for which time series data were available is included (23 countries in Europe and Central Asia [ECA], 16 countries in the Organisation for Economic Co-operation and Development [OECD], 11 countries in Latin America and the Caribbean [LAC], 7 countries in the Middle East and North Africa [MENA], 7 countries in East Asia and Pacific [EAP], 5 countries in Sub-Saharan Africa [SSA], and 3 countries in South Asia [SA]). Brackets show standard errors.

to older people, younger men and women also express higher aspirations for gender equality and control over their lives, including getting more education, having fewer children, and marrying later. However, the relaxation of gender norms can also trigger physical and other forms of violence against women as reminders of repressive traditions, as shown through qualitative interviews conducted in 20 countries for the *World Development Report 2012: Gender Equality and Development* (Muñoz Boudet et al. 2013).

Three sets of views regarding gender equality are considered: whether university education is more important for a boy than a girl, whether men have more right to jobs when jobs are scarce, and whether men make better political leaders than women. As table 5.2 shows, each of these attitudes mediates an important element of social inclusion. For instance, education of girls is crucial in determining their future opportunities. Attitudes regarding women's right to having a job when jobs are scarce may reflect norms of masculinity that emphasize the role of men as breadwinners and have an impact on women's economic empowerment and access to markets.

Attitude surveys indicate that there has been a favorable shift in attitudes toward women's education but negative attitudes are still widespread and correlated with actual education outcomes. Chapter 4 highlighted the huge expansion in education across the board and the fact that gender differentials in education have narrowed considerably. In some regions, women's educational outcomes are better than those of men.

The World Values Surveys ask respondents whether they think university education is more important for boys than for girls. The results show that a number of countries, including the Islamic Republic of Iran, Mali, and Iraq, display the most discriminatory attitudes, with more than half of respondents in the Islamic Republic of Iran saying that university education is more important for boys. These responses are generally in keeping with objective measures of educational outcomes across countries. Figure 5.6 shows that there is a negative relationship between the gross tertiary school enrollment rate for women and the percentage of survey respondents who think that higher education is more important for men than for women. By contrast, in countries where female tertiary school enrollment is almost universal, discriminatory attitudes toward access to higher education are very low: almost no one in Sweden, Andorra, or Norway believes that men should have greater access to higher education than women.

Figure 5.6 Countries and Areas in Which People Say University Education Is More Important for Boys Than Girls Have Lower Tertiary School Enrollment Rates for Women

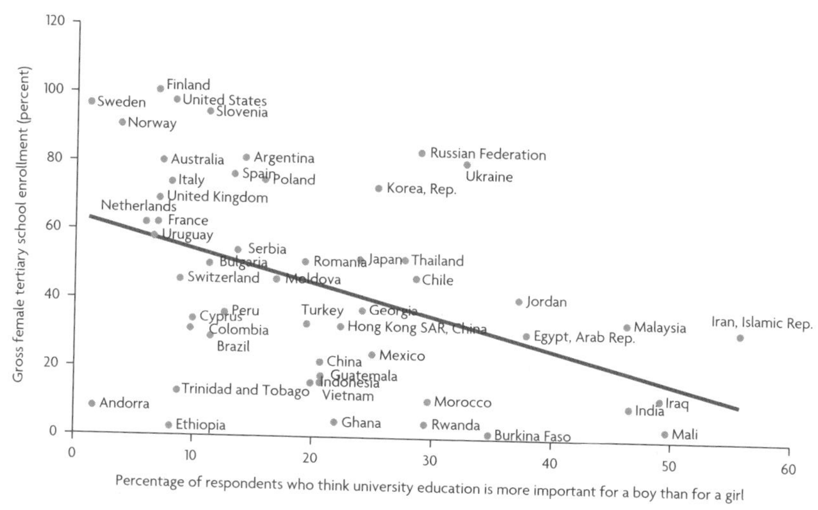

Source: World Bank, based on data from the World Values Surveys 2005–08 (attitudes) and World Development Indicators 2005–08 (tertiary education).

Note: Values are included for all countries and areas for which data for both variables were available within a period of two years. Latest data available are used.

Responses in the World Values Surveys to women's access to jobs show greater conservatism. The literature on discrimination against women in jobs has documented that a mix of labor market conditions, women's reproductive roles, and active discrimination have been responsible for women's lower outcomes compared with men. The World Values Surveys ask respondents whether they think men should be given preference for jobs when jobs are scarce in the economy. Respondents in the vast majority of countries believe that men should be given preference. The most discriminatory attitudes are found in countries that have the lowest female labor force participation rates (less than 25 percent), including the Arab Republic of Egypt, the Islamic Republic of Iran, Jordan, and Iraq, with 90 percent of respondents in Egypt and Jordan believing that men should get preference (figure 5.7). Jordan presents a peculiar paradox. Despite a strong supply-side push for female education, which has increased educational attainment for girls and women relative to other countries in the region, labor market outcomes remain poor. Figures 5.6 and 5.7 show that public attitudes to both equal education and jobs are very discriminatory

Figure 5.7 Countries and Areas in Which People Say Men Have More Right to Jobs Have Lower Labor Force Participation Rates for Women

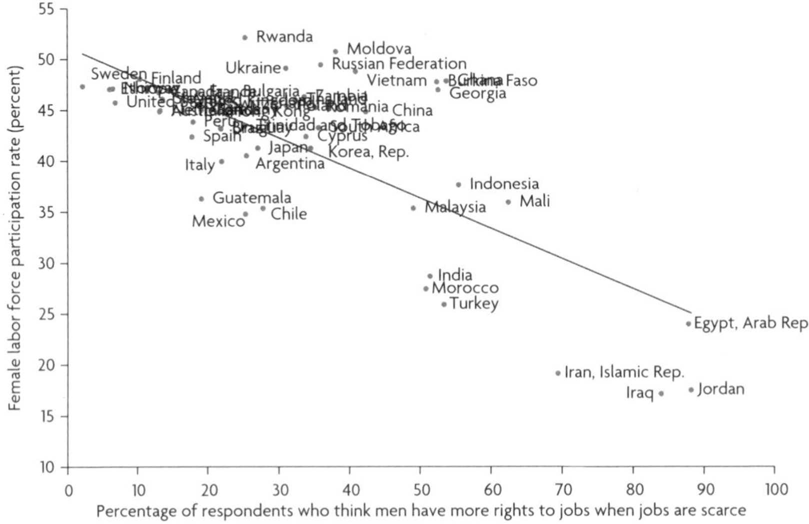

Source: World Bank, based on data from the World Values Surveys 2005–08 (attitudes) and World Development Indicators 2005–08 (female labor force participation rate).

Note: Values are included for all countries and areas for which data for both variables were available within a period of two years. Latest data available are used.

(in chapter 6, the case of Jordan is discussed in more detail). Countries that have the least discriminatory attitudes are Sweden, Norway, Finland, and Ethiopia. Ethiopia stands out among African countries in terms of both high female labor force participation rate and attitudes toward women's right to jobs in a tight labor market.

Discriminatory attitudes about women pertaining to the labor market have eased in almost all countries where the same question was asked at least twice in the World Values Surveys. The exceptions are Mexico, Turkey, India, Argentina, and China, where discriminatory attitudes toward women participating in the labor market seem more entrenched (figure 5.8). More than half of respondents in Turkey and India, and more than 40 percent in China, believed that men should be given preference when jobs are scarce (see figure 5.7). Interestingly, these countries have seen robust growth rates during the last decade or so, and there are reports of increasing jobs. In India, the National Sample Survey also shows fairly flat trends in female labor force participation during a period of relatively high growth. However, both the baselines and end lines for

Figure 5.8 Attitudes to Jobs Became Less Gender Discriminatory in Most Countries and Areas between 1989 and 2008

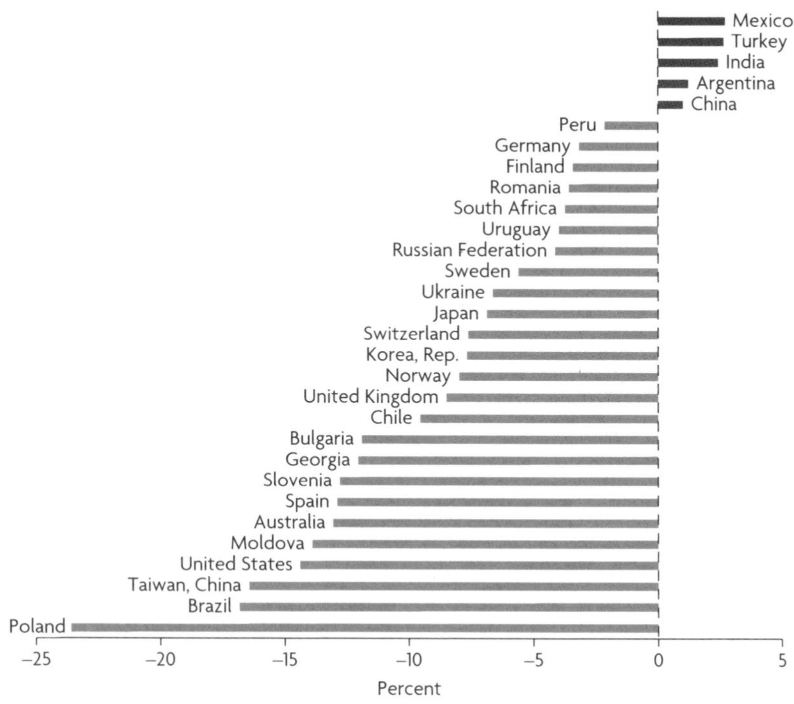

Source: World Bank, based on data from the World Values Surveys 1989–2008.
Note: Change between earliest and latest data available is estimated. Negative axis shows change toward more liberal attitude.

individual countries in figure 5.8 are different and may not reflect the most recent attitudes.

A final indicator of gender equality that has received considerable attention is the distribution of leadership positions between men and women. Since the mid-1990s, the share of women in parliaments and legislative bodies has been used as one of the indicators to measure women's leadership status.[10] The discourse around women in leadership positions has recently gained momentum, and representation of women in private sector board rooms and higher echelons of civil services and politics are very much on women's rights agendas. Discussion around women's leadership roles has been accompanied in recent decades by overall improvements in women's roles in high-level politics.

Attitudes toward women holding leadership positions are even more conservative than those regarding women's education and employment. The World Values Surveys ask respondents whether they think men make better political leaders than women. About 80 percent of respondents in Egypt, Iraq, Jordan, the Islamic Republic of Iran, Ghana, and Mali believe that men make better political leaders. On the other side of the spectrum, Sweden, Andorra, Norway, Canada, and Switzerland display the most open attitudes, with less than 15 percent of respondents saying that men make better political leaders. These attitudes are negatively related to the share of seats held by women in national parliaments, with the first set of countries having the lowest share of women parliamentarians and the second set of countries having the highest (figure 5.9). A notable exception is Iraq, where more than 25 percent of the postwar parliament were women but attitudes toward women's leadership are strongly negative. Rwanda, interestingly, is split 50-50 on both accounts. Across regions, attitudes toward women's leadership are also negatively associated with the number of female leaders in top executive positions.

Figure 5.9 Countries in Which People Say Men Make Better Leaders Have Low Proportions of Women in Parliament

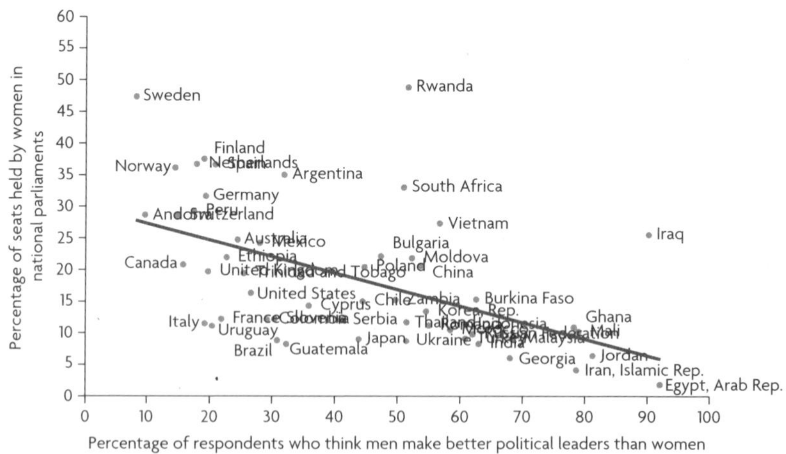

Source: World Bank, based on data from the World Values Surveys 2005–08 (attitudes) and World Development Indicators 2005–08 (parliamentary seats held by women).

Note: Values are included for all countries for which data for both variables were available within a period of two years. Latest data available are used.

Perceptions of Inequality and Fairness

Both the experience and the perception of inequality and fairness are important in assessing the extent to which social inclusion has resulted and the fruits of growth have filtered across societies.[11] The last decade has seen a spate of global protests against what is broadly considered unfairness or lack of accountability and transparency. These protests are usually against the state but also against business leaders, landowners, and other agglomerates. The uprisings in many parts of the Middle East and North Africa are believed to be more than just a reaction to unemployment—they are regarded as uprisings against the state. Reich and Satz (2011), writing about the Occupy Movement, discuss not merely the lack of opportunity, their central proposition, but also the perceived injustice of inequality. These growing protests have caused considerable anxiety to governments and, in some countries, led to crackdowns against protest.

People's acceptance of inequality is, to a large extent, rooted in historical circumstances. History plays a large role in people's preferences about the society in which they live (Verme 2009). For example, precolonial and colonial institutions affect the extent to which citizens accept or legitimize inequality and exclusion. DiJohn and Putzel (2009) highlight the fact that the inclusionary political settlement in Botswana was successful because colonial institutions did not have a tight hold on the country's institutions, which led to a more equitable distribution of mineral wealth. The Brazil case is also instructive. In an analysis based on a survey conducted in 2000, Scalon and Cano (2008) find that Brazilians were very aware of the high levels of income inequality in their country but that there was an implicit acceptance of this inequality across income groups. They argue that the "selective modernization" of Brazil, which retained traditional values on the one hand and introduced modern institutions on the other, enabled the acceptance of large, and at the time of their analysis, growing, inequalities:

> For many people, it is difficult to understand how it is possible that in a highly unequal country, a perception also exists—even among those who are at the bottom and thus most affected by inequality—that people must be unequally rewarded for their unequal assets and talents. But one must also ask how a country could accept extraordinary gaps in equality for decades without adopting an ideology that permits and legitimizes this inequality. This seems perverse, and it is: unequal societies tend to be more tolerant toward inequality, which in turns perpetuates that

inequality.... A shared political culture that is complicit with the acceptance of inequality makes it hard to break patterns in a society. (Scalon and Cano 2008, 95)

Given differences in the historical circumstances of each country, the relationship between actual and perceived inequality is mixed. The analysis of the World Values Surveys data for 2005 suggests a nonlinear relationship between "aversion to inequality" and observed inequality across countries (figure 5.10). Australia and many countries in Europe, for example, have low inequality alongside a low appetite for it. In contrast, some countries in Latin America (such as Chile, Argentina, Uruguay, and to some extent Colombia and Brazil) have high levels of measured inequality, but their inequality aversion is similar to that of countries with lower levels of inequality. This pattern is most likely driven by the colonial and precolonial institutional structure of these countries.

Acceptance or aversion to inequality may also depend on the type and extent of social stratification in a country. Societies that have highly hierarchical

Figure 5.10 Perceptions and Actual Levels of Inequality Are Not Always Related

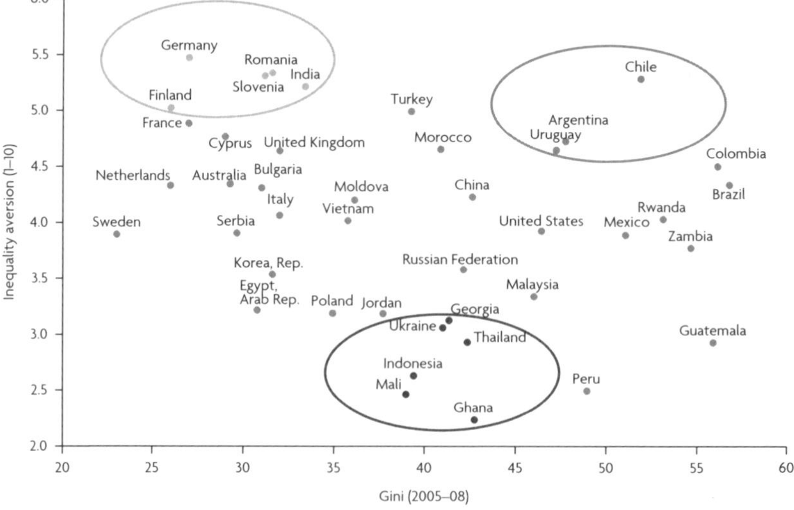

Source: World Bank, based on data from the World Values Surveys 2005–08 (attitudes), WIID2C, and PovcalNet (Gini coefficient).

Note: Attitudes toward inequality were collected at different times between 2005 and 2008. Gini coefficients are either from the same year as the attitude variable or from the closest period within a span of one year. Circles distinguish countries that cluster at similar intersections.

stratification systems seem to have higher levels of acceptance of inequality. Take the case of India, which has low levels of measured inequality but high acceptance of it (despite a small increase in the Gini coefficient in the last two decades) (see figure 5.10).[12] The public rhetoric against inequality and social exclusion in India is pervasive, linked to both Gandhian and Nehruvian visions of an ideal society. Yet the caste system, while having morphed into a political category, is still intact. In this respect, India presents an interesting conundrum. On the one hand, the public ideology of a modern India is implicitly linked to the demise of caste; on the other, an elaborate religious ideology supports the existence of caste. Socioreligious reformers have historically tried to counter this oppressive ideology, but caste-based beliefs and stereotypes remain pervasive in people's private lives.

Citizens' views about the extent of fairness in their country often reflect deeper issues of inclusion and exclusion in society. The sharper focus on the measurement of subjective well-being promises to serve as an avenue for citizens, especially those who feel they are not being heard, to voice their grievances. Herian et al. (2012) argue that fairness in formal institutions is judged against four main criteria: the ability of individuals to express their opinions, the consistency of the authority in its application of processes and transparency of its decisions, respectful treatment of individuals, and the perceived trustworthiness of the authority. Whether people consider the policies and decisions of state authorities as legitimate is related to whether they perceive them as fair and impartial (Tyler 2006; Gilley 2009). More generally, people may perceive situations as unjust if they are denied participation and active citizenship and do not feel respected by authority (Sampson 1983; Marc et al. 2012). In short, citizens' perception of the fairness of the way the state treats them is, to some extent, also a measure of their feelings of being excluded by the state.

Perceived fairness is often related to the extent of opaqueness and corruption. Linde (2012) shows, for instance, that public support for the political system in postcommunist democracies is determined to a large extent by what citizens perceive the degree of corruption is among public officials and the level of fairness they expect when they deal with them. In a similar vein, the Afrobarometer asks respondents how often they feel they are being treated unequally by the state. Although it is a bit farfetched to expect too many people to think of any state as being "never unfair," the results can be indicative of feelings of injustice (figure 5.11).

At the top of the list is Botswana, where 43 percent of respondents indicate that people are never treated unequally and another 25 percent report

Figure 5.11 How Often Do You Think People in Your Country Are Treated Unequally?

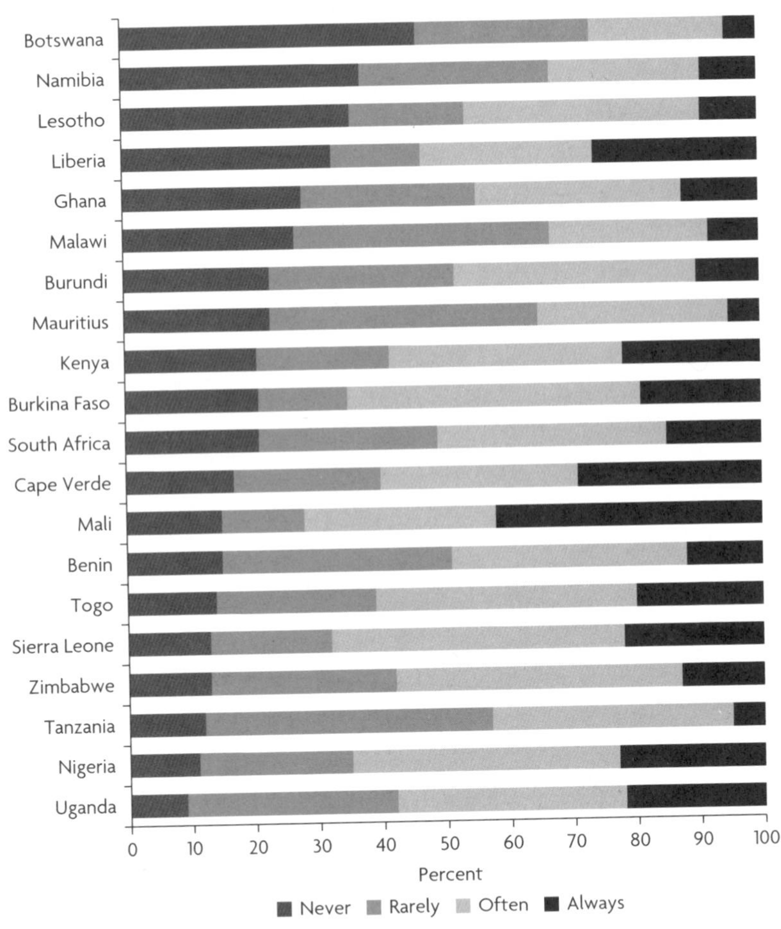

Source: World Bank, based on data from Afrobarometer Round 5 (2010–12).
Note: Based on responses to the question, "In your opinion, how often, in this country, are people treated unequally under the law?"

that people are rarely treated unequally. It is followed by Namibia, where 38 percent of respondents report that people are never treated unequally and 30 percent report that people are rarely treated unequally. Other countries where respondents did not report strong feelings of unequal treatment under the law include Burundi, Lesotho, Liberia, Ghana, Malawi, and Mauritius. By contrast, more than two-fifths of respondents in Sierra Leone (45 percent),

Zimbabwe (44 percent), Burkina Faso (43 percent), and Nigeria (41 percent) report that people are often unequally treated, and 13–23 percent report that people are always unequally treated by their state.

That the majority of citizens feel that people in their country are treated unequally may be indicative of the fact that the state is perceived as catering to the needs of a small section of society and that exclusion is a problem for many rather than a few. Africa's economic growth over the past decade has been in substantial measure from mineral extraction, with the benefits concentrated among a few. Economic power is closely related to political power and representation in decision making, which in turn affects the allocation of public expenditure and can lead to disparities in opportunities. Income inequality, too, rose considerably in the last three decades throughout Sub-Saharan Africa. In 2010, Africa was the second most unequal region in the world (after Latin America), and 6 of the world's 10 most unequal countries worldwide were located in Southern Africa (AfDB 2012). The increasingly visible contrast between rich and poor may be one of the driving forces behind feelings of unequal treatment.

There also seems to be a decline in approval ratings of what governments are doing about inequality in many African countries. The Afrobarometer surveys ask respondents whether they approve their governments' efforts to narrow the gap between rich and poor. In no country in the sample did approval ratings exceed 50 percent, although it is unclear whether respondents wanted their governments to do more or less. Moreover, the periods 2005/06–2008/09 and 2008/09–2011/12 saw a decline or no change in approval in the sampled countries, except in Botswana, Malawi, and Zimbabwe (figure 5.12). The increase in approval was highest in Malawi, where respondents changed their approval ratings from 19 percent to 44 percent in the period 2005/06–2008/09 (followed by a slight decline to 41 percent in 2011/12). The largest drop observed was in Senegal (from 34 percent to 7 percent) in the period 2005/06–2008/09 and in Tanzania (from 35 to 13 percent) and Namibia (from 42 to 28 percent) in the period 2005/06–2011/12.

Recent reports suggest that new divisions may be emerging across Africa, as countries are adopting new strategies for growth. Take the case of Uganda. Expert opinions point to growing concerns that the majority of the population views itself as excluded from economic prosperity. A recent study notes that a minority that belongs to the "right groups" is systematically provided better opportunities economically, politically,

Figure 5.12 Most African Countries Show a Decline in Approval of Government's Effort to Narrow the Gap between Rich and Poor

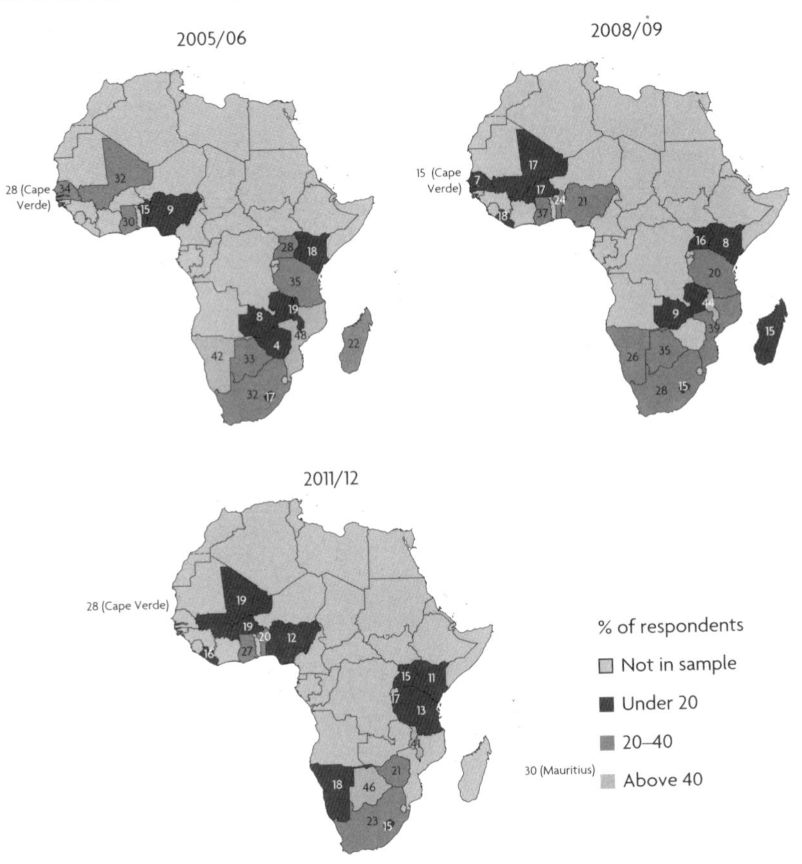

Source: World Bank, based on data from Afrobarometer 2005–12.

and socially. Patronage and corruption have become the processes by which groups are included or excluded from taking their share of the national wealth (Awori 2012). In line with this argument, only 9 percent of Ugandan respondents said their country never treats people unequally, whereas 58 percent say people are always or often unequally treated (see figure 5.11). In 2012, the most common reason that respondents cited for not reporting corruption was that they "knew no action would be taken." This finding clearly signals a sense of powerlessness with respect to perceived injustices taking place in state institutions.

Concluding Reflections

Attitudes and perceptions matter for the behavior and actions of individuals and groups. They can influence the terms on which some groups are included and affect the way groups access opportunities. They are intrinsic to the dignity and respect accorded to many groups. They change over time, can be correlated with both country-level and global changes, and are likely to be responsive to new incentives. Paying attention to attitudes and perceptions and changes in them is therefore important, because they can throw light on what can be done to foster positive change.

Subjective reports of how people regard their situation and that of others could well have to do with whom people compare themselves with and what they aspire to. Negative subjective reports are often indicative of unfulfilled aspirations for social mobility and a sense that "others are doing better than us." Subjective well-being is also a reflection of the way in which society treats its members and the extent to which people feel they can access opportunities. Measuring perceptions allows excluded groups and groups with little voice to make themselves heard. Perceptions of the way the state treats its citizens can be a reflection of the extent of exclusion. They can be rooted in long-term grievances against the state and against the rule of a few.

Notes

1. For example, the Scottish Social Attitudes Survey, conducted three times since 2002, examines views on whether different groups of people are equally suitable for employment as a primary school teacher and compares the responses with views about these same groups marrying into a person's family. It also explores gender stereotyping in attitudes toward parental leave, attitudes to older people working, and perceived labor market competition from particular groups. The aim of this survey is specifically to provide inputs into policy to address discrimination (see Das 2012).
2. Classical economists and philosophers, such as Jeremy Bentham, John Stuart Mill, and Adam Smith, incorporated the pursuit of happiness in their writings. However, as economics grew more technical as a discipline, more parsimonious definitions of welfare, underpinned by decision making by a utility-maximizing rational individual, became more common; subjective perceptions became secondary to observed objective measures.
3. For a comprehensive review of the interdisciplinary literature on relative deprivation, see Walker and Smith (2002).

4. Detailed information about sampling and fieldwork and the exact text of each question can be found at http://www.worldvaluessurvey.org.
5. Certain negative attitudes tend to be widely held, showing some tendency to soften with advances in education. However, the dominant type of negative attitude, and how strong it is, depends largely on the country in which a respondent is living (Lakhani, Sacks, and Heltberg 2012).
6. This view seems unfounded, as international migration of skilled workers relative to unskilled workers has been rising since the 1970s for every developing region of the world (Docquier 2006).
7. Certain conjectures popularly held about migrants underpin exclusionary attitudes toward them. Pritchett (2006) calls these conjectures "immovable ideas" or "self-interested arguments," which are often made by the elite. They must be shifted if the issue of exclusion of immigrants is to be tackled in a comprehensive manner.
8. An increase from 5 percent of a society that rejects migrants to 15 percent can be expected to have a far more significant impact on the policy debate and discourse than an increase from 60 percent to 70 percent, despite the fact that both are 10 percentage-point increments. Because of this nonlinear effect, changes in the ratio may be more meaningful for the purpose of empirical analysis.
9. The latest round of the World Values Surveys (2010–12) shows that one of the most notable exceptions to the generally negative relationship between attitudes toward homosexuals and attitudes toward people with HIV/AIDS is Zimbabwe. Respondents in Zimbabwe are severely against homosexuality but not HIV/AIDS. Zimbabwe saw one of the sharpest declines in HIV prevalence within a decade; coverage of ARV treatment among adults rose from 15 percent in 2007 to 80 percent in 2010 (WHO, UNAIDS, and UNICEF 2011).
10. The Gender Empowerment Measure (GEM), for example, was one of the indicators introduced by the United Nations' 1995 Human Development Report. It consists of three indicators: male and female shares of parliamentary seats; male and female shares of administrative, professional, technical, and managerial positions; and power over economic resources, as measured by women's and men's estimated earned income.
11. See, for instance, the indicators for a Rule of Law Index created by Agrast et al. (2008) for the American Bar Association.
12. The low levels of observed inequality are in part related to measurement issues (see World Bank 2011 for a discussion).

References

AfDB (African Development Bank Group). 2012. "Income Inequality in Africa." Briefing Note 5. http://www.afdb.org/fileadmin/uploads/afdb/Documents

/Policy-Documents/FINAL%20Briefing%20Note%205%20Income%20Inequality%20in%20Africa.pdf (accessed April 5, 2013).

Agrast, M. D., J. C. Botero, A. Ponce Rodriguez, and C. Dumas. 2008. "The World Justice Project Rule of Law Index: Measuring Adherence to the Rule of Law around the World." Paper presented at the World Justice Forum, Vienna, July 3.

Awori, T. 2012. "All for One or One for All? The Imperative for Social Inclusion in Uganda." Background paper draft, World Bank, Washington, DC.

Baker, W., S. Howell, A. C. Lin, A. Shryock, A. Jamal, and R. Stockton. 2009. *Citizenship and Crisis: Arab Detroit after 9/11*. New York: Russell Sage Foundation Press.

Basu, K. 2003. "The Economics and Law of Sexual Harassment in the Workplace." *Journal of Economic Perspectives* 17 (3): 141–57.

Campbell, C., M. Skovdal, C. Madanhire, O. Mugurungi, S. Gregson, and C. Nyamukapa. 2011. "We, the AIDS People… How Antiretroviral Therapy Enables Zimbabweans Living with Aids to Cope with Stigma." *American Journal of Public Health* 101 (6): 1004–10.

Campos, N. F., and V. S. Kuzeyev. 2007. "On the Dynamics of Ethnic Fractionalization." *American Journal of Political Science* 51 (3): 620–39.

Das, M. B. 2012. "Stubborn Inequalities, Subtle Processes: Exclusion and Discrimination in the Labor Market." Background paper for *World Development Report 2013*, World Bank, Washington, DC.

DFID (U.K. Department for International Development). 2007. *Taking Action against HIV Stigma and Discrimination: Guidance Document and Supporting Resources*. http://www.icrw.org/publications/taking-action-against-hiv-stigma-and-discrimination (accessed October 7, 2013).

Diener, E., and R. Biswas-Diener. 2005. "Psychological Empowerment and Subjective Well-being." In *Measuring Empowerment: Cross-Disciplinary Perspectives*, ed. N. Deepa, 125–40. Washington, DC: World Bank.

DiJohn, J., and J. Putzel. 2009. "Political Settlements." GSDRC Issues Paper, University of Birmingham, Governance and Social Development Resource Centre, Birmingham, United Kingdom.

Docquier, F. 2006. "Brain Drain and Inequality across Nations." IZA Discussion Paper 2440, Institute for the Study of Labour, Bonn.

Easterlin, R. A. 2010. "Well-Being, Front and Center: A Note on the Sarkozy Report." *Population and Development Review* 36 (1): 119–24.

Foa, R. 2012. "Trends in Tolerance of Social Minorities across the World." Background paper draft, World Bank, Washington, DC.

Gilley, B. 2009. *The Right to Rule: How States Win and Lose Legitimacy*. New York: Columbia University Press.

Graham, C. 2011. "Adaptation amidst Prosperity and Adversity: Insights from Happiness Studies from around the World." *World Bank Research Observer* 26 (1): 105–37.

Graham, C., and S. Pettinato. 2002. "Frustrated Achievers: Winners, Losers and Subjective Well-Being in New Market Economies." *Journal of Development Studies* 38 (4): 100–40.

Guild, M. 2013. "Migrating North: Crisis Pushes European Integration in Unexpected Ways." *Financial Sense,* March 20. http://www.financialsense.com/contributors/guild/migrating-north-crisis-pushes-european-integration-in-unexpected-ways (accessed April 20, 2013).

Herian, M. N., J. A. Hamm, A. J. Tomkins, and L. M. P. Zillig. 2012. "Public Participation, Procedural Fairness, and Evaluations of Local Governance: The Moderating Role of Uncertainty." *Journal of Public Administration Research and Theory* 22 (4): 815–40.

Jalalzai, F., and M. L. Krook. 2010. "Beyond Hillary and Benazir: Women's Political Leadership Worldwide." *International Political Science Review* 31 (1): 5–21.

Kleemans, M., and J. Klugman. 2009. "Understanding Attitudes towards Migrants: A Broader Perspective Human Development." Human Development Report Research Paper 2009/53, United Nations Development Programme (UNDP), New York. http://w.rrojasdatabank.info/HDRP_2009_53.pdf.

Lakhani, S., A. Sacks, and R. Heltberg. 2012. "Unwelcome Neighbors: Understanding Social Exclusion." Background paper draft, World Bank, Washington, DC.

Life in Transition Survey (LiTS) (database). 2006, 2010. World Bank and European Bank for Reconstruction and Development. http://www.ebrd.com/pages/research/analysis/publications/transition/data.shtml.

Linde, J. 2012. "Why Feed the Hand That Bites You? Perceptions of Procedural Fairness and System Support in Post Communist Democracies." *European Journal of Political Research* 51 (3): 410–34.

Marc, A., A. Willman, G. Aslam, M. Rebosio, and K. Balisuriya. 2012. *Societal Dynamics and Fragility: Engaging Societies in Responding to Fragile Situations.* Washington, DC: World Bank.

Marcus, R., S. Espinoza, L. Schmidt, and S. Sultan. 2013. "Social Exclusion in Africa: Towards More Inclusive Approaches." Background paper draft, World Bank, Washington, DC.

Muñoz Boudet, A. M., P. Petesch, C. Turk, and A. Thumala. 2013. *On Norms and Agency: Conversations about Gender Equality with Women and Men in 20 Countries.* Washington, DC: World Bank.

Narayan, D., L. Pritchett, and S. Kapoor. 2009. *Moving Out of Poverty: Success from the Bottom Up*, vol. 2. Washington, DC: World Bank and Palgrave Macmillan.

Norris, P. 2005. *Radical Right: Voters and Parties in the Electoral Market.* New York: Cambridge University Press.

———. 2009. "The Globalization of Comparative Public Opinion Research." In *Handbook of Comparative Politics*, ed. T. Landman and N. Robinson, 522–40. London: Sage.

Pickens, J. 2005. "Attitudes and Perceptions." In *Organizational Behavior in Health Care*, ed. N. Borkowski, 43–75. Sudbury, U.K.: Jones and Bartlett Publishers. http://healthadmin.jbpub.com/borkowski/chapter3.pdf.

Plonka, B. 2013. "Social Inclusion in Poland." Background paper draft, World Bank, Washington, DC.

PovcalNet: An Online Poverty Analysis Tool. World Bank, Washington, DC. http://iresearch.worldbank.org/PovcalNet/index.htm.

Pritchett, L. 2006. *Let Their People Come: Breaking the Gridlock on Global Labor Mobility.* Washington, DC: Center for Global Development.

Reich, R., and D. Satz. 2011. "Ethics and Inequality." *Boston Review*, November 28.

Robins, S. 2006. "From 'Rights' to 'Ritual': AIDS Activism in South Africa." *American Anthropologist* 108 (2): 312–23.

Robins, S., and B. von Lieres. 2004. "AIDS Activism and Globalisation from Below: Occupying New Spaces of Citizenship in Post-Apartheid South Africa." *IDS Bulletin* 35 (2): 84–90.

Sampson, E. E. 1983. *Justice and the Critique of Pure Psychology*. New York: Plenum Press.

Scalon, M. C., and I. Cano. 2008. "Legitimization and Acceptance: How Brazilians Survive Inequalities." In *Social Exclusion and Mobility in Brazil*, ed. E. Gacitúa-Marió and M. Woolcock, 81–97. Washington, DC: World Bank.

Serajuddin, U., and P. Verme. 2012. "Who Is Deprived? Who Feels Deprived? Labor Deprivation, Youth and Gender in Morocco." Policy Research Working Paper 6090, World Bank, Washington, DC.

Stouffer, S. A., E. A. Suchman, L. C. DeVinney, S. A. Star, and R. M. Williams Jr. 1949. *The American Soldier*, vols. I and II. Princeton, NJ: Princeton University Press.

TAC (Treatment Action Campaign). n.d. "About the Treatment Action Campaign." http://www.tac.org.za/about_us (accessed December 18, 2012).

Tyler, T. R. 2006. "Psychological Perspectives on Legitimacy and Legitimation." *Annual Review of Psychology* 57 (1): 375–400.

UNAIDS (Joint United Nations Programme on HIV/AIDS). 2012. "High-Level Taskforce for Women, Girls and HIV Calls for Accelerated Efforts to Protect the Rights and Wellbeing of Young Women and Girls in South Africa." October 31. http://www.unaids.org/en/resources/presscentre/featurestories/2012/october/20121031sataskforce/.

Verme, P. 2009. "Happiness, Freedom and Control." *Journal of Economic Behavior and Organization* 71 (2): 146–61.

Walker, I., and H. J. Smith. 2002. "Fifty Years of Relative Deprivation Research." In *Relative Deprivation: Specification, Development, and Integration*, ed. I. Walker and H. J. Smith, 1–13. Cambridge, U.K.: Cambridge University Press.

WHO (World Health Organization), UNAIDS (Joint United Nations Programme on HIV/AIDS), and UNICEF (United Nations Children's Fund). 2011. *Global HIV/AIDS Response. Epidemic Update and Health Sector Progress towards Universal Access*. Progress Report. Geneva: WHO.

WIID2C (UNU-WIDER World Income Inequality Database). United Nations University/World Institute for Development Economics Research, Version 2.0c, May 2008. http://www.wider.unu.edu/research/Database.

World Development Indicators (database). World Bank, Washington, DC. http://data.worldbank.org/data-catalog/world-development-indicators.

World Bank. 2011. *Perspectives on Poverty in India: Stylized Facts from Survey Data*. Washington, DC: World Bank.

World Values Surveys (database). World Values Survey Association. http://www.worldvaluessurvey.org.

PART III

CHANGE IS POSSIBLE

CHAPTER 6

Change toward Social Inclusion

Cultures are made of continuities and changes, and the identity of a society can survive through these changes. Societies without change aren't authentic; they're just dead.

—KWAME ANTHONY APPIAH, *COSMOPOLITANISM: ETHICS IN A WORLD OF STRANGERS* (2007)

Change is inevitable. It happens by stealth or by design. It happens through discrete events, as well as through gradual processes that culminate over time. It is inevitably a complex process. For example, its impacts on groups can vary, and what is considered costly today may have positive outcomes in the future or vice versa. Attempts to make change inclusive may involve trade-offs, creating both winners and losers. For these reasons, change toward social inclusion is almost always political and occurs through the dialectic between different power groups in society. There can be push-back from the dominant groups when previously subordinate groups feel included and break the norms. Push-back can come with active retaliation, which can set the process of change back. So change is hardly ever linear or clear-cut.

Despite its messiness or complexity, the process of change can be influenced toward social inclusion. Although it is true that social inclusion is hampered by, among other things, culture, norms, and history, the impacts are not immutable. Examples of change toward inclusion abound in history. South Africa, for example, moved from institutionalized segregation toward an ideal of a "rainbow nation" in a matter of two decades. Foot-binding, an ancient tradition in China, was curtailed and eventually eliminated, following an intense social campaign and prohibition by law.

The articulation of social exclusion in Brazil that started with a widespread belief in a "racial democracy" led to acceptance of the notion that discrimination on the basis of race has held some groups back. The exclusionary system of informal local justice in Bangladesh (the *shalish*) has been transformed by greater voice and participation. In a region where women's role in society is confined to the private sphere, higher educational attainment among women in Jordan has become the rule rather than the exception.

This chapter focuses on the manner in which change can take place and the political processes that underpin it. Before presenting a variety of policies and programs that have been used for tackling social inclusion in the next chapter, it is important to start with a few pointers regarding the process of change. The first section of this chapter gives examples of different areas in which change toward social inclusion has been possible. The second section then reflects on the actors who can propel change toward social inclusion, based on the cases reviewed and other literature. The third section argues that change toward social inclusion is conditioned by the nature of the social contract, the extent of a shared vision in society, and the strength of institutions. The final section concludes. The chapter provides the foundation for assessing the nature of policies and programs that can lead to social inclusion, discussed in chapter 7.

Change in What?

Bangladesh: Changes in Local Justice Institutions

Access to justice in Bangladesh, as in several other countries, is limited by long delays in the formal court system and poor access by various excluded groups, particularly women. Countries often have a range of local justice mechanisms, with varying degrees of formality, which serve as substitutes for formal institutions. That such traditional dispute resolution systems are often also undemocratic and exclusionary has been well documented.

In Bangladesh, the traditional *shalish* is an informal institution delivering justice, while formal courts are at the other end of the spectrum. The literature documents the tension between the *shalish* as a fast and inexpensive mechanism for resolving local and family disputes and its character as the enforcer of often retrogressive norms. The literature on the *shalish* has underscored its elitist character and the hazard that it perpetuates existing power structures. For example, few women are invited to serve as *shalishkars* (mediators) in the traditional *shalish*, making them less likely to approach it for justice. The dearth of women as mediators is important because the large majority of cases that women would like to see resolved are family based, many of them related to domestic and spousal violence. Another key aspect of exclusion is that *shalish* decisions tend to enforce established social norms and in that sense may also deter women from participating. Such norms perpetuate the lower status of women and the poorest people in relation to the rich and more powerful (Bode and Howes 2002; Golub 2003; Guirguis 2004; Jahan 2007; World Bank 2008).

In many parts of rural Bangladesh, the *shalish* has been transformed into a more participatory and representative local justice institution. This transformation has been concurrent with an improvement in women's status across the board through expansion of education, better health outcomes, and steep fertility decline. Women in Bangladesh are now much more visible in public spaces and are able to make their voices heard (World Bank 2008). These developments have coincided with efforts by nongovernmental organizations (NGOs) and been supported by international donors in an environment that encouraged local democracy. The reformed *shalish* includes an equal number of women as *shalishkars* and often addresses injustices to women such as violence, dowry demands, abandonment, and maintenance. NGOs assist parties in accessing the formal system when *shalish* is either not appropriate or not satisfactory. The Bangladesh Rural Advancement Centre (BRAC) runs one of the largest informal justice systems in the world. The activities of BRAC and legal aid organizations (Bangladesh Legal Aid and Services Trust, Ain-o-Shalish Kendro, and Nagorik Uddyong), which also run the reformed *shalish,* have been documented.

The reach of the reformed *shalish* is speculative, although one report estimates its coverage at 30 percent of the country (Asia Foundation 2007). Local governments in Bangladesh—known as Union Parishads (UPs)—have embraced the changes in the local justice landscape. Their role in conducting the *shalish* has also expanded. Some of this change in local government involvement could be related to the growing political importance of the UPs and the lack of commensurate discretionary power and resources available to them. It is likely therefore that UPs use their role as new elites in mediation—something that gives them added political power. It is also likely that with the increasing push toward decentralization, the contact of UPs with higher levels of administration has increased. The rising importance of elected representatives of the UPs, the increasing penetration of NGO-sponsored dispute resolution, and the movement toward legal empowerment of the poor has created new social and political dynamics. Elites and institutions are competing for spaces and spheres of influence. Traditional elites are reimagining themselves, and new elites are carving out their roles (Das and Maru 2011).

Brazil: Changes in Framing Issues of Inclusion

Afro-descendants (counted as the "negro" and "black" categories in the census) made up 7.6 percent of Brazil's population in 2010. In the 1970s, at a time when the dominant discourse in Brazil emphasized tolerance and social harmony across racial groups, Thomas Skidmore, a sociologist from Brown University, wrote about discrimination against Afro-Brazilians. He focused on the "whitening thesis," by which "Brazilian intellectuals of the late 19th and early 20th centuries managed their racial and nationalist anxieties by interpreting miscegenation as a dynamic process that would dilute Brazil's black population" (Davila, Morgan, and Skidmore 2008). Skidmore's analysis was met with negative reaction from what Skidmore termed the "elite" in Brazil, which comprised policy makers and academics alike. To them, Skidmore was attacking the very foundation of Brazil's famed "racial democracy." However, until recently, racially disaggregated data were only partially available from Brazilian official statistics.

Using qualitative evidence, Skidmore argued that there are systematic differences in labor market and human development outcomes of Afro-Brazilians and other Brazilians, most notably whites. These differences generated much interest in differential outcomes between blacks and whites in other arenas as well, leading in turn to a body of empirical evidence and simultaneous education of the Brazilian public and elite about these differentials as well as the discrimination that underlies them.

Later, Telles (2006) carefully analyzed the differential outcomes in the labor market and in education by race. His main conclusion was that there is a high degree of social harmony across racial groups in Brazil, which is marked by deep and meaningful social interactions, intermarriage, interdining, and co-residence. However, this apparent social harmony masks high levels of inequality across racial groups.

By the turn of the 21st century, there was increasing acceptance in policy circles in Brazil that Afro-Brazilians were discriminated against and deserved special treatment. In its 2003 report to the United Nations (UN) Committee on the Elimination of Racial Discrimination, Brazil recognized that "for many decades, the myth of a nationality characterized by the harmonious and perfect fusion of three races, responsible for the construction of a 'racial democracy' in the country, was propagated. Over a long period of time, the Brazilian State and society, acting on behalf of this myth, revealed themselves incapable of implementing effective mechanisms to incorporate Afro-descendants, indigenous individuals, and members of other discriminated groups into the larger society" (CERD 2003, 5). More recently, Brazil put in place quotas for Afro-Brazilians that guarantee them seats in public educational institutions. These quotas are being seen as a game changer for these groups. In sum, there is an emerging consensus that the fight against poverty in Brazil cannot be disassociated with the recognition of race as a marker of inequality and that without specific policies targeted at reducing race-based inequality, improvements will occur too slowly for this group (Gacitúa-Marió and Woolcock 2008).

China: Changes in Egregious Social Practices

Foot-binding was a centuries-old custom in China that required that women tie their feet so that they would be small and pretty. This conception of beauty was tied to control over female bodies. The interesting thing about foot-binding was how soon it came to an end, propelled most strongly by the power of external actors in the form of missionaries and Chinese elites (Mackie 1996; Appiah 2006).

The movement that overturned the ancient and revered practice of foot-binding was propelled by Christian missionaries. In 1875, Rev. John Macgowan, of the London Missionary Society, called a meeting of Christian women in Xiamen and asked them to sign a pledge to abandon the practice. At first, nine women did. Quickly, growing numbers joined, other groups were founded, and membership of anti-foot-binding organizations was in the tens of thousands. A national movement for change had started. The campaigners against foot-binding did not necessarily have new arguments: the Chinese had long known that foot-binding produced suffering and debility. Nevertheless, bound feet had continued to be regarded as an important status symbol and instrument for enforcing the chastity of women—or as Appiah (2006) puts it, foot-binding had simply become the normal thing to do.

The leaders of the movement against foot-binding were careful not to impose their ideas but to change minds instead through respectful engagement and knowledge-building: they set up newspapers and magazines such as *Review of the Times* (founded in 1868), which gave the Chinese elite access to ideas and events from abroad. They also republished anti-foot-binding essays by Chinese writers. Beyond changing the minds of people, campaigners also created role models who helped change the shared commitments of society: members of anti-foot-binding societies not only pledged to stop binding their own daughters' feet, they also pledged not to allow their sons to marry women with bound feet.

Jordan: Changes in Women's Educational Attainment

The success of Jordan in expanding education services to its citizens, particularly women, is widely acknowledged. Since the late 1980s, the government has spent more than 5 percent of its annual domestic product on education, a larger share than any other lower-middle-income country (World Bank 2005). Education policies were supported by active participation of civil society organizations, especially in regard to early childhood education, illiteracy, and vocational training programs. Between 1980 and 2002, literacy rates for adult men increased from 82 percent to 96 percent (a 14 percentage point increase), while rates for adult women increased from 55 percent to 86 percent (a 31 percentage point increase). The performance of women also improved in higher education: between 1988 and 1999, the number of female university students in Jordan quadrupled; their share of the student body increased from 39 percent to 45 percent; and in 1998, for the first time in history, more than half of university admissions were women (Jansen 2006).

Although education is a necessary condition for gender equality, it is far from sufficient. Despite improvements in female educational attainment, there are significant barriers to gender equality in Jordan, both in the education system and after women enter the labor market. For example, the education system reinforces traditional gender roles and implicitly directs young women into "appropriate" professions (such as art, the humanities, teaching) thereby segregating women into certain kinds of jobs even before they enter the labor market. In 2005, the World Bank's gender assessment of Jordan described a paradox. It documented that female labor force participation in Jordan stood at about 28 percent, which was 50 percent of its potential when taking into account women's educational level, reductions in the fertility rate, and the age structure of the population (World Bank 2005). Public attitudes about gender equality are still very conservative, as chapter 5 shows.

Some of the gender disparities in Jordan reflect an underlying attitudinal and policy bias against women. Although Jordanian women enjoy legal equality with men on many issues (for example, health care, education, and political participation), they suffer from discriminatory statutes on nationality and citizenship law, family law, and provisions of pensions and social security benefits. Legislation aimed at protecting women's health, safety, and "modest standing in society" has had the effect of constraining their ability to find employment. Finally, Jordan has deeply entrenched patriarchal norms, although from 2004 until the end of 2009, the women's movement in Jordan made a number of important gains that led to new laws and expanded access to services. However, some women, such as divorced women, the elderly, and widows, are still constrained from participating fully in society. They are most likely to experience poverty and deprivation, often depending on relatives, friends, or welfare support.

South Africa: Changes in Income Inequality

South Africa's success in reducing racial inequalities presents an interesting conundrum. Postapartheid policies sought to aggressively equalize the historical burden that the apartheid era had left on a range of outcomes. South Africa still has high levels of income inequality (measured by a Gini coefficient of 0.63), but inequality is driven primarily by within-race inequalities, which account for about 59 percent of overall income inequality. This pattern is likely to continue in the future, confounded by the fact that the share of black South Africans in the population will rise. Therefore, going forward, attempts to address intragroup inequalities will drive South Africa's quest for greater inclusion more than intergroup disparities.

Despite this important shift, economic disparities across groups remain the major drivers of social exclusion. Although the Reconciliation Barometer survey shows significant progress—in 2012 the survey found that two-thirds of South Africans are willing to "forget about apartheid" and "move forward together as a country" (Lefko-Everett 2012)—issues of "material justice" seem to stand in the way. Low levels of economic inclusion and slow transformation remain important concerns: 43.1 percent of the Reconciliation Barometer survey participants believe that "reconciliation" and "improved social relationships between South Africans" are impossible when people who were disadvantaged under apartheid are still poor. Levels of disagreement vary with age: across all racial categories, youth are more likely than adults to disagree that progress has been made. Racial differences are particularly evident in relation to two survey items related to restitution and the economic legacy of apartheid. About one-third of white (31.1 percent) and Indian/Asian (34.2 percent) youth feel that economic justice and greater equality are not necessary preconditions for reconciliation. A significant share of white youth (29.5 percent) also opposes the idea that the government should continue to support apartheid victims. This share is much larger than it is among white adults (14.5 percent).

The Propellers of Change toward Social Inclusion

The preeminent role of the state as the driver and propeller of change toward inclusion is well recognized. The state can intervene for social inclusion through three conduits. The first is to create an enabling environment for social inclusion, such that citizens have the freedom to exercise their choice and innovate for better outcomes and processes. The second is to design legislation, policies, and programs that directly or indirectly affect social inclusion. The third is to ensure implementation and enforcement of the legal and policy framework. All these roles are underpinned by the nature of the state, the degree of openness of the polity, and the vision that the state and citizens share. The strength of both formal and informal institutions is critical for the success of state-led actions. Strong institutional contexts with a clear vision of social inclusion lead to better outcomes (Acemoglu and Robinson 2012). Chapter 7 discusses policies and programs for social inclusion in greater detail.

The state, however, does not act suo moto; a host of nonstate actors are active drivers of social inclusion. The impact of state-led actions, in

> I know that we should participate in politics and leadership at all levels. We have a right to property; we have a right to education. But men do not like this and I think that they are wrong: they have enjoyed too much because everything was theirs. Now these laws are saying that not everything is theirs. If I were the one in their position, I would not like the laws either. My husband told me one time when we finished the seminar with World Vision on the rights of women and we were talking about female circumcision: "rights of women, yes, but what about the rights of men"? I like the question of rights, but sometimes I think that many women get more problems when they talk about their rights and they are abandoned by their husbands as stubborn women and bad women. Men get other women.
>
> —Female focus group participant in Chibelela, Tanzania, Moving Out of Poverty study (World Bank)

fact, is contingent upon other actors and their stakes in making the change successful. Similarly, processes led by nonstate actors often need buy-in from powerful groups, such as the political elite. Together, these actors build coalitions and shape the course of change.

Catalysts and champions of change toward social inclusion often come from among the elite. The movements to end slavery in the United States, foot-binding in China, and apartheid in South Africa were all led by elites, whether from among the excluded groups (as in South Africa) or dominant groups (as in the United States). Appiah draws parallels between the processes that ended foot-binding in China to the processes that led to the abolition of female genital mutilation in Senegal. Both began with respectful elites assembling a core of supporters and organizing a program of commitment to new practices that were sensitive to traditions of the community. In contrast, the top-down criminalization of genital mutilation by the Senegalese government a few years earlier backfired, leading to the cutting of many girls in deliberate violation of the law. Dani and de Haan (2008b) point out that although "modernizing elites" and colonial traditions were early drivers of change, over time, with the increasing influence of international organizations, NGOs and international actors have assumed more prominence in driving change agendas. The role of NGOs and international actors is probably greater in highly aid-dependent contexts.

The role of business leaders in promoting social inclusion is also well recognized and has a long history in both developed and developing countries. Private foundations have both the political clout and the financial resources to influence change toward social inclusion. A large number of private foundations address the goals of social inclusion by supporting services such as health or education. Few of them invest in nondiscrimination, citizenship, or diversity, although these inclusionary outcomes are often externalities of successful service delivery programs. Organizations like the Open Society Foundation have funded a range of projects, including media campaigns, to change public attitudes and advocacy to influence policy. These campaigns are explicitly aimed at combating discrimination and xenophobia against a broad range of excluded groups, such as the Roma and Muslims in Europe; lesbian, gay, bisexual, and transgender people; asylum seekers and refugees; people with disabilities; and stateless people (Open Society Foundation 2012).

Social movements and collective action have historically pushed agendas for social inclusion by taking up specific wrongs that society needs to correct.

Most large social reforms have had at least some element of public support. The end of foot-binding in China and the acceptance of race as an axis of exclusion in Brazil had strong elements of social movements. In addition, collective action by excluded groups that lobby for rights are forms of social movements that build coalitions for change. The more impressive strategies of subversion are at the group level and usually involve political coalition building. Not all of them, however, as Appiah notes, are claims for recognition; some are demands for participation in different spheres of life.

The media can help in creating awareness about exclusion and in changing mindsets. Awareness campaigns are usually based on getting information to the public, especially when stereotypes and misinformation are rife. In the cases discussed earlier, the importance of awareness in China and of new data in Brazil had a positive impact on bringing new facts to the agenda.

The use of soap operas in changing attitudes and behaviors is increasingly being recognized. In a particularly innovative move, the U.S. Census used Telemundo, the Spanish-language television company, to run messages during a popular soap opera. The aim was to encourage Latinos to participate in the U.S Census of 2010 in the face of strong anti–U.S. government feeling among Latinos and a potential boycott of the census. Trujillo and Paluck (2012) randomly assigned Latino participants in Arizona, Texas, and New Jersey during a period of either contemplated or passed anti-immigration legislation to compare people who had seen the pro-census scenes and those who had viewed scenes featuring the soap opera characters but not the census information. Compared with control viewers, census viewers expressed more positive attitudes toward the U.S. government and more behavioral support for the census (wearing pro-census stickers and taking informational flyers). Affinity with the soap opera character was associated with stronger effects. However, there were no positive effects in Arizona, where anti-immigration legislation had directly affected participants. Similar changes in attitudes have been noted with respect to HIV/AIDS, contraceptive use, and girls' education in developing countries. But the obverse is also true: the media can be used effectively to spread misinformation about excluded groups and events.

The Importance of Shared Goals and Strong Institutions

Policies and programs that seek to enhance social inclusion are rooted, first and foremost, in the nature of the social contract. As Sen (2001, 74) writes,

"Inclusion is characterized by a society's widely shared social experience and active participation, by a broad equality of opportunities and life chances for individuals and by the achievement of a basic level of well-being for all citizens." This shared vision about what it means to be included in society is crucial, as it underlines support for or opposition to inclusionary measures. Shared ideals are usually laid out in constitutions; upheld through laws; refocused through vision documents, plans, and manifestos; and put in practice through policies, programs, and projects. Ideals such as fundamental rights and, often, nondiscrimination are common in modern constitutions. Vision documents and national plans serve to reiterate these ideals and focus attention on them. Kenya's Vision 2030 is intended to create a "just and cohesive society enjoying equitable social development in a clean and secure environment"; Malawi's Vision 2020 aspires for the country to be "secure, democratically mature, environmentally sustainable, self-reliant with equal opportunities for and active participation by all"; the Uganda National Resistance Movement's manifesto for 2011–15 is entitled "prosperity for all" (Marcus et al. 2013). Although such higher-order ideals are the core of the social contract, their actualization is usually the real challenge.

When different groups in a population have a shared vision of society that is based on a common identity, actions for social inclusion are likely to be more successful. Qualitative interviews conducted as part of an ongoing World Bank poverty and social impact analysis of the hill state of Himachal Pradesh in India reveal a shared sense of pride among Himachalis from all caste groups when it comes to their rich environmental heritage. Their shared vision of progress accords equal weight to economic progress and environmental sustainability.

Research on Bangladesh points to a remarkable congruence between the ideals and vision of the elite on the one hand, and of ordinary people on the other, regarding poverty and development at the national level (Hossain 2005). It also notes that elites in Bangladesh are relatively new and still maintain their links with their rural roots, because the cultural ethos of the elites and the people are remarkably similar. Such shared vision allows for policies that address poverty and target other positive social outcomes.

Identification with a shared vision of society is often related to whether citizens regard their national identity or their parochial identity to be preeminent. Societies that have diverse groups with strong ethnic identities are often regarded as prone to fragmentation. In Uganda, despite

Table 6.1 Half of Ugandans Identify Themselves Equally as Ugandan and as Members of Their Ethnic Group

Identify	Percentage of respondents
Only in terms of ethnicity	6.0
More in terms of ethnicity than Ugandan	15.4
Equally in terms of ethnicity and Ugandan	53.4
More Ugandan than in terms of ethnicity	9.4
Only Ugandan	16.0

Source: World Bank, based on data from 2008 Afrobarometer.

a strong association between ethnicity and access to services, as indicated in chapter 3, the majority of Ugandans do not identify only with their ethnic group. About half the Ugandans surveyed by the Afrobarometer identify themselves equally as Ugandan and as a member of their ethnic group (table 6.1). At the multivariate level, only food security, education, and cell phone use are statistically significant predictors of identity, but the size of the effects is small for all except education. Religion, for instance, has a very weak effect on individuals' national versus ethnic identity, and access to services seems to have no effect at all. Certain ethnic groups, however, are more likely to give higher weight to ethnicity than to national identity. People who belong to the same ethnicity as the ruling elite tend to identify themselves as Ugandan more than those who do not belong to the ruling elite.

Shared vision builds support for public expenditures toward social inclusion. Consider again the case of Brazil, which has one of the largest income transfer programs in the world. Bolsa Família evolved from a small pilot to a sophisticated program that is credited with, among other things, partially propelling the recent decline in income inequality. Chapter 5 discussed the reasons for Brazil's relatively high tolerance for inequality. By the turn of the millennium, when Brazil came to be held up as the negative outlier in income inequality, there was a strong current of public opinion that believed that not just poverty but inequality needed tough policy intervention. A range of initiatives were launched at the federal, state, and municipal levels, of which the expansion of the benefits of Bolsa Família was one. Figure 6.1 indicates that even though people believe that Bolsa Família may be a handout, they realize its importance for ending hunger and poverty. This response holds across regions but manifests itself most strongly in the poorest areas of the North and Northeast. There is also little support for the perception

Figure 6.1 Support for Bolsa Família Is Remarkably Consistent across Regions in Brazil

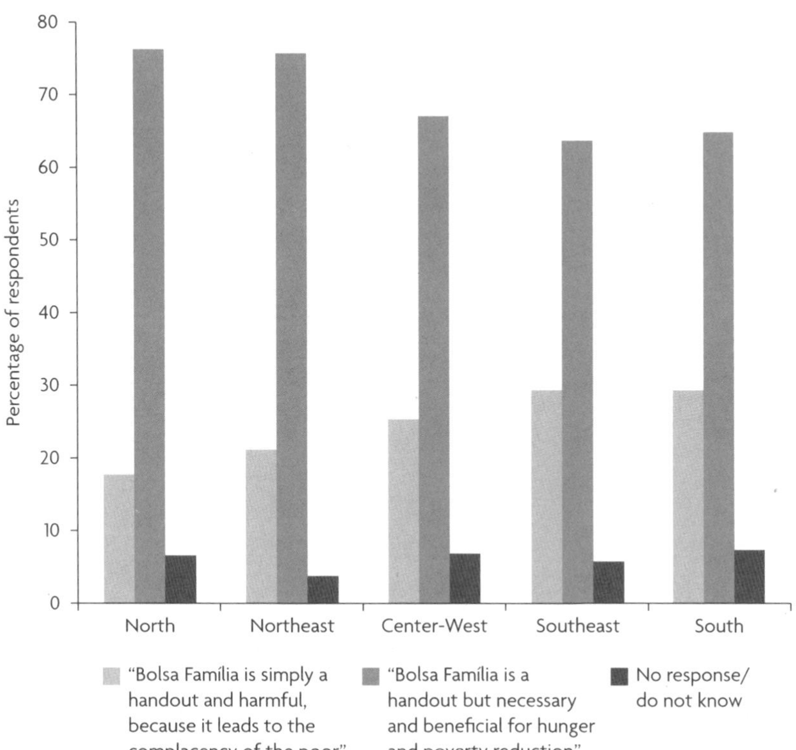

Source: Government of Brazil 2009.

that the program leads to complacency among the poor, with less than 20 percent of respondents in the poorest regions and 30 percent in the richest thinking so. Overall, many ingredients contributed to the success of Bolsa Família, but it probably would not have succeeded without the shared support for public expenditure.

Public approval of inclusion measures can vary by social group and age. Figure 6.2 shows responses from the 2012 South African Reconciliation Barometer, a representative survey that sampled 3,565 people, asking respondents how they felt about various positive discrimination measures in employment and in monitoring. Only half the respondents agreed that the government should use racial categories to measure the impact of policy and programming. But differences were evident by racial group. Although

Figure 6.2 Attitudes toward Social Policy in South Africa Vary by Age and Race, 2012

Agree		White	Indian/Asian	Colored	Black	Total
Government should use race categories to measure progress	Youth (15–34)	19	45	36	55	51
	Adults (35 and older)	31	51	31	53	47
	Total	28	49	34	54	49
Workforce should be representative of race	Youth (15–34)	68	62	53	58	58
	Adults (35 and older)	61	61	49	58	57
	Total	63	62	51	58	58
Workforce should be representative of gender	Youth (15–34)	72	64	54	64	64
	Adults (35 and older)	68	67	53	62	62
	Total	69	66	54	63	63
Workforce should be representative of disability	Youth (15–34)	81	54	58	65	65
	Adults (35 and older)	73	64	55	60	62
	Total	75	61	56	62	63
Black economic empowerment is an effective policy for ensuring black participation in the economy	Youth (15–34)	35	41	39	54	51
	Adults (35 and older)	35	39	43	49	46
	Total	35	40	41	52	49
Equity in employment policies has succeeded in creating a representative workforce	Youth (15–34)	24	33	29	49	46
	Adults (35 and older)	39	38	37	46	43
	Total	34	36	34	48	45

■ Youth (15–34) ■ Adults (35 and older) ■ Total

Source: Lefko-Everett 2012.

more than half of black South Africans agreed, only a little over a third of "colored" and just over a quarter of white South Africans supported the idea. The divergence was particularly salient by age. Black (55 percent) and "colored" (36 percent) youth expressed stronger support than adults that government should use apartheid race categories for tracking progress; support was much lower among white youth (19 percent). In contrast, support for representation by disability status and gender was high overall, at 63 percent. Interestingly, white South Africans were most likely to support the view that the workforce should be representative of race, gender, and disability status. Responses were much more instructive when broken down by age. Both gender equality and disability status in the workforce were more important for black and "colored" youth than their adult counterparts. Black economic empowerment policies and employment equity policies received low overall approval ratings, with only about half of all respondents agreeing that they are effective policy instruments. Support for these policies among black respondents, although stronger than among other racial groups, was still lukewarm.

Although shared vision is important, strong institutions are the foundation for realization of higher-order goals such as social inclusion. The strength of institutions lies in large part in the agility and malleability with which they can address new needs of social inclusion. The report *Inclusive States* (Dani and de Haan 2008a), for instance, addresses how legal and judicial institutions can contribute to inclusion. *Societal Dynamics and Fragility* (Marc et al. 2012) analyzes how interactions between different institutions, state as well as customary, can undermine the effectiveness of these institutions in fulfilling their role, such as governing access to land or providing a functioning legal system, thereby reinforcing divisions and conflict between different groups in society.

Take the case of Sweden, often held up as a shining example of social inclusion but currently grappling with the challenges of immigration. The country's institutions, which have historically responded positively to social and economic challenges, now need ways to accommodate a more heterogeneous population than Sweden has been used to. *The Economist* recently reported that only 51 percent of non-Europeans in Sweden have a job, compared with more than 84 percent of native Swedes. Poverty and incarceration rates are also higher among non-Europeans. Sweden recently relaxed rules for immigration of more skilled workers and put in place several measures to accommodate foreigners, such as housing, language training, and help to negotiate the complexities of the welfare state. Although the impact of these measures is unclear, it is evident that Sweden has been able to respond to the issue of immigration with alacrity because of its institutions combined with a shared vision of a just society (*The Economist* 2012). The status of Sweden as a positive outlier in terms of social attitudes is evident in the data presented in chapter 5.

BOX 6.1

The Inclusion-Exclusion Nexus in Botswana's Institutional Development

Drivers of More Inclusive Development

A central plank of Botswana's progress has been its construction of institutions, which have protected private property rights, and the presence of various incentives for economic and political elites to support a relatively redistributive state structure. Some key aspects of the bargains made with elites include the following. First, there was a close alliance between the Botswana Democratic Party (BDP)—which has dominated politics since independence—and cattle owners, who, after independence, were the most important economic interest group and were politically influential. A significant share of infrastructure investment since 1966 favored cattle-ranching regions. Second, Botswana possessed relatively inclusive precolonial institutions, placing constraints on political elites. The effect of British colonialism on Botswana was minimal and did not destroy these institutions. Third, a system of checks and balances to contain corruption emerged after independence, It comprised measures such as the holding of primary elections within the party, which resulted in significant rotation of officials; a high degree of press freedom, allowing for criticism of policies and politicians; and competing ideological factions within the BDP, which enhanced political competition. All of these measures led to a party with relatively inclusive patronage structures, which accommodated urban elites and the middle class, as well as the main rural elites (chiefs and cattle herders). Fourth, as a result of the generally inclusive coalition of the BDP, diamond rents were widely distributed in the form of infrastructure and social service delivery, which reduced the incentives of elites to rock the boat. Finally, presidential decisions helped maintain political stability. For instance, the decision by Sereste Khama, Botswana's first president, to reduce the political power of tribal chiefs with respect to land allocation just after independence is thought to have reduced tribal cleavages and conflicts.

(*continued next page*)

BOX 6.1 *(continued)*

The Exclusion Side of the Coin

Although the political settlement in Botswana was inclusive of most economic elites, it was still exclusionary toward nonelite groups and classes. This development can in part be explained by the political sociology of the ruling party—the fact that it was dominated largely by cattle barons and traders, for instance, meant that limited effort went toward protecting the most destitute and excluded groups, such as the Sans (bushmen). Various analyses find that the drought relief program increasingly came to serve the interests of large landholders and cattle owners and did not address the fact that a pressing problem for the destitute and the Sans was their lack of formal land rights.

Source: de Waal 1997; Good 1999; Acemoglu, Johnson, Robinson 2003; Hickey 2007; Putzel and Di John 2012; O'Meally and Ramshaw 2012.

Reflecting on the Trajectory of Change

Change from exclusion to inclusion is a long-term agenda; attention to timing is important when initiating reform. Lasting "one stroke of the pen" changes are few. Change is usually preceded by a series of processes or events. Processes, practices, and outcomes that take centuries to aggregate to egregiousness are usually not undone in a few years of inclusive policy, especially when very exclusionary or hierarchical institutions are sought to be reformed. Further, undoing the past often entails more than just reversing negative impacts. It also requires overcoming negative beliefs and stereotypes about excluded groups, which is usually a long-term endeavor that requires multifaceted interventions. Timing is of the essence. The impacts of some changes may be felt years into the future and may well be the unintended consequences of policy or other developments.

Depending on the extent of support, change can be a nonlinear process. Some changes may be unintended. Jordan is the exemplar among lower-middle-income Muslim countries in the expansion of female education, but women's labor market outcomes remain poor, partly because of the unintended consequences of education policies, which lead to segregation of women into certain occupations or constrain their ability to find employment. It is important for policy makers to be cognizant of the way the society will receive and react to policies. So it is important to have a long-term view of change. Efforts made today are likely to yield important payoffs down the road.

Discrete actors and processes can spur change. Although the state is often the main propeller and its actions the most potent and effective, implementation or acceptance by society depends to a large extent on institutional and political economy factors as well as public support for change. The best kind of change is change that builds inclusive settlements and creates incentives for all actors to partake in the change.

Finally, social inclusion is often a work in progress. For example, racial inequality in South Africa is decreasing, but within-group inequality is increasing. Bangladesh's informal justice systems have become more inclusive of women, but access to formal justice is still out of reach for many, especially poor and young women. In China, foot-binding may have stopped completely, but urbanization, internal migration, and other trends pose new areas for social inclusion, as discussed in chapter 4. And so on. Social inclusion is and will always be a work in progress, as some challenges of inclusion are met even as others arise.

References

Acemoglu, D., S. Johnson, and J. A. Robinson. 2003. "An African Success Story: Botswana." In *In Search of Prosperity: Analytical Narratives on Economic Growth*, ed. D. Rodrik. Princeton, NJ: Princeton University Press.

Acemoglu, D., and J. A. Robinson. 2012. *Why Nations Fail: The Origins of Power, Prosperity, and Poverty*. New York: Crown Business.

Appiah, K. A. 2006. "The Politics of Identity." *Daedalus* 135 (4): 15–22. http://www.scribd.com/doc/163184582/The-Politics-of-Identity-Appiah.

——. 2007. *Cosmopolitanism: Ethics in a World of Strangers*. New York: Norton.

Asia Foundation. 2007. *Promoting Improved Access to Justice: Community Legal Service Delivery in Bangladesh*. Dhaka: Asia Foundation.

Bode, B., and M. Howes. 2002. "The Northwest Institutional Analysis." CARE Bangladesh, Dhaka.

CERD (United Nations Committee on the Elimination of Racial Discrimination. 2003. "Report Submitted by States Parties under Article 9 of the Convention, Seventeenth Periodic Reports of States Parties due in 2002, Addendum, Brazil." CERD/C/431/Add.8, October 16. Office of the United Nations High Commissioner for Human Rights, Geneva, Switzerland.

Dani, A. A., and A. de Haan, eds. 2008a. *Inclusive States: Social Policy and Structural Inequalities*. Washington, DC: World Bank.

———. 2008b. "Social Policy in a Development Context: Structural Inequalities and Inclusive Institutions." In *Inclusive States: Social Policy and Structural Inequalities,* ed. A. Dani and A. de Haan, 3–38. Washington, DC: World Bank.

Das, M. B., and V. Maru. 2011. "Framing Local Conflict and Justice in Bangladesh." Policy Research Working Paper 5781, World Bank, Washington, DC.

Davila, J., Z. R. Morgan, and T. E. Skidmore. 2008. "Since Black into White: Thomas Skidmore on Brazilian Race Relations." *The Americas* 64 (3): 409–23.

de Waal, A. 1997. *Famine Crimes: Politics and the Disaster Relief Industry in Africa*. Bloomington, IN: Indiana University Press.

Economist, The. 2012. "Immigrants: The Ins and Outs." February 2. http://www.economist.com/news/special-report/21570836-immigration-and-growing-inequality-are-making-nordics-less-homogeneous-ins-and.

Gacitúa-Marió, E., and M. Woolcock, eds. 2008. *Social Exclusion and Mobility in Brazil*. Washington, DC: World Bank.

Golub, S. 2003. "Non-state Justice Systems in Bangladesh and the Philippines." Paper prepared for the Department for International Development, London. http://gsdrc.org/docs/open/DS34.pdf (accessed October 7, 2012).

Good, K. 1999. "The State and Extreme Poverty in Botswana: The San and Destitutes." *Journal of Modern African Studies* 37 (2): 185–205.

Government of Brazil. 2009. "Pesquisa Quantitativa Regular Bimestral" (First Regular Bimonthly Survey), July. http://www.secom.gov.br/sobre-a-secom/acoes-e-programas/pesquisas/relatorios/pesquisa/impressao_view (accessed October 7, 2013).

Guirguis, C. 2004. "Village Governance: Conflict Resolution and the Poorest." Draft report. BRAC Research and Evaluation Department, Dhaka.

Hickey, S. 2007. "Conceptualising the Politics of Social Protection in Africa." Working Paper 4, Brooks World Poverty Institute, University of Manchester, Manchester, U.K.

Hossain, N. 2005. *Elite Perceptions of Poverty in Bangladesh*. Dhaka: University Press.

Jahan, F. 2007. "From Rule of Law to Legal Empowerment for the Poor in Bangladesh." Unpublished. Dhaka, Bangladesh.

Jansen, W. 2006. "Gender and the Expansion of University Education in Jordan." *Gender and Education* 18 (5): 473–90.

Lefko-Everett, K. 2012. *Ticking Time Bomb or Demographic Dividend? Youth and Reconciliation in South Africa*. SA Reconciliation Barometer Survey: 2012 Report. Institute for Justice and Reconciliation, Cape Town.

Mackie, G. 1996. "Ending Footbinding and Infibulation: A Convention Account." *American Sociological Review* 61 (6): 999–1017. http://www.polisci.ucsd.edu/~gmackie/documents/MackieASR.pdf.

Marc, A., A. Willman, G. Aslam, M. Rebosio, and K. M. Balasuriya. 2012. *Societal Dynamics and Fragility: Engaging Societies in Responding to Fragile Situations*. Washington, DC: World Bank. https://openknowledge.worldbank.org/handle/10986/12222.

Marcus, R., S. Espinoza, L. Schmidt, and S. Sultan. 2013. "Social Exclusion in Africa: Towards More Inclusive Approaches." Background paper draft, World Bank, Washington, DC.

O'Meally, S., and G. Ramshaw. 2012. "The Political Economy of Social Inclusion." Background paper draft, World Bank, Washington, DC.

Open Society Foundation. Roma Initiatives Office. http://www.opensocietyfoundations.org/about/programs/roma-initiatives-office.

———. 2012. "Statelessness." February 7. http://www.opensocietyfoundations.org/projects/statelessness.

Putzel, J., and J. Di John. 2012. *Meeting the Challenges of Crisis States*. Crisis States Research Centre Report. London: London School of Economics and Political Science.

Sen, A. 2001. *Development as Freedom*. Oxford: Oxford University Press.

Telles, E. E. 2006. *Race in Another America: The Significance of Skin Color in Brazil*. Princeton, NJ: Princeton University Press.

Trujillo, M. D., and E. L. Paluck. 2012. "The Devil Knows Best: Experimental Effects of a Televised Soap Opera on Latino Attitudes toward Government and Support for the 2010 U.S. Census." *Analyses of Social Issues and Public Policy* 12 (1): 113–32.

World Bank. Moving Out of Poverty (research initiative). http://www.worldbank.org/en/topic/poverty.

———. 2005. *The Economic Advancement of Women in Jordan: A Country Gender Assessment*. Washington, DC: World Bank.

———. 2008. *Whispers to Voices: Gender and Social Transformation in Bangladesh*. Bangladesh Development Series 22. Dhaka: World Bank.

CHAPTER 7

Propelling Social Inclusion

Koh har qadar beland baashad, sar-e khod raah daarad.
(Even a very high mountain has a path to the top.)

—AFGHAN PROVERB

Chapter 6 showed that change toward social inclusion is possible and that the state plays a preeminent role in propelling such change. Its role is both direct, in terms of putting in place policies, programs, and institutions, and indirect, in terms of creating conditions that enable inclusion.

This chapter addresses some of the ways in which social inclusion has been promoted in diverse contexts. It looks at actions and interventions that have enhanced social inclusion across the three domains of the conceptual framework, namely, markets, services, and spaces (figure 7.1). These domains represent both barriers to and opportunities for inclusion. Underlying the discussion is an explicit caveat: the set of policies and programs presented is not a prescription. Rather, it is a tentative menu of options to choose from, depending on need, opportunities, culture, budget, politics, and institutional capacity.

No single set of policies or programs can be classified as "social inclusion policies" or "social inclusion programs." In fact, depending on the "wrong" that needs to be addressed, or the "right" that needs to be deepened, a range of interventions could be employed. This realization then leads to the question: How do policies that have social inclusion at their core differ from ordinary social policies? The question is a difficult one to answer. In essence, policies that place social inclusion at the core do not necessarily do more but do things differently. This chapter provides a

Figure 7.1 Propelling Social Inclusion through Markets, Services, and Spaces

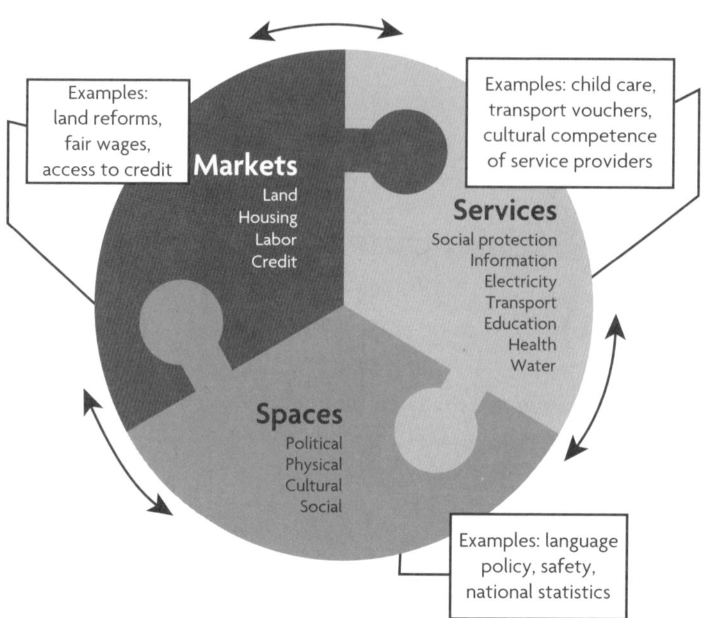

few examples of interventions within a broad typology, but any policy or program can be designed and implemented with a social inclusion focus.

Often the same policy or program can cut across different domains—market, services, and spaces. Although it is somewhat of a truism to say that policies toward social inclusion need to be "connected" or "cross-sectoral," the truism deserves repeating. Social exclusion is a multidimensional process in which practices in one domain lead to or reinforce exclusion in another. Policies to address social exclusion therefore require what Silver (2013) calls "a dynamic sequence of interventions." Illustrating her argument with the case of the homeless, she argues that their inclusion in society requires a "continuum of care" starting from transitional housing, labor market training, and (possible) drug and alcohol treatment to (eventually) permanent housing, perhaps with long-term supportive services to help the homeless stay housed. This chapter categorizes interventions into the domains of markets, services, and spaces, recognizing that the domains overlap and that intervening in one domain can have effects in others.

An intervention can have an impact on social inclusion by affecting ability, opportunity, and dignity simultaneously and incrementally.

During the construction of a large thermal power plant, for instance, initial consultations can enhance dignity and voice, the use of local labor for civil works can enhance opportunities, and the delivery of electricity to households can enhance ability. One of the components of Barrios de Vereda (Real Neighborhood), an urban infrastructure project in Bolivia, was the construction of indoor sanitation facilities and street lighting to improve pedestrian mobility and women's security. These features helped increase women's ability to access spaces. The project also constructed child care centers, which gave women opportunities to improve their participation in the labor market (World Bank 2010b).

Designing the right instrument means first understanding the real problem. The real test of moving toward social inclusion is not to accept that some people and groups are overrepresented among the poor or have worse human development outcomes. The real work of social inclusion is to persevere with questions, to ask why certain outcomes obtain for certain groups. The narrative that is so constructed provides the wherewithal for the design of the right policy. Moving too quickly to the repertoire of policies for answers entails the risk of using a blunt or wrong instrument to address a particular problem.

This chapter presents examples of policies and programs that can lead to social inclusion. The first three sections provide examples of interventions in the domains of markets, services, and spaces. The fourth section discusses policies that cut across these domains (for example, affirmative action and conditional cash transfers) and are commonly used to promote inclusion. The last section takes one specific indicator of exclusion—poor maternal health among indigenous women in India—and walks the reader through steps to come up with solutions.

Intervening for Social Inclusion through Markets

> With the ban on untouchability, we can now directly approach (officials) to complain about being a victim of untouchability. We can force the officials to punish those who practice it. Now, people in the local community have started using some respectful and decent words to address us, instead of degrading and humiliating us like (they did) earlier.
>
> —Participant from a historically disadvantaged caste (Damai) in a discussion group in Khotang, Nepal (World Bank 2011b)

Land redistribution can play an important role in combating structural disadvantages. Although land reforms by themselves are not a panacea for exclusion or inequality, societies that have carried them out tend to be more inclusionary, because the agrarian structure is an important axis of exclusion, especially in countries that are still heavily dependent on agriculture or have large rural populations, as pointed out in chapter 3. Many countries and states that have opted for land reforms (for example, Costa Rica, the state of West Bengal in India) were either never very unequal to begin with or saw declines in inequality after land reforms.

But merely undertaking a reform does not ensure that it will stand the test of time. Additional measures may be necessary if inclusion obtained through the initial impacts of land reforms is to be sustained. In her thesis on the experience of land reforms in Brazil, for instance, Lindemann (2010) finds that although such reforms increased access to land by people considered outside settlers, those settlers continued to face resistance from the original inhabitants of the land, who claimed that their use of the land was illegitimate or economically unsustainable. Deininger, Narayan, and Sen (2009) show that in West Bengal, only households that made complementary investments in inputs, such as seeds and technology, benefited from the reforms.

Providing land titles to women and granting de facto recognition of the communal land use patterns of indigenous populations can be effective in creating opportunity and enhancing dignity. Women in many societies do not traditionally own land. Making them joint landholders in land redistribution or resettlement projects or reserving land use quotas can increase their access to opportunities (in agriculture, for example) while also empowering them. Deininger, Goyal, and Nagarajan (2010), for instance, find that giving women joint ownership to property can have a salutary effect on the education of girls in the household. Evidence from Argentina and Peru shows that giving land titles to women can also boost women's labor force participation, leading to lower fertility, better chances for children's education, lower child labor, and better housing (Field 2003; Galiani and Schargrodsky 2009, cited in Todd 2012). Similarly, recognizing the customary rights of indigenous populations over their native lands and strengthening their representation in land negotiations is as much about creating opportunity for these groups to use the land as it is about recognition. For example, Mozambique's 1997 land law allows oral evidence to be used as part of land tribunals. As illiteracy rates are high among poor and marginalized groups in rural areas, this measure proved critical in enabling their participation in land registration procedures (FAO 2010). In Kenya, the decision of the African Commission on Human and Peoples' Rights to recognize the ownership rights of Endorois (agro-pastoralists) helped these communities gain unrestricted access to their ancestral lands around the Lake Bogoria Game Reserve, traditionally used for cattle grazing, and to perform their religious and cultural rites (Abraham 2012).

Programs offering skills development can enhance women's labor market outcomes (box 7.1). Both women's labor force participation rates and their wages are lower than those of men, even after controlling for a range of individual and household-level factors (World Bank 2012b, 2013b). Many women cannot work because of their family responsibilities, yet child care in most places is costly and scarce. Programs providing subsidized child care not only can help women improve their labor market outcomes, they can have other positive externalities as well.

Attanasio and Vera-Hernandez (2004), cited in Todd (2012), evaluate the impact of one such initiative—the Hogares Communitarios, Colombia's largest welfare program—which provides child day care to poor households in rural Colombia. They find large positive impacts: the probability of female employment increased from 0.12 to 0.37, and the number of hours worked by women increased by 75 a month. The study also finds statistically significant effects of the program on children's height and, over the longer term, school attendance and grades. Even if the impact had been reflected exclusively in increased leisure time, this could well influence a range of other outcomes for women and their families.

Inclusion in financial markets, which advances access to appropriate and affordable financial services, is crucial to inclusive growth. New alternatives to traditional banking are allowing millions of people who would otherwise be excluded from the formal financial system to perform financial transactions cheaply and securely. The widespread availability of mobile phones, for instance, has created a new gateway for financial transactions. Mobile money has achieved its broadest success in Sub-Saharan Africa, where in 2011 about 16 percent of adults reported having used a mobile phone in the past 12 months to pay bills or send or receive money (Demirgüç-Kunt and Klapper 2012). In Kenya, M-PESA, a mobile money service, has provided about 70 percent of all adults with access to financial services. Crucially, about 43 percent of Kenyan adults who reported having used mobile money in the past 12 months did not have a formal account.

BOX 7.1

Including Women in the Labor Market in Liberia

Youth unemployment is one of the main obstacles to development in Liberia. The situation of young women is particularly challenging. To help improve the employability of young women, the Liberian Ministry of Gender and Development launched the Economic Empowerment of Adolescent Girls and Young Women (EPAG) project in 2009. A three-year pilot initiative undertaken in partnership with the World Bank, the project included a six-month classroom training course, followed by six months of placement and support, including microenterprise advisory services, internship, and job placement assistance. The objective was to facilitate the transition from the classroom to wage or self-employment for women between the ages of 16 and 24. The project targeted women who were not attending day school but had basic numeracy and literacy skills.

Training was delivered in two rounds in nine communities. About 70 percent of participants were trained in business development skills and 30 percent were provided with job skills. All job skills trainees also received training in entrepreneurship. In addition, all participants received life skills training specifically designed for Liberian women. They received small stipends contingent upon classroom attendance and were assisted in opening savings accounts at local banks. Women who completed the training were awarded a small bonus ($20) and targeted to sectors with high demand. The project also included a capacity-building component for the Ministry of Gender and Development, which resulted in the creation of a new unit within the ministry, the Adolescent Girls Unit, which now helps mainstream gender-sensitive programming and policies in Liberia.

Preliminary results from a randomized impact evaluation (baseline and midline surveys) are encouraging. The program led to a 50 percent increase in employment among women who started training in round 1 (the treatment group) compared with women assigned to round 2 (the control group). Before the first round of training, outcomes for the treatment and control groups were similar: about 38 percent of young women in both groups reported being engaged in at least one income-generating activity. Both groups improved by the midline, but the change was significantly larger for the treatment group. For a young woman from the control group, the likelihood of working improved by nearly 20 percent (from 38 percent to 45 percent), whereas that of a young woman from the treatment group improved by more than 70 percent (from 39 percent to 67 percent).

(*box continues next page*)

BOX 7.1 (*continued*)

Figure B7.1.1 Increase in the Likelihood of Working Was Larger for Young Women Receiving Skills Training in Liberia

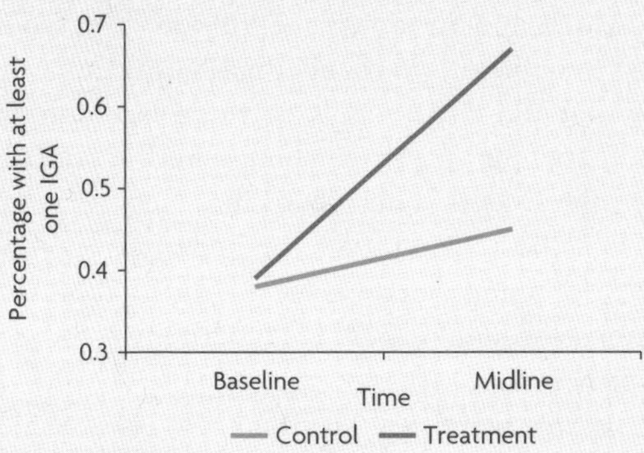

Note: IGA = income-generating activity.

The positive employment outcome was stronger among the business skills trainees. The employment rate at midline was 76 percent among business skills trainees and 52 percent among job skills trainees. Business skills graduates were also more likely to be involved in self-employment at the time of the midline survey than in wage employment. At midline, 87 percent of business skills graduates were self-employed, and only 12 percent were wage-employed. In comparison, 50 percent of job skills graduates who reported working were self-employed (the other 50 percent were engaged in wage employment).

Source: World Bank 2013a.

Intervening for Social Inclusion through Services

Perhaps the most important route to social inclusion is through the enhancement of human capital, which can be achieved through better and more dignified access to services. Take the example of disability services in the United States, which are provided across an individual's life cycle. Rights of people with disabilities are underpinned by the Americans with Disabilities Act (ADA) of 1990, which has gone through several amendments. The law says that "physical or mental disabilities in no way diminish a person's right to fully participate in all aspects of society." It then goes on to provide a set of rules and makes it incumbent upon federal and state entities to abide by them. The law is buttressed by strong enforcement mechanisms, and each entity is responsible for ensuring that it does its part in upholding the provisions of the ADA.

In Mozambique and Tanzania, Braille and sign language are used to ensure that HIV messages reach young people with visual and hearing impairment. In Uganda, the Sustainable Clubfoot Care Project improves the detection and rehabilitation of children with clubfoot by raising public awareness that the condition is correctable, improving the provision of orthotics, training health personnel, and subsidizing transport costs. Examples in the United States, Australia, New Zealand, and some other countries from the Organisation for Economic Co-operation and Development (OECD) stand out because of their cross-sectoral nature and the mechanisms through which accountability is sought from the state and service providers.

Minorities at risk can be targeted through programs that are tailored to them. Box 7.2 highlights the way in which services are tailored to the Maori (the indigenous people of New Zealand) and the manner in which the services simultaneously enhance ability, opportunity, and dignity.

Ethiopia has made substantial investment in ensuring that groups most at risk of being excluded from education are targeted. Some civil society innovations address barriers faced by minorities and subordinate groups. They include mobile schools and libraries for pastoralist children and a system of introductory letters facilitating children's movement between Alternative Basic Education Centres (ABECs) if their family migrates to new pasturelands. ABECs are intended to provide flexibly scheduled, informal education in the mother tongue with a "relevant and compressed curriculum" to out-of-school children, who then transition into the second primary education cycle (Jennings et al. 2011). The number of students attending ABECs in Ethiopia doubled since 2005, and ABECs have accounted for 15 percent of enrollment in pastoral areas of Ethiopia. Recruiting qualified women facilitators has been a challenge, which may explain the lower enrollment of girls at ABECs in some regions (for example, Afar and Gambella). Improving quality is another ongoing challenge, as is more flexible scheduling to fit in with families' daily and seasonal farming and animal husbandry activities.

Subsidized fares targeted to excluded groups and accessible transport services can help improve physical access and inclusion. In many cities in developing countries, the poor live on the outskirts. They depend on public

BOX 7.2

Inclusion through Tailored Services: Reaching the Maori in New Zealand

Although overall development outcomes for Maori have improved considerably in the last few decades, Maori continue to lag behind non-Maori. To address this problem, the government of New Zealand tailors services and benefits to respond to the particular needs of Maori. Tailored programs are designed so that intended beneficiaries are most likely to access the program or service but—unlike targeted services—they are not exclusive to specific beneficiaries.

Tailoring not only provides separate, alternative Maori services, such as immersion education and Maori health providers; it also tries to better fit mainstream services to Maori. For instance, Maori are now more involved in policy making and service delivery, as members of school boards and representatives on district health boards and primary care organizations. Service provision is devolved to Maori organizations. For example, there has been growth in alternative Maori health providers, who provide services that are responsive to Maori health needs and the Maori *kaupapa* (philosophy). The Maori language is used in consultations, in health promotion materials, and in the provision of Maori healing services.

Maori immersion education serves several goals: it helps preserve the Maori language and culture, and it also strengthens Maori ownership of education and self-determination. The first *kōhanga reo* (language nest) was set up in New Zealand in 1981. The *kōhanga reo* movement spread rapidly: within 12 months, 107 centers had been established with government funding; seven years later, more than 600 *kōhanga* were in operation, and in 2004 there were 513 centers, with 10,319 students. The *kōhanga reo* movement has also influenced mainstream education: many non-Maori have sent their children to *kōhanga reo*.

Maori providers seem to do well in reaching poorer populations. For example, 77 percent of their patients come from poorer areas, where nationally 56 percent of Maori live. Patients are also more likely to have a community services card, an indicator of low income.

Source: Ringold 2008.

transport and have long commutes across multiple administrative jurisdictions. To address the problem, the city of São Paolo chose flat fares as an alternative to distance-based fares, in order to cross-subsidize the poor. Fare systems are also built so that they are valid across multiple modes or trips on one journey.

Some groups, such as women and people with disabilities, face additional barriers to using transport (inadequate street lighting leading to concerns about safety, transport that is inaccessible to people with disabilities and so forth). Here, too, countries are experimenting with innovative methods to address the challenges these groups face. Some cities in Liaoning Province, China, are constructing new sidewalks that can be used by residents with vision impairment or limited mobility. Women-only subways, buses, and train cars are being used to combat aggression toward and harassment of women in a number of countries, including Belarus, Brazil, the Arab Republic of Egypt, India, Japan, Mexico, and the Philippines. Several urban transport projects financed by the World Bank now include indoor sanitation facilities and street lighting in their design, to improve pedestrian mobility and women's security (World Bank 2010a).

Stereotypes that are often ingrained in service providers can have a damaging effect on the way they treat their clients, but these issues are not insurmountable, as discussed in Part I. A growing practice focuses on "cultural competencies" among service providers. This practice is particularly advanced in health and social work, and it is growing in education and other sectors. Holding providers accountable not merely for their presence and their technical skill but for cultural competence as a performance indicator is likely to go a long way toward ensuring that cultural minorities feel comfortable in accessing services. Box 7.3 summarizes recent advances in building cultural competencies.

Judicial services can be made inclusionary by making the principle of law more broadly applicable. Brinks and Gauri (2012) find that the impact of courts is positive and pro-poor in two of the five countries they study (India and South Africa), neutral in two others (Brazil and Indonesia), and sharply anti-poor in one (Nigeria). They attribute the success of India and South Africa to the fact that litigation there took the form of broadly binding erga omnes (toward everyone) decisions rather than purely inter partes (between the parties) decisions. As a result, the decisions of the court were applicable to everyone (not just the people petitioning), thereby making them largely nonexcludable. It helped that the highest courts in these countries are strong and have records of aggressive rulings on rights. In 2004, for instance, the South African Constitutional Court interpreted the constitutional right to health to require a recalcitrant Mbeki government to launch a major program to prevent the transmission of HIV from mothers to infants (Heywood 2009). India has a strong "right to information," which litigants use to demand information from their governments.

BOX 7.3

Cultural Competence Training to Health Care Professionals

Training health care professionals in cross-cultural communication—what is referred to as "cultural competence training"—is one way to address racial and ethnic disparities in health care. There are two approaches to such training. The first is a categorical approach, in which health practitioners are taught about attitudes, values, beliefs, and behaviors of specific social groups. Such distinctions may deepen stereotypes about these groups and lead health providers to oversimplify rather than respect the complexity of a culture. The second—and preferred—approach is to train professionals so that they "hear" all individuals, irrespective of group identities.

Some key principles for cultural competence training have evolved over time. First, buy-in of the health care provider is important. Second, training needs to be integrated into medical courses. Although there can be a separate module for cross-cultural care and communication, it should be stressed that it is not an add-on but is essential to delivering quality medical care. Third, the module needs to be built through the entire duration of medical education (graduate and postgraduate), with the first few years focusing on basic skills (for example, awareness about beliefs of certain groups) and the last few focusing on techniques for reaching specific groups that are more discipline specific. Finally, the key to addressing culturally rooted demands of certain groups is to understand their sociocultural background. In other words, just as physicians must ask certain questions that lead to a diagnosis, they can also ask questions that provide a glimpse of the sociocultural profile of their patients and the factors that may have led to their illness, without sounding paternalistic.

Randomized control evaluations of cultural competence training, though rare, show that such training can improve the attitudes of health care providers and improve patient satisfaction. Factors that need to be considered in an evaluation are the group being targeted (for example, Latinos in the United States); the medical condition (for example, asthma); the skills or screening tool used to diagnose that condition; the diagnosis offered; patient satisfaction; and other controls.

Source: Betancourt and Green 2010.

Intervening for Social Inclusion through Spaces

The idea of "spaces" is at once real and symbolic. Perhaps the first step to inclusion is to recognize the existence of individuals or groups and to make them visible in state records. Many countries have weak systems of birth and death registration. Initiatives to correct the problem may not immediately conjure up images of social inclusion. But without such registration, children may be unable to attend school and family members may be unable to gain access to property following a death in the family. Often, the poorest and the most excluded groups cannot access benefits because they do not have identification or any means to prove that they indeed exist. Such literal recognition can come from initiatives that provide identity cards or that create electronic databases or make social efforts to count people at risk of remaining invisible. Brazil's efficiency in implementing the Bolsa Família and related cash transfer programs is partly the result of the Cadastro Único, an electronic database of program participants. Similarly, censuses can undercount ethnic minorities because they themselves may inaccurately report their ethnicity out of fear of being unfairly treated. This is the case for the Roma, whose itinerant lifestyle and tendency to hide their identity so that they can meld in leads to an underestimation of their real numbers.

Interventions that work at the cusp of social and physical space can be transformative. The city of Medellín, Colombia, stands as a unique and innovative example of how cities can become inclusive for their citizens through both infrastructure planning and citizen engagement. Infamously known for its drug cartel, which used the city as a base for operations, the city undertook wide-ranging police and military action between 2003 and 2006 that resulted in the dismantling of the cartel and a significant decline in the number of homicides. It transformed its transportation system, with cable cars running between *comunas* (municipalities or councils) previously at war (Romero 2007). Among the urban development initiatives undertaken was the creation of new public spaces—for example, the Parque Biblioteca España and new museums—to encourage social interaction. A large part of Medellín's municipal budget is now spent on social investments, targeted at vulnerable sections of the population, including older people. Several programs work on organizing youth and older adults into community action groups. These groups, which come with elected positions, help the vulnerable put forth their interests before the municipalities (especially at the time of budgetary planning) and enable them to hold government entities accountable.

Inclusion in physical spaces can be deepened through improvements in security and services. Inspired by Medellín's success, the state government of Rio de Janeiro launched Unidades de Polícia Pacificadora (UPP), an innovative program to regain control of areas previously in the hands of drug gangs and militias. The program was conceived as a first step in providing residents of *favelas* with the same rights and opportunities available to the rest of the city. The UPP police intervention was followed by the work of its social arm, UPP Social, which aims to promote social and economic integration in a divided city through the coordination of policies and services in these communities. Estimates by Cano (2012) point to large reductions in lethal violence (75 percent) and thefts (50 percent) after implementation of the UPP.[1] Residents also report being able to move more freely within and across communities as a result of the "pacification."[2] Qualitative evidence also points to a reduction in stigma in "pacified" communities, reflected by use of residents' real addresses in job applications (previously, they had concealed where they lived to avoid being identified as *favelados*) (Cano 2012). Also, 72 percent of residents said they felt more respected by people outside their communities after the UPP (Instituto Brasileiro de Pesquisa Social 2012). At the same time, residents regard stigma as positive, as it could prevent their land from being taken over by real estate developers (World Bank 2012a).

Language is an important aspect of identity and claims to political and cultural space. Language policy can thus be an important driver of both exclusion and inclusion (box 7.4). The status of certain languages as official for government or education has symbolic, political, and practical consequences. Symbolically, official status suggests that certain ethno-linguistic groups and their cultures are more valuable than others. Practically, not speaking an official language can prevent excluded groups from participating in democratic processes or making use of public services. Furthermore, the disadvantage may be passed on over generations, with children of linguistically excluded groups facing barriers accessing learning and jobs. Language policy can therefore lead to an important grievance against which groups have mobilized politically and militarily.

Respect for a language constitutes respect for a people. Although it is sometimes controversial, bilingual education can improve children's language and cognitive development as well as strengthen their identity and self-confidence (Cooper et al. 2004; Hall and Patrinos 2006). Education programs in which teachers speak the same language as their students, teachers are prepared to teach in a bilingual classroom environment, and parents and the community participate in the design of curricular materials have had good results. In Guatemala, indigenous students enrolled in bilingual schools tend to have higher attendance and promotion rates

BOX 7.4

Inclusion of the Immigrant Population: The Way to Norway

Immigrants feel less discriminated against in Norway than in any other European OECD country: only about 14 percent—compared with more than 30 percent in Greece and Austria and more than 20 percent in Portugal, Spain, the Netherlands, and France—report feeling discriminated against. Inclusion of migrants has been a long-standing issue on the Norwegian policy agenda—and their integration in the labor market is considered an essential part of it.

Since 2006, the government of Norway has put in place a range of policies under its Action Plan for Integration and Social Inclusion of the Immigrant Population. One focus concerns language and cultural training, which is promoted in several ways:

- All migrant children (including irregular migrants) have a right to primary and secondary education. Students who are not sufficiently proficient in Norwegian to attend regular schools have a right to mother tongue instruction or bilingual subject teaching.
- Adult immigrants are provided free Norwegian language training by municipalities, which receive grants from the central government. They also receive training in information and communication technology skills. Participants who cannot read or write in their mother tongue are eligible for basic literacy training.
- Refugees and people granted residence on humanitarian grounds are entitled to an introduction benefit of NKr 164,244 (twice the basic annual amount of the National Insurance Scheme) while taking part in language training. Training also includes a 50-hour social studies module (in a language the immigrant understands) to familiarize the migrant with life in Norway.

There is little doubt that host language skills are an important factor for integration, although further research is needed to assess the precise nature of benefits. The same holds for the effect of the introduction program. Preliminary research suggests that the program has increased the labor market prospects of immigrant men but not women. In November 2010, 55 percent of people who finished the program in 2009 were employed or participated in education.

In 2008, the Norwegian government started a two-year pilot of moderate affirmative action for immigrants applying for public administration positions. Where candidates have equal or approximately equal qualifications, a candidate with an immigrant background is to be preferred. Managers taking part in the project say it has made them more aware of diversity. Between 2008 and 2013, the public sector has also contributed

(*box continues next page*)

BOX 7.4 *(continued)*

disproportionately to higher employment among non-OECD migrants who have been in Norway longer. Although it is challenging to assess the precise impact of such measures, Norway has achieved a representation of immigrants in the public sector that is broadly at par with their overall presence in the labor market.

Sources: Norwegian Ministry of Labour and Social Inclusion 2006; Kavli, Hagelund, and Bråthen 2007; OECD 2009, 2012a, 2012b; IMO n.d.

and lower repetition and dropout rates relative to nonindigenous students. Although bilingual education comes with high cost associated with teacher training and materials, in the long term it may save resources, through lower grade repetition. In Guatemala, for instance, in 1996, the cost savings associated with lower grade repetition were estimated at $5 million, an amount sufficient to provide primary education to 100,000 students. There is considerable debate, however, over the quality of bilingual education, particularly its effect on achievement as measured by standardized test score results and returns to schooling (Parker, Rubalcava, and Teruel 2005).

Programs that seek to promote multiculturalism have had mixed impact, with programs having a long-term view faring better. Evidence from prejudice-reduction interventions show that positive attitude changes resulting from such interventions quickly weaken or disappear (Katz and Zalk 1978, cited in Turner and Brown 2008; Bigler 1999; Hill and Augoustinos 2001).

The evaluation of the impact of the Friendship Project in Kent, in the United Kingdom, by Turner and Brown (2008) is illustrative. Designed to improve primary school children's attitudes toward refugees, the program separated participants into two groups: children who received four weekly lessons based on the program and children who received no lessons. All participants completed attitude measures before and after implementation of the program. Half the participants completed the test one week after completion of the program, the other half completed the test seven weeks after its completion.

The evaluation showed only modest impact. The modest impact could be explained in part by limitations of the project and the context in which it was conducted. Participants who took part in the project lived in a region where they had long been exposed to hostile community attitudes toward refugees as well as media coverage of refugees that was typically extremely negative. Also, the program lasted for just four classes over a period of four weeks. The intervention was probably too brief to have been able to counteract the ongoing impact of such an environment.

Ultimately, focusing on extended positive contact between members of different groups can reduce intergroup prejudice more effectively than can merely learning about the other group (box 7.5). Such a strategy, when combined with other interventions, serves to emphasize the importance of social inclusion as a long-term agenda.

Symbolic acts can go a long way toward reconciliation of people who have been historically excluded. In 2010, the U.S. Congress offered its first bipartisan "apology to Native Peoples of the United States." The statement

BOX 7.5

Innovations in Inclusion: Poland's Post-Accession Rural Support Project

The World Bank–supported Post-Accession Rural Support Project (PARSP) in Poland was implemented between 2006 and 2011. It targeted the most excluded groups in 500 poor rural communities (*gminas*). Unique to the design of the project was participation of local communities in the identification and planning of what was called their own social inclusion strategy. Service delivery was tailored to reach groups considered excluded in each community. Some *gminas* organized activities for children, offering them opportunities to develop social and creative skills outside the school setting. Others designed programs that allowed the elderly to participate in community life, to help them overcome social isolation.

The project is estimated to have reached nearly 230,000 children and youth, 74,000 elderly people, 42,000 people with disabilities, 25,000 victims of violence, and 59,000 homemakers. Nearly 60 percent of project beneficiaries were women.

As a result of the program, the majority of *gminas* decided to start cultural and sport activities that changed perceptions about socially excluded people, such as people with disabilities. The village of Byszow, for example, started organizing races for people with disabilities, in an effort to change perceptions about them in the village. The project also helped build the capacity of local *gmina* offices in resource management, strategic planning, and program delivery. Municipalities are now leveraging this investment in order to access external funding, particularly from the European Union.

Source: Plonka 2013.

apologized for "the many instances of violence, maltreatment, and neglect inflicted on Native Peoples by citizens of the United States."[3] In Australia, the aboriginals are now symbolically referred to as the "indigenous custodians of this country." Constructing memorials to victimized groups may serve as a reconciliatory mechanism for addressing past wrongs. In conflict settings, truth commissions (or restorative justice bodies) are a common means of achieving reconciliation and compromise between the perpetrators of crimes and their victims. Although there is no right or wrong way to achieve reconciliation, evidence suggests that transitional justice processes come with their own attendant risks and may not necessarily provide effective reconciliation solutions for the long term. Truth commissions in Africa, for instance, offer restorative justice but have been largely unsuccessful in acting as a deterrent to human rights violations. To be truly effective, reformists argue, transitional justice mechanisms need to take into account victims' voices and the local circumstances that led to the conflict in the first place. Creating informal channels for restoring peace (for example, indigenous forms of reconciliation) may also help.

Cross-Cutting Approaches Spanning Many Domains

There is an age-old tension between policies and programs that seek to provide universal access and those that target specific groups. Targeting can range from area-based approaches (often called "geographic targeting") to the targeting of certain individuals or groups. Targeting criteria can include poverty status, age, disability status, gender, or a mix of these criteria. In addition, programs can include conditions—such as sending one's children to school—that create incentives for increasing the demand for certain services, such as education and health care.

Affirmative action policies can be viewed as a form of targeting in which certain groups, by virtue of their historical exclusion, are given special treatment to enable them to catch up with the average in the population. Affirmative action can come in various forms; quotas are just one type of affirmative action. In the United States, for instance, affirmative action implies a range of interventions, from unspecified quotas for minorities in educational institutions to overt quotas in some institutions. Laws that ensure equal opportunity in employment, credit, housing, and education are another form of affirmative action. The constitutions of several countries, including Bolivia, India, Malaysia, Nepal, South Africa, and Uganda, allow for preferential policies for excluded groups to redress historical imbalances. Intended to enhance opportunities and level the playing field, these policies reserve places in public educational institutions, public employment, or legislative bodies (box 7.6). The target groups vary by country: India has provisions for Scheduled Castes and Scheduled Tribes, Malaysia's affirmative action policy rests on preferential treatment of the *bumiputras* (native Malays). Northern Ireland has a statute that provides quotas for Catholics in police hiring. Because membership in a group determines access to these preferential measures, these policies tend to be highly politicized (Weiner 1983).

Preferential policies often create issues and concerns. One issue is whether countries want to name groups and thereby "affirm" the divide. In Brazil, for instance, quotas for Afro-Brazilians were preceded by an intense debate over whether establishing them would mean implicitly recognizing race as a marker of discrimination—an idea that ran contrary to Brazil's construct of a "racial democracy," as discussed in chapter 6. France has opted for geographical targeting of socioeconomically deprived areas rather than naming ethnic groups living in those areas. China has made impressive advances in the reduction of poverty and social exclusion by good geographical targeting. In the EU accession countries, the Roma are not specifically acknowledged in affirmative action legislation but are subsumed under the overarching term of "disadvantaged groups" (Silver 2013). A second issue is how to ensure that entrenched elites do not skim the benefits of quotas when resources are scarce. A related issue is how to prevent perverse incentives for other groups to show "weakness" and hence entitlement for affirmative action. A final concern is that positive discrimination policies can build resentment among dominant groups, who may question the qualifications of candidates who receive preferential treatment, thereby intensifying their stigma.

The evidence on whether affirmative action results in positive or negative outcomes for the excluded is ambiguous. The positive impact of affirmative action on the self-confidence of the excluded cannot be ignored. In India, there is new evidence to suggest that the policy of reserving local council seats for women has weakened gender stereotypes in both the domestic and public spheres by creating role models. In villages that had had the experience of a female leader, aspirations about educating girls and girls' test scores were higher than they were in villages that had not had a female leader. Men in villages that had been led by women spoke about the competence of female leaders in an unbiased way (Bhavnani

2009; Beaman et al. 2012). But there are reports of mixed impacts as well. In Malaysia, for instance, the New Economic Policy and its successor, the New Development Policy, reduced interethnic inequalities but increased inequality among Malays (Jomo and Hui n.d.). And affirmative action policies in the South African labor market reduced wage inequalities only at the top of the wage distribution (Burger and Jafta 2006).

BOX 7.6

Electoral Quotas for Women in Sub-Saharan Africa

Rwanda is the only country in the world where women parliamentarians outnumber men. But a number of other African countries have significant representation of women among their parliamentarians. These gains have been achieved through the adoption of quotas.

In Rwanda, the use of reserved seats in the 2003 elections led to women constituting 48 percent of representatives in the lower house and 30 percent in the upper house (Ward 2006). The reservation principle is enshrined in the (postgenocide) 1996 constitution. As of November 2011, women constituted 56 percent of parliamentarians and held a third of Cabinet positions, including some top positions, such as that of speaker (Ghosh 2012). Women parliamentarians and observers credit the high level of political representation to changes such as laws that enshrine women's property rights, including land rights, greater availability of contraception, and much greater attention to sexual offenses (Boseley 2010).

South Africa rapidly increased women's parliamentary representation, from 2.4 percent before democratization (which began in 1993) to 33 percent in 2004 (Ward 2006). In 1994, after the first democratic elections, women held 15 percent of Cabinet positions and 56 percent of deputy ministerial positions. Since 1994, women have held a number of "hard" portfolios, including trade and finance (Piron and Curran 2005).

In Tanzania, there are 33 percent quotas for women in local elections and 20 percent in national elections. Interestingly, the "quota MPs" are not identified with particular constituencies—that is, they are, in principle, understood as Members of Parliament with a national rather than local constituency (Ward 2006). In an attempt to widen the basis of its political representation and bring a wider range of society into national decision making, Tanzania's main political party has also put in place quotas for youth, members of the armed forces, and workers.

Source: Marcus et al. 2013.

Social protection programs can have benefits that far exceed their original intent. They can enhance self-esteem of subordinate groups and their "capacity to aspire" as well as the attitudes of others toward them. In Lesotho, for example, recipients of social pensions indicated an increase in respect for them in society once the national social pension was introduced. The pension also contributed to greater self-esteem, because recipients were able to make larger financial contributions to their grandchildren's upbringing and education. HelpAge International (2004, cited by Marcus et al. 2013) suggests that social pensions are often valuable to older women, who often lack assets because of discriminatory inheritance or property rights laws. A World Bank (2011b) study reports similar responses from the elderly who receive social pensions in Nepal. They cite having greater dignity, economic independence, and self-esteem in the family as a result of the pension. Box 7.7 reports the results of an impact evaluation of a conditional cash transfer program in Nicaragua that had unforeseen positive impacts on women's leadership and community role models.

Social grants and transfers can play a role in reducing historical disparities. In preapartheid South Africa, the beneficiaries of social grants were primarily whites and "colored" people; black people received a minor share of the benefits. The postapartheid government instituted reforms such that social grants would target blacks, who were hugely overrepresented among the poor but were not receiving the transfer (Leibbrandt, Woolard, and Woolard 2007).

Mexico's well-targeted Oportunidades program, in addition to benefiting a much larger proportion of the population in indigenous than in nonindigenous municipalities (figure 7.2), also decreased gender gaps in employment and reduced levels of domestic violence. Angelucci (2008), cited in Todd (2012), finds that on average, the program led to a 13-fold increase in the income of married women, who had almost no income before the program, given their low rates of formal labor market participation. Participation in the program also led to a decrease in the share of household income earned by the husband, from 97 percent to 62 percent. For households receiving relatively small transfers, the program led to a 15 percent decrease in alcohol abuse and a 37 percent decrease in drunken violence. But in households in which wives received larger grants (because of higher eligibility), the husband had less education, and the age gap between husband and wife was large, the chances of violence and aggressive behavior were higher.

Community-driven development is an approach that gives community groups control over planning decisions and investment resources for local

BOX 7.7

Positive Spillovers of Social Protection Programs: The Case of Nicaragua

In their study on the impact of social protection in Nicaragua, Macours and Vakis (2009) find that the aspirations of participants in a social protection program were enhanced through social interactions with successful and experienced individuals, which in turn positively influenced the attitudes and behaviors of the people surrounding them. The authors studied a two-stage randomized short-term transfer program in Nicaragua that randomly allocated 3,000 households to one of three conditional cash transfer packages as part of the Atención a Crisis program implemented by the Ministry of the Family. The first package was a basic conditional cash transfer aimed at protecting investments in human capital. The second package also included a scholarship component for occupational training. The third package consisted of the basic package plus a special grant for productive investments. The design of the program created opportunities to enhance interactions among beneficiaries, particularly women, who were the recipients of the cash transfers and were given a leading role in the implementation of different components of the program.

The evaluation focused on the additional impact of the program (that is, the impact above being assigned to the treatment group) on beneficiaries who lived near female leaders who received the productive investment package. The female leaders were generally younger and more educated than the average beneficiary; they were required to develop a business development plan outlining the objectives of their business initiatives and investments in new livestock or nonagricultural income-generating activities. These requirements were supported through technical assistance and business-skills training workshops.

Source: Macours and Vakis 2009.

development projects. Recent evidence on the impact of such programs suggests that when implemented well, they can improve service delivery in sectors such as health and education, increase resource sustainability, and help communities build lower-cost and better-quality infrastructure (Wong 2012; Mansuri and Rao 2013). Furthermore, by virtue of targeting mostly the poor and vulnerable, these programs can help bring the voice of such groups to the policy table. An impact evaluation of Indonesia's Kecamatan Development Program (KDP), for instance, finds widespread participation of beneficiaries in program meetings, with poorer and female-headed households as likely to attend as others (Barron et al. 2009).

Figure 7.2 Mexico's Oportunidades Program Benefited Indigenous People Much More Than It Did Nonindigenous People

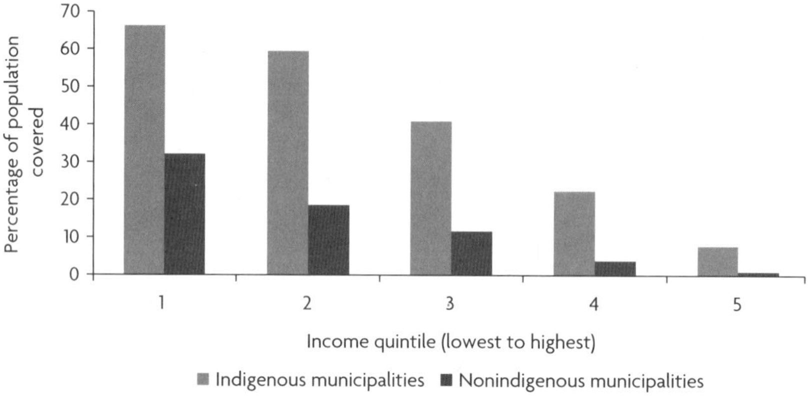

Source: Hall and Patrinos 2006.

What Can Social Inclusion Mean in Practice?

This section shifts the discussion to the level of practice. It uses the example of high numbers of maternal deaths among tribal women in India to argue that an intervention or change toward inclusion in any domain needs to start with the right diagnosis. Once the underlying reasons for exclusion are known, mitigating measures can be tailored accordingly, followed by innovations in monitoring and grievance redress.

Step 1: Diagnose: Ask Why

An understanding of who is excluded, and how, is often the first step toward designing the right policies and programs. Yet the quest among practitioners is too often for answers, before articulating the question clearly. Getting at the question is hard and complex. It is also often political.

Take the case of the tribal women from India introduced in chapter 2. The National Family Health Survey of India 2004/05 reports that 80 percent of tribal women in India give birth at home, compared with 60 percent of all Indian women. When asked why they opt to deliver their children at home, 72 percent of tribal women say they do not consider it necessary to deliver in a health facility. This finding often leads health authorities to conclude, incorrectly, that there is low demand for institutional births among tribal women and that this low demand is a result of cultural factors and ignorance. However, what masquerades as low demand may reflect an assertion of dignity and a rejection of bad treatment by service providers. When probed on why they think institutional births are unnecessary, 1 percent of tribal women say they deliver at home because there is no female provider at the health center, 2 percent say they do so because they do not trust the facility, 5 percent say that they are held back by their husbands and family, 5 percent complain of the facility not being open, 17 percent speak of it being too far and inaccessible because of no transport, and 23 percent say it is too costly. Only 7 percent say it is not customary to opt for an institutional birth (World Bank 2011a).

Underlying the proximate reasons for poor outcomes are complex phenomena that are not immediately visible. Staying with the example of high numbers of maternal deaths among tribal women in India, this report argues that the poor health of a tribal woman is rooted in the low power she has relative to almost everyone else. Issues of land and forests are central to her situation. Once viewed in this way, it is clear that a supply-side push for better health facilities is a blunt instrument with which to address high levels of maternal mortality.

An intervention would benefit from "asking why" at different steps of the diagnosis of a poor outcome (figure 7.3). Questions could include the following:

- What is the wrong or the intractability that is being addressed, or what went right that needs to be deepened? Why?
- Whom does the intervention or service seek to include, or who is at risk of being left out? Why?
- Why are those groups or areas at risk of being left out? What are the channels through which inclusion can take place? Why?
- What innovations can be put in place to ensure inclusion? What can be done differently?

There are several ways to ask the right questions and identify the channels through which to intervene. In some cases, an ex ante analysis can help. For example, a Poverty and Social Impact Analysis (PSIA) of charcoal sector reforms in Tanzania found that a rise in charcoal prices could result in cutbacks in both food and nonfood expenditures in households, with particularly negative impacts on women and children. It therefore suggested putting the burden of higher prices on the dealer-transporter-wholesaler networks, which could cope with them.

In other cases, program or project managers can opt for consultations with the group to explore why they think a problem (such as high mortality

Figure 7.3 Ask Why! Why Are Maternal Deaths among Tribal Women in India High?

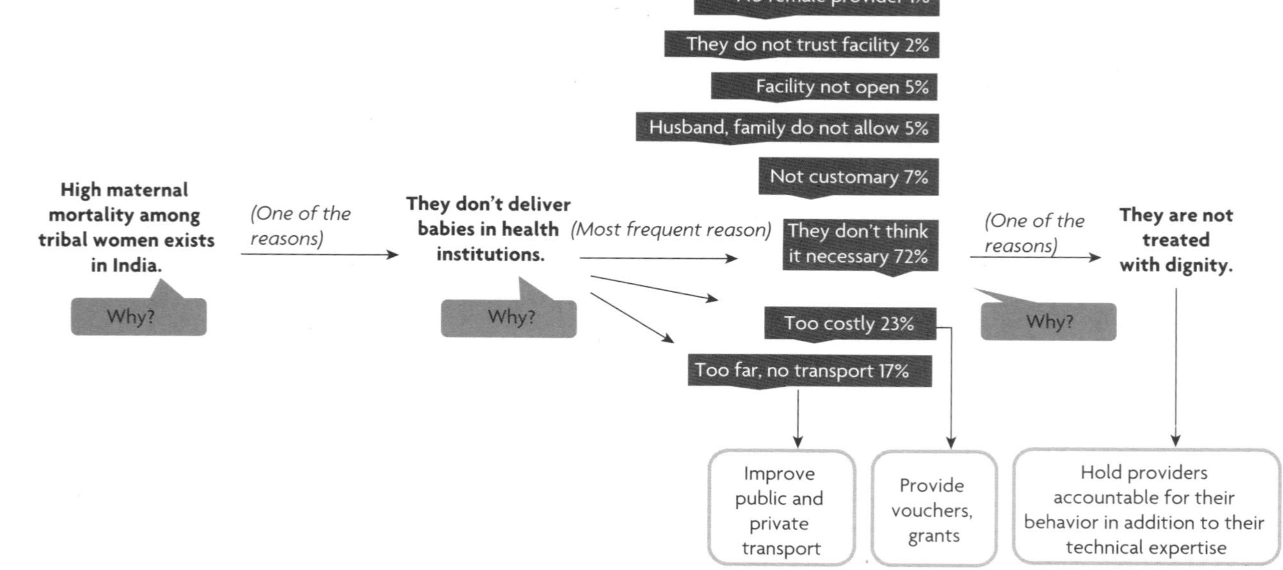

Source: Adapted from World Bank 2011a, which is based on the National Family and Health Survey of 2005.

Note: Percentages show multiple responses of tribal women who delivered their babies at home to a question asking why they did not deliver at health institutions.

rates among indigenous children) exists. In Peru, for example, interviews conducted as part of the RECURSO program found that indigenous women rejected formal health facilities for delivery because they found them "inappropriate" and not respectful of their cultural preferences and standards.[4] The study accordingly recommended that health centers in indigenous areas imbue their staffs with greater sensitivity to the cultural preferences of women regarding how they would like to give birth (for example, allowing a family member to be present during birth, providing staff who can communicate in indigenous languages, facilitating the process of giving birth in a vertical position, and accommodating traditional preferences regarding the disposal of the placenta).

Innovative methods such as using information and communication technology to solicit anonymous responses to questions have become increasingly popular. In Tanzania and South Sudan, for instance, two pilot initiatives referred to as "Listening to Africa" have been highly successful in collecting panel data through mobile phone interviews. Evaluations suggest that the method is cost-effective, with low attrition rates even after more than 30 rounds of interviews (Croke et al. 2012). In other cases, there may already be a strong body of research that can be synthesized and tailored to the issue at hand.

Consultations are the cornerstone of diagnosing problems and building support for interventions. A consultation, as distinct from a dialogue, commits the provider to active listening and to carefully considering the comments, ideas, and recommendations of beneficiaries about what is bothering them and why. Building such consultations into projects and programs can help organizations frame key questions and identify the right channels for intervention. The key is to hold consultations early in the project cycle, so that findings can feed into project design. Consultations segregated by gender and other groups can also help project teams understand why group characteristics matter and how they can be addressed for good results.

Step 2: Design

Once the underlying reasons for exclusion are identified, interventions to address them can be designed accordingly. To go back to the example of high numbers of maternal deaths in India, the issue of too few female providers can be addressed by training local birth attendants from tribal communities (figure 7.4). Family restrictions on using a facility can be worked around through education and awareness campaigns using local languages and idioms. Tribal communities can be involved in the surveillance of health

Figure 7.4 How to Include: Addressing the High Numbers of Maternal Deaths among Tribal Women in India

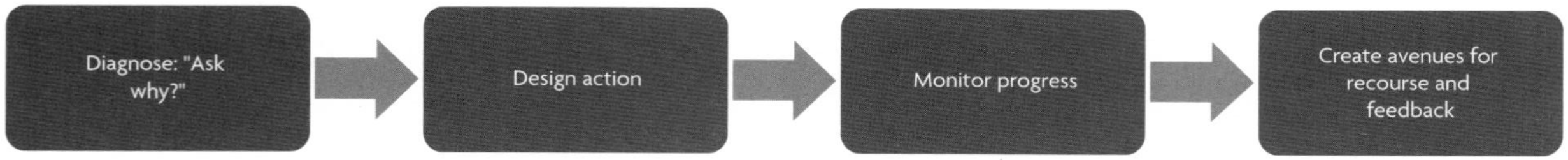

Diagnose: "Ask why?"

- Why do a large majority of tribal women say they don't think it's necessary to give birth in health facilities?
- If the reason is poverty, why are these women overrepresented among the poor?
- If the reason is lack of knowledge, why are they not better informed?
- If the reason is remoteness, why are they not connected?

Through:

- Conducting innovative ex ante analysis
- Holding meaningful consultations, including through the use of information and communications technology (ICT) to allow women to respond to questions anonymously

Design action

- Provide vouchers, grants, and culturally appropriate incentives
- Launch education/awareness campaigns in local language and idiom
- Register births and deaths
- Involve the community in health surveillance
- Use tribal systems of knowledge of health
- Establish links to other programs
- Make innovative use of private providers, including private transport agencies
- Hire more female staff from tribal communities
- Require cultural competency training for service providers
- Hold providers accountable for their behavior as well as technical skills
- Create incentives for providers to reside in remote areas

Monitor progress

- Establish a monitoring framework that can be accessed by tribal people
- Create community monitoring mechanisms
- Establish third-party monitoring mechanisms
- Use social audits and hold public meetings
- Conduct "verbal autopsies"
- Mandate citizen report cards
- Publicly disclose results of monitoring, including through electronic channels
- Use ICT to solicit anonymous feedback

Create avenues for recourse and feedback

- Establish an empowered ombudsman-like institution that enforces tribal rights
- Empower tribal women through legislation and provide them with legal assistance
- Create independent help lines
- Establish local tribal health committees with access to district administration
- Form empowered grievance redress committees
- Establish systems to report back to communities on action taken

facilities, monitoring their opening and closing hours as well as the amenities and infrastructure available. Simultaneously, incentives can be given to service providers to reach and stay in remote areas. Private transport agencies, transport vouchers, and other culturally appropriate incentives can be made available to get tribal people to bridge distances and reach formal health facilities.

Deepening trust among the excluded of a system that discriminates against them or humiliates them may be tricky and require sensitive handling. In the case of health services, it can be achieved through cultural competence training of health providers (see box 7.3) and tracking of performance based not just on attendance but also on behavioral parameters. Trust can also be deepened by incorporating tribal people's own indigenous systems of health into formal practices of health care delivery.

Step 3: Monitor Progress

There can be several methods to monitor progress. The most effective ones are those that involve communities themselves, such as social audits (verification of government data by people in public meetings); citizen report cards (users' assessments of the availability and quality of services); and the

BOX 7.8

Questions Used in a Third-Party Monitoring Initiative in Nigeria

Third-party monitoring reports by civil society organizations in Nigeria shed light not only on whether projects are being implemented and services delivered but also on why things are working the way they are. Some questions they addressed included the following:

- Why are there gaps in service delivery even though facilities and mechanisms are in place?
- Why doesn't information reach citizens, despite efforts to communicate about the project?
- Why are certain groups not benefitting, despite project team efforts to reach them?
- Why are project inputs not used or misused? Is it as a result of citizens' lack of understanding?
- Are there barriers to access?

Source: World Bank 2013b.

use of information and communications technology to solicit anonymous feedback.

In the case of maternal deaths among tribal women, progress can be tracked through "verbal autopsies"—interviews with a member of the family, preferably the caregiver, of the deceased. This method is used to collect cause-specific mortality information in areas where people may not access health services before death or where vital registration systems for birth and death are weak. A third party may undertake the monitoring; what is essential is that the indicators used be made available in a language the people being interviewed speak and that the results of monitoring be disclosed publicly to create pressure for change. Metropolitan transit authorities in Argentina, for instance, regularly survey citizens to receive inputs on the regularity and efficiency of transit services. They now want to analyze the data through a gender lens to better serve underserved populations and understand women's travel patterns better. Compañía Minera Poderosa, a private mining company, conducts surveys of women in communities near its mines to find out how they feel about the social programs funded by the company, about members of their family working for the company, and so forth. These questions have given the company a sense of how it scores on women's satisfaction with the company's performance and, therefore, the extent to which the company is having an influence on local development (Ward and Strongman 2010).

Step 4: Create Avenues for Recourse and Feedback Loops

For the most part, exclusion is manifested in everyday processes that are ingrained in local realities. Grievances related to them therefore also need to be tackled at the local level. Grievances about child mortality, for instance, can be resolved through local tribal health and grievance redress committees that have access to district administration. Mobile phones can be used to establish help lines that provide information on available services. All grievance redress or dispute resolution mechanisms need to be linked back to systems that can enable reporting back to communities on action taken.

Establishing a feedback loop helps projects adapt for better outcomes. What do projects do with the information they get from evaluation surveys, midterm appraisals, and ongoing analysis and consultations? The best ones usually integrate the lessons into implementation. Repeater projects provide a formal mechanism to integrate learning from previous phases. For instance, data from the first phase of the World Bank–supported LACOSREP project in Ghana showed that the project had not adequately addressed capacity building of water user associations and women's access to land and water. The second phase was therefore designed to systematically and rigorously grant women access to dry season irrigation plots by involving them in water user associations and giving them a quota in plot allocation.

Countries can also set up specialized agencies and institutions that enforce nondiscrimination laws. The U.S. Equal Employment Opportunity Commission (EEOC) and the Brazilian Special Secretariat for Policies and Promotion of Racial Equality are two examples of institutions with teeth that have furthered the nondiscrimination agenda. The EEOC enforces federal laws that make it illegal to discriminate against a job applicant or an employee because of the person's race, color, religion, gender (including pregnancy), national origin, age, disability, or genetic information. It is also illegal to discriminate against a person because the person complained about discrimination, filed a charge of discrimination, or participated in an employment discrimination investigation or lawsuit. Equal employment laws cover most employers with at least 15 employees (20 in age discrimination cases). Most labor unions and employment agencies are also covered. The laws apply to all types of work situations, including hiring, firing, promotion, harassment, training, wages, and benefits.

Brazil's Special Secretariat for Policies and Promotion of Racial Equality promotes initiatives against racial inequalities. It is committed to the construction of a government policy that takes into consideration the interests of the black population and other discriminated-against ethnic groups, such as "the gypsies." It involves, promotes, and monitors the implementation of cooperation programs with public and private, domestic and foreign entities for the protection of the rights of individuals and racial and ethnic groups affected by discrimination.

In New Zealand, Te Puni Kōkiri (the Ministry for Maori Development) leads Maori public policy and advises on policies affecting Maori wellbeing. It monitors policy and legislation and recognizes the importance of Maori achieving success without compromising what it means to be Maori. It also maintains close and interactive connections with Maori through a strong network of regional offices.

All of these institutions, in addition to acting as enforcement agencies, help coordinate the multisector interventions needed to address exclusion. More importantly, they raise the profile of inclusion issues and the urgency of addressing them within a country.

What should excluded groups do when their rights are violated? Vulnerable groups often have no legal recourse when they do not receive their entitlements or their rights are violated. One of the most effective ways to provide legal assistance is simply to increase awareness about it. A study by AusAID on access and equity in Indonesian religious courts shows that there are differences in access between regular court users and female household heads. As a follow-up to the study, the World Bank–supported Justice for the Poor program, implemented in partnership with a local nongovernmental organization, worked with a community empowerment program that trained paralegals to disseminate legal information, provided assistance to village women, and supported grassroots policy advocacy. Building on the results of the program at the district level, the government of Indonesia decided to implement reforms in religious courts nationwide. The effort resulted in a 14-fold increase in the number of poor clients able to access such courts (as a result of court fee waivers) and a 4-fold increase in the number accessing circuit courts in remote areas. Experiences with and the importance of local, informal judicial institutions such as religious courts in Indonesia and the *shalish* in Bangladesh have compelled countries to look beyond state legal systems to improve access to legal recourse for the vulnerable (Tamanaha, Sage, and Woolcock 2012).

Notes

1. The study also observes increases in all other types of crimes (including rape, domestic violence, and threats), which could be explained by the end of the authoritarian order previously established by the drug lords.
2. The term *pacification* and its variants are not intended as pejoratives. They are the translations of Portuguese terms indicating control by the state rather than violent gangs.
3. Department of Defense Appropriations Act, 2010, H.R. 3326, 111th Congress (2010).
4. RECURSO is a multiyear program of analytical and advisory activity of the World Bank that focuses on strengthening accountability and results in the social sectors. The programmatic title is derived from the Spanish acronym, Rendimiento de Cuentas para los Resultados Sociales.

References

Abraham, K. S. 2012. *Kenya at 50: Unrealized Rights of Minorities and Indigenous Peoples*. London: Minority Rights Group International.

Angelucci, M. 2008. "Love on the Rocks: Aggressive Behavior and Alcohol Abuse in Rural Mexico." Working Paper, Department of Economics, University of Arizona, Tucson.

Attanasio, O., and M. Vera-Hernandez. 2004. "Medium and Long Run Effects of Nutrition and Child Care: Evaluation of a Community Nursery Programme in Rural Colombia." Working Paper 04/06, Institute for Fiscal Studies, University College, London.

Barron, P., M. Humphreys, L. Paler, and J. Weinstein. 2009. *Community-Based Reintegration in Aceh: Assessing the Impacts of BRA-KPED*. Washington, DC: World Bank.

Beaman, L., E. Duflo, R. Pande, and P. Topalova. 2012. "Female Leadership Raises Aspirations and Educational Attainment for Girls: A Policy Experiment in India." *Science* 335: 582–86.

Betancourt, J. R., and A. R. Green. 2010. "Commentary: Linking Cultural Competence Training to Improved Health Outcomes: Perspectives from the Field." *Academic Medicine* 85 (4): 583.

Bhavnani, R. 2009. "Do Electoral Quotas Work after They Are Withdrawn? Evidence from a Natural Experiment in India." *American Political Science Review* 103 (1): 23–35.

Bigler, R. S. 1999. "The Use of Multicultural Curricula and Materials to Counter Racism in Children." *Journal of Social Issues* 55 (4): 687–705.

Boseley, S. 2010. "Rwanda: a Revolution in Rights for Women." *Guardian*, May 28. http://www.guardian.co.uk/world/2010/may/28/womens-rights-rwanda (accessed December 14, 2012).

Brinks, D., and V. Gauri. 2012. "The Law's Majestic Equality? The Distributive Impact of Litigating Social and Economic Rights." Policy Research Working Paper 5999, World Bank, Washington, DC.

Burger, R., and R. Jafta. 2006. "Returns to Race: Labour Market Discrimination in Post-Apartheid South Africa." Working Paper 4, Stellenbosch University, Department of Economics, Stellenbosch, South Africa.

Cano, I. 2012. *Os donos do morro: Uma avaliação exploratória do impacto das Unidades de Polícia Pacificadora (UPPs) no Rio de Janeiro.* (*The Owners of the Hill: An Exploratory Evaluation of the Impact of Pacifying Police Units (UPP) in Rio de Janeiro*). Rio de Janeiro, Brazil: LAV/UERJ e Fórum Brasileiro de Segurança Pública.

Cooper, G., V. Arago-Kemp, C. Wylie, and E. Hodgen. 2004. *Te Rerenga a Te Pirere: A Longitudinal Study of Kohanga Reo and Kura Kaupapa Maori Students.* New Zealand Council for Educational Research, Wellington.

Croke, K., A. Dabalen, G. Demombybes, M. Giugale, and J. G. M. Hoogeveen. 2012. "Collecting High Frequency Panel Data in Africa Using Mobile Phone Interviews." Policy Research Working Paper 6097, World Bank, Washington, DC.

Deininger, K., A. Goyal, and H. Nagarajan. 2010. "Inheritance Law Reform and Women's Access to Capital: Evidence from India's Hindu Succession Act." Policy Research Working Paper 5338, World Bank, Washington, DC.

Deininger, K., D. Narayan, and B. Sen. 2009. "Politics of the Middle Path: Agrarian Reform and Poverty Dynamics in West Bengal." In *Moving Out of Poverty: The Promise of Empowerment and Democracy in India,* ed. D. Narayan, 286–348. Washington, DC: World Bank.

Demirgüç-Kunt, A., and L. Klapper. 2012. "Measuring Financial Inclusion: The Global Findex Database." Policy Research Working Paper 6025, World Bank, Washington, DC.

FAO (Food and Agriculture Organization). 2010. *Africa's Changing Landscape: Securing Land Access for the Rural Poor.* Accra, Ghana: FAO Regional Office for Africa. http://www.fao.org/docrep/012/al209e/al209e00.pdf (accessed January 20, 2013).

Field, E. 2003. "Entitled to Work: Urban Property Rights and Labor Supply in Peru." *Quarterly Journal of Economics* 122 (4): 1561–1602. http://qje.oxfordjournals.org/content/122/4/1561.short.

Galiani, S., and E. Schargrodsky. 2009. "Property Rights for the Poor: Effects of Land Titling." Ronald Coase Institute Working Paper 7, St. Louis, MO.

Ghosh, P. 2012. "Rwanda: The Only Government in the World Dominated by Women." *International Business Times*, January 3. http://www.ibtimes.com/rwanda-only-government-world-dominated-women-213623 (accessed December 14, 2012).

Hall, G., and H. A. Patrinos, eds. 2006. *Indigenous Peoples, Poverty, and Human Development in Latin America.* New York: Palgrave Macmillan.

HelpAge International. 2004. *Age and Security. How Social Pensions Can Deliver Effective Aid to Poorer People and Their Families.* London: HelpAge International.

Heywood, M. 2009. "South Africa's Treatment Action Campaign: Combining Law and Social Mobilization to Realize the Right to Health." *Journal of Human Rights Practice* 1 (1): 14–36.

Hill, M. E., and M. Augoustinos. 2001. "Stereotype Change and Prejudice Reduction: Short And Long Term Evaluation of a Cross–Cultural Awareness Programme." *Journal of Community and Applied Social Psychology* 11 (4): 243–62.

IMO (International Migration Organization). n.d. *International Migration 2011–2012. IMO Report for Norway.* Report prepared for the OECD reporting system on migration.

Instituto Brasileiro de Pesquisa Social. 2012. *Pesquisa sobre a percepção acerca das Unidades de Polícia Pacificadora (Research on the Perceptions of the Pacifying Police Units).* Rio de Janeiro, Brazil: Instituto Brasileiro de Pesquisa Social 2012.

Jennings, P. A., K. E. Snowberg, M. A. Coccia, and M. T. Greenberg. 2011. "Improving Classroom Learning Environments by Cultivating Awareness and Resilience in Education (CARE): Results of Two Pilot Studies." *Journal of Classroom Interaction* 46 (1): 37–48.

Jomo, K. S., and W. C. Hui. n.d. "Affirmative Action and Exclusion in Malaysia: Ethnic and Regional Inequalities in a Multicultural Society." http://www.jomoks.org/research/other/rp002.htm (accessed October 7, 2013).

Katz, P., and S. Zalk. 1978. "Modification of Children's Racial Attitudes." *Developmental Psychology* 14: 447–61.

Kavli, H., A. Hagelund, and M. Bråthen. 2007. "With the Right to Learn and the Duty to Participate." Report 2007/34, Fafo, Oslo.

Leibbrandt, M., I. Woolard, and C. Woolard. 2007. "Poverty and Inequality Dynamics in South Africa: Post-apartheid Developments in the Light of the Long-Run Legacy." Paper prepared for a workshop sponsored by the International Poverty Centre and the David Rockefeller Center for Latin American Studies, Brasilia, January 11–13.

Lindemann, C. 2010. "'Landless Peasant' Activism in Brazil: Fighting for Social Inclusion through Land Reform." PhD thesis, University of Melbourne, School of Philosophy, Anthropology and Social Inquiry (PASI), Melbourne, Australia.

Macours, K., and R. Vakis. 2009. "Changing Households' Investments and Aspirations through Social Interactions: Evidence from a Randomized Transfer Program in a Low-Income Country." Policy Research Working Paper 5137, World Bank, Washington, DC.

Mansuri, G., and V. Rao. 2013. *Localizing Development: Does Participation Work?* Washington, DC: World Bank.

Marcus, R., S. Espinoza, L. Schmidt, and S. Sultan. 2013. "Social Exclusion in Africa: Towards More Inclusive Approaches." Background paper draft, World Bank, Washington, DC.

Norwegian Ministry of Labour and Social Inclusion. 2006. *Action Plan for Integration and Social Inclusion of the Immigrant Population and Goals for Social Inclusion.* Oslo: Ministry of Labour and Social Inclusion.

OECD (Organisation for Economic Co-operation and Development). 2009. *Jobs for Immigrants: Labour Market Integration in Norway.* Paris: OECD Publishing.

———. 2012a. *Jobs for Immigrants, vol. 3. Labour Market Integration in Austria, Norway and Switzerland.* Paris: OECD Publishing.

———. 2012b. *Settling In: OECD Indicators of Immigrant Integration 2012.* Paris: OECD Publishing.

Parker, S. W., L. Rubalcava, and G. Teruel. 2005. "Schooling Inequality and Language Barriers." *Economic Development and Cultural Change* 54 (1): 71–94.

Piron, L.-H., and Z. Curran. 2005. *Public Policy Responses to Exclusion: Evidence from Brazil, South Africa and India.* Overseas Development Institute, London.

Plonka, B. 2013. "Social Inclusion in Poland." Background paper draft, World Bank, Washington, DC.

Ringold, D. 2008. "Accounting for Diversity: Policy Design and Maori Development in New Zealand." In *Inclusive States: Social Policy and Structural Inequalities,* ed. A. Dani and A. de Haan, 271–94. Washington, DC: World Bank.

Romero, S. 2007. "Medellin's Nonconformist Mayor Turns Blight to Beauty." *New York Times*, July 15. http://www.nytimes.com/2007/07/15/world/americas/15medellin.html?pagewanted=all (accessed October 7, 2013).

Silver, H. 2013. "Framing Social Inclusion Policies." Background paper draft, World Bank, Washington, DC.

Tamanaha, B. Z., C. M. Sage, and M. J. Woolcock, eds. 2012. *Legal Pluralism and Development: Scholars and Practitioners in Dialogue*. Cambridge, U.K.: Cambridge University Press.

Todd, P. 2012. "Effectiveness of Interventions Aimed at Improving Women's Employability and Quality of Work: A Critical Review." Policy Research Working Paper 6189, World Bank, Washington, DC.

Turner, R. N., and R. Brown. 2008. "Improving Children's Attitudes Toward Refugees: An Evaluation of a School-Based Multicultural Curriculum and an Anti-Racist Intervention." *Journal of Applied Social Psychology* 38: 1295–328. http://www.academia.edu/676317/Improving_childrens_attitudes_towards_refugees_An_evaluation_of_a_multicultural_curricula_and_anti-racist_intervention (accessed April 28, 2013).

Ward, B., and J. Strongman. 2010. *Gender-Sensitive Approaches for the Extractive Industry in Peru: Improving the Impact on Women in Poverty and Their Families*. Washington, DC: World Bank.

Ward, E. 2006. "Real or Illusory Progress: Electoral Quotas and Women's Political Participation in Tanzania, Eritrea and Uganda." *Trocaire Development Review* 73–95 (Dublin).

Weiner, M. 1983. "The Political Consequences of Preferential Policies: A Comparative Perspective." *Comparative Politics* 16 (1): 35–52.

Wong, S. 2012. *What Have Been the Impacts of World Bank Community-Driven Development Programs? CDD Impact Evaluation Review and Operational & Research Implications*. World Bank, Sustainable Development Department, Washington, DC. http://www-wds.worldbank.org/external/default/WDSContentServer/WDSP/IB/2012/06/14/000386194_20120614062031/Rendered/PDF/695410WP0SW0CD00Box370017B00PUBLIC0.pdf.

World Bank. Moving Out of Poverty (research initiative). http://www.worldbank.org/en/topic/poverty.

———. 2010a. "Mainstreaming Gender in Transport: Operational Guidance for World Bank Staff." *Transport Papers 28*, World Bank, Washington, DC.

———. 2010b. *Social Development and Infrastructure: Making Urban Development Work for Women and Men: Tools for Task Teams*. Washington, DC: World Bank.

———. 2011a. *Poverty and Social Exclusion in India*. Washington, DC: World Bank.

———. 2011b. "Social Safety Nets in Nepal." Draft report, World Bank, Washington, DC.

———. 2012a. *O Retorno do Estado às Favelas do Rio de Janeiro* (*The State Return to the Slums of Rio de Janeiro*). World Bank, Brasília.

———. 2012b *World Development Report 2012: Gender Equality and Development*. Washington, DC: World Bank.

———. 2013a. *Adolescent Girls Initiative Brief*. Washington, DC: World Bank.

———. 2013b. *World Development Report 2013: Jobs*. Washington, DC: World Bank.

Social Inclusion

- The process of improving the terms for individuals and groups to take part in society
- The process of improving the ability, opportunity, and dignity of people, disadvantaged on the basis of their identity, to take part in society

CHAPTER 8

Concluding Reflections

I am fundamentally an optimist. Whether that comes from nature or nurture, I cannot say. Part of being optimistic is keeping one's head pointed toward the sun, one's feet moving forward. There were many dark moments when my faith in humanity was sorely tested, but I would not and could not give myself up to despair.

—NELSON MANDELA, *LONG WALK TO FREEDOM*

This report puts boundaries around the idea of social inclusion and develops a framework for moving towards it. It argues that inclusion has both intrinsic and instrumental value: it is integral to human well-being and social justice, but it also matters because the exclusion of individuals and groups has substantial social, political, and economic costs. The idea of social inclusion takes poverty analysis beyond identifying correlates to uncovering its underlying causes.

Exclusion can take place through practices and processes that are embedded in norms and values, restricting people's access to markets, services, and spaces (figure 8.1). The report argues that inclusion in these three interrelated domains can be wrought by enhancing abilities, opportunities, and dignity of disadvantaged individuals and groups.

The report emphasizes that policy matters and asks how policies that are effective in addressing social inclusion differ from other policies. It argues that such policies do not necessarily do more but that they do things differently.

No single set of policies or programs can be classified as "social inclusion" policies or programs. Depending on the "wrong" that needs to be addressed, or the "right" that needs to be deepened, a range of interventions

Figure 8.1 Propelling Social Inclusion: A Framework

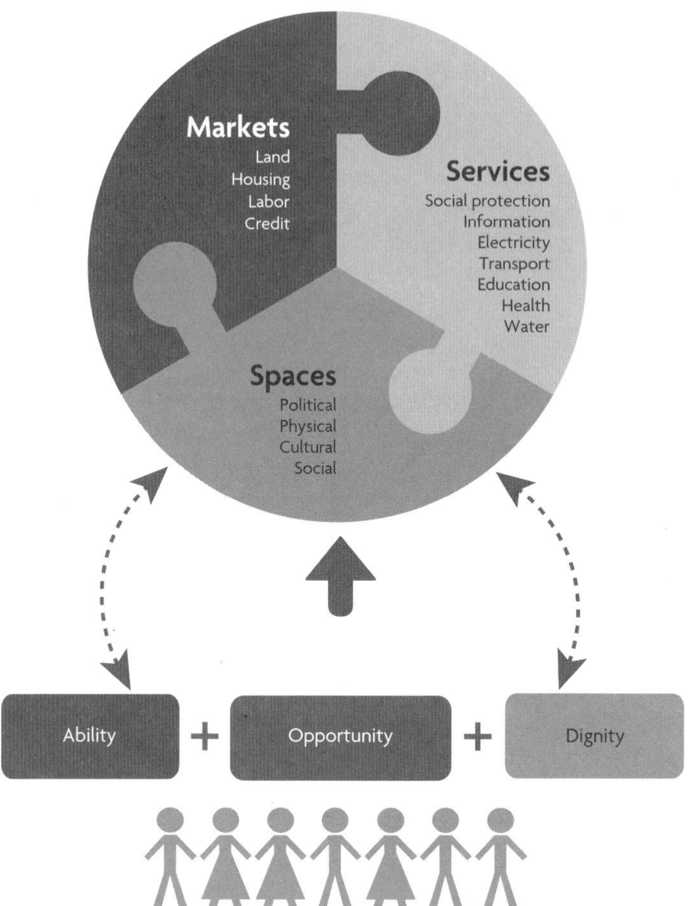

could be employed. The report therefore discusses the ways in which different countries have practiced social inclusion. In the process, it presents a menu of options that can help policy makers start addressing issues of inclusion and exclusion rather than proposing a set of prescriptions.

Going forward, the changing global context is expected to make social inclusion issues more relevant. Many societies have been and will continue to be reshaped by profound transformations, such as changing age structures and the influx and outflow of migrants. These transitions can lead to new forms of exclusion, but they can also create new opportunities for inclusion. They often have an effect on attitudes and perceptions, which in turn affect the way people act and feel. Feelings of being included and respected by others, or being heard by the state, are central to shaping people's abilities, their sense of dignity, the opportunities they access, the way in which they take part in society, and the way the state responds to them. In the post-2015 development context—where the underlying drivers of poor outcomes in some countries will be explored in parallel with the new and complex issues affecting virtually every country—influencing change toward social inclusion will be an important piece of the puzzle.

What Does This Report Mean for Practitioners of Development?

This report is at once an input into the global discussion of the post-2015 agenda and a contribution to the new goals of the World Bank Group of ending extreme poverty and promoting shared prosperity. A sustainable path of development and poverty reduction, as articulated in the World Bank Group's goals (World Bank 2013), is one that manages the resources of the planet for future generations, *ensures social inclusion*, and adopts fiscally responsible policies that limit future debt burden.

Although its contribution to the world of ideas is an important objective, the report will be a larger public good only if it influences the world of policies, programs, and projects. What are the potential contributions of this report to the design and implementation of policies, programs, and projects? How does it highlight a new agenda on social inclusion?

This report speaks to practitioners in the following broad ways:

- It is an exhortation to practitioners and researchers alike to use the term *social inclusion* with careful attention to meaning and boundaries. Too many programs use the terms *inclusive* or *inclusion* without adequate attention to how they are different from *inequality* or *poverty*. This report makes those distinctions, which although far from watertight, bring out the distinguishing characteristics of *social inclusion*. If indeed social inclusion is the overreaching goal of a policy, program, or project, the expectation should be that processes, practices, stereotypes, attitudes, perceptions, and behaviors that produce exclusion are given due attention.
- It brings some ideas from the realms of philosophy and theory into the realm of practice. For instance, the fact that subjective reports can be important drivers of success or failure is not generally recognized in the

design and implementation of policies and programs. Leaders of programs and projects would do well to pay attention to public opinions and perceptions, which, when combined with objective indicators, can be a good proxy for the performance of a project or program.

- It highlights the gaps in the understanding of social inclusion. The report brings new ideas, such as the importance of dignity, into the mainstream discourse of the World Bank Group, but it relies mainly on secondary evidence in highlighting the importance of such concepts for development practice. There is much more work to be done to understand how ideas of dignity and respect, for instance, play out in improving outcomes for excluded groups in markets, services, and spaces. Do interventions that address these issues stand the test of effectiveness, as borne out through empirical rigor? What can be efficient starting points for infusing a program or project with elements of social inclusion? How do aspirations affect participation in programs? These are some of the questions that deserve greater empirical understanding if these issues are to be integrated into program design.
- It underscores the importance of additional work on measuring social inclusion. The report cautions that metrics are only a first point of defense against exclusion, that they are flags. Yet, it emphasizes the importance of measurement to establish the extent and depth of exclusion and to monitor progress toward inclusion. Efforts at measuring social inclusion are still in the developing stage. Appendix B lays out a number of initiatives that broadly address social inclusion, but the report notes that measurement is challenging and needs additional resources, creative thinking, and a consensus among academics, policy makers, implementing agencies and civil society.
- It emphasizes the importance of "asking why," of understanding why poor outcomes continue to persist for some groups. It highlights the fact that practitioners may be using blunt instruments to tackle difficult issues if they do not undertake good ex ante analysis of the problem. There are a number of ways by which such analysis can take place. Mixed methods are important, as is hearing the voices of people who have poor outcomes or who are at risk of being excluded.
- It draws attention to the fact that monitoring change toward social inclusion needs innovation and that such innovation needs to be incorporated into practice. Examples of innovations include the creative use of information and communications technology, third-party monitoring,

grievance redress, and feedback from program participants, which are being tried in a number of places. These efforts need to find space in mainstream monitoring mechanisms and results frameworks.

References

Mandela, Nelson. 1995. *Long Walk to Freedom: The Autobiography of Nelson Mandela*. Boston: Little Brown, and Company.

World Bank. 2013. *The World Bank Group Goals: End Extreme Poverty and Promote Shared Prosperity.* Washington, DC: World Bank. http://www.worldbank.org/content/dam/Worldbank/document/WB-goals2013.pdf.

APPENDIX A

Usage of Terms *Social Inclusion* and *Social Exclusion*

Table A.1 Usage of the Term *Social Inclusion* and Its Variants

Definition	Key concepts
Social inclusion is a process which ensures that those at risk of being left out gain opportunities and resources necessary to participate fully in economic, social, political and cultural life and enjoy a standard of well-being that is considered normal in the society in which they live. It ensures that they have a voice in decisions which affect their lives and access to markets, public services, and their fundamental rights (European Commission 2004).	• Participation in society • Well-being • Voice • Fundamental rights
A socially inclusive society is one in which all Australians feel valued and have the opportunity to participate fully in the life of our society (Hayes, Gray, and Edwards 2008).	• Feeling valued • Opportunity • Participation in society
Social inclusion and exclusion refer to the extent that individuals, families and communities are able to fully participate in society and control their own destinies (Stewart 2000).	• Participation in society • Control over one's own destiny
Social inclusion refers to a set of policies and institutions (broadly conceived to include organizations, norms and codes of behavior) that support pro-poor growth and social equity (Bennett 2002).	• Institutions • Norms • Behavior • Pro-poor growth • Social equity
Inclusive economic institutions ... are forged on foundations laid by inclusive political institutions, which make power broadly distributed in society and constrain its arbitrary exercise. Such political institutions also make it harder for others to usurp power and undermine the foundations of inclusive institutions. Those controlling political power cannot easily use it to set up extractive economic institutions for their own benefit (Acemoglu and Robinson 2012).	• Institutions • Power • Extraction versus inclusion

(*continued next page*)

Table A.1 Usage of the Term *Social Inclusion* and Its Variants (*continued*)

Definition	Key concepts
Social inclusion is the removal of institutional barriers and the enhancement of incentives to increase the access of diverse individuals and groups to development opportunities (World Bank 2011).	• Institutions • Opportunity
A socially inclusive society is defined as one where all people feel valued, their differences are respected, and their basic needs are met so they can live in dignity (Cappo 2002).	• Feeling valued • Respecting differences • Meeting basic needs • Living with dignity
Social inclusion is based on the belief that we all fare better when no one is left to fall too far behind and the economy works for everyone. Social inclusion simultaneously incorporates multiple dimensions of well-being. It is achieved when all have the opportunity and resources necessary to participate fully in economic, social, and cultural activities which are considered the societal norm (Boushey et al. 2007).	• Equality • Well-being • Opportunity • Participation in society
Social inclusion is not what does it mean, but what do we mean by it—or rather what is meant by it, by whom? How is this metaphor used, by whom, and for what purpose? And how might it be used, perhaps for other purposes? What are the political consequences or possibilities of this particular metaphor? What kind of society is actually, or can be, implied by the term *social inclusion*? Factors that might be seen as part of an inclusion agenda include, for example, discrimination on the grounds of gender, ethnicity, disability, age, religion, and sexuality. [Inclusion] addresses not equality in a distributive sense, but equal opportunities. Other aspects of inclusion concern questions of rights and questions of recognition, and inclusion in the processes of decision-making rather than simply the outcomes of those decisions (Levitas 2003).	• Context specificity • Political nature of the term • Opportunity • Rights • Recognition • Voice

Table A.2 Usage of the Term *Social Exclusion*

Definition	Key concepts
Social exclusion can [thus] be constitutively a part of capability deprivation as well as instrumentally a cause of diverse capability failures. The case for seeing social exclusion as an approach to poverty is easy enough to establish within the general perspective of poverty as capability failure.... The helpfulness of the social exclusion approach does not lie, I would argue, in its conceptual newness, but in its practical influence in forcefully emphasizing—and focusing attention on—the role of relational features in deprivation (Sen 2000, 5, 8).	• Capability • Social relations
Social exclusion is a rupturing of the social bond. It is a process of declining participation, access, and solidarity. At the societal level, it reflects inadequate social cohesion or integration. At the individual level, it refers to the incapacity to participate in normatively expected social activities and to build meaningful social relations (Silver n.d., 4411).	• Participation • Access • Solidarity • Social cohesion • Integration • Social relations/social bonds
The concept (social exclusion) takes us beyond mere descriptions of deprivation, and focuses attention on social relations and the processes and institutions that underlie and are part and parcel of deprivation (de Haan 2000, 26).	• Social relations • Processes • Institutions
Disadvantage results in social exclusion when the various institutional mechanisms through which resources are allocated and value assigned operate in such a way as to systematically deny particular groups of people the resources and recognition which would allow them to participate fully in the life of that society (Kabeer 2000, 9).	• Institutions • Resources • Recognition • Participation
Social exclusion is the process through which individuals or groups are wholly or partially excluded from full participation in the society within which they live (European Foundation for the Improvement of Living and Working Conditions 1995, 4, cited in de Haan and Maxwell 1998, 2).	• Participation
Social exclusion is a process whereby certain individuals are pushed to the edge of society and prevented from participating fully by virtue of their poverty, or lack of basic competencies and lifelong learning opportunities, or as a result of discrimination. This distances them from job, income and education opportunities as well as social and community networks and activities. They have little access to power and decision-making bodies and thus often feel powerless and unable to take control over the decisions that affect their day-to-day lives (European Commission 2004).	• Participation • Opportunities • Discrimination • Networks • Access • Power • Control
Social exclusion ... refers not only to material deprivation, but to the inability of the poor to fully exercise their social, cultural and political rights as citizens (Powell 1995, 22–23).	• Rights • Citizenship

(continued next page)

Table A.2 Usage of the Term *Social Exclusion* (*continued*)

Definition	Key concepts
The European Commission emphasizes the idea that each citizen has the right to a certain basic standard of living and a right to participate in the major social and occupational institutions of the society—employment, housing, health care, education and so on.... Social exclusion occurs when citizens suffer from disadvantage and are unable to secure these social rights (Bhalla and Lapeyre 1997, 415).	• Rights • Participation • Institutions
Lack of power, or unequal power relations, is at the root of every type of exclusion (Stewart et al. 2006, 4).	• Power
Exclusion from social, political and economic institutions resulting from a complex and dynamic set of processes and relationships that prevent individuals or groups from accessing resources, participating in society and asserting their rights (Beall and Piron 2004, cited in Stewart et al. 2006, 4).	• Institutions • Processes • Access • Resources • Participation • Rights
Social exclusion occurs when the institutions that allocate resources and assign value operate in ways that systematically deny some groups the resources and recognition that would allow them to participate fully in social life (Zeitlyn 2004, cited in Stewart et al. 2006, 4).	• Institutions • Resources • Recognition • Participation
A concoction (or blend) of multidimensional and mutually reinforcing processes of deprivation, associated with progressive dissociation from social milieu, resulting in the isolation of individuals and groups from the mainstream of opportunities society has to offer (Vleminckx and Berghman 2001, 46).	• Multidimensionality • Isolation from society • Opportunities
Social exclusion is manifested "in recurrent patterns of social relationships in which individuals and groups are denied access to the goods, services, activities, and resources which are generally associated with citizenship" (Gore and Figueiredo 1997, 8, cited in Jackson 1999, 127–28).	• Social relations • Access • Resources • Citizenship

References

Acemoglu, D., and J. A. Robinson. 2012. *Why Nations Fail: The Origins of Power, Prosperity, and Poverty*. New York: Crown Business.

Beall, J., and L. H. Piron. 2004. *DfID (Department for International Development) Social Exclusion Review*. London: London School of Economics and Overseas Development Institute.

Bennett, L. 2002. "Using Empowerment and Social Inclusion for Pro-poor Growth: A Theory of Social Change." Background paper for the Social Development Sector Strategy Paper, World Bank, Washington, DC.

Bhalla, A., and F. Lapeyre. 1997. "Social Exclusion: Towards an Analytical and Operational Framework." *Development and Change* 28 (3): 413–33. http://www.oit.org/wcmsp5/groups/public/---ed_dialogue/---actrav/documents/meetingdocument/wcms_161351.pdf.

Boushey, H., S. Fremstad, R. Gragg, and M. Waller. 2007. "Social Inclusion for the United States." Center for Economic and Social Inclusion, London. http://inclusionist.org/files/socialinclusionusa.pdf (accessed August 10, 2013).

Cappo, D. 2002. "Social Inclusion Initiative. Social Inclusion, Participation and Empowerment." Address to Australian Council of Social Services National Congress, Hobart, November 28–29.

de Haan, A. 2000. "Social Exclusion: Enriching the Understanding of Deprivation." *Studies in Social and Political Thought* 2 (2): 22–40.

de Haan, A., and S. Maxwell. 1998. "Editorial: Poverty and Social Exclusion in North and South." *IDS Bulletin 29* (1): 1–9.

European Commission. 2004. "Joint Report on Social Inclusion." Report 7101/04, European Commission, Brussels.

European Foundation for the Improvement of Living and Working Conditions. 1995. *Public Welfare Services and Social Exclusion: The Development of Consumer Oriented Initiatives in the European Union.* Dublin: European Foundation for the Improvement of Living and Working Conditions.

Gore, C., and J. B. Figueiredo. 1997. *Social Exclusion and Anti-Poverty Policy: A Debate.* Geneva: International Institute of Labour Studies.

Hayes, A., M. Gray, and B. Edwards. 2008. "Social Inclusion Origins, Concepts and Key Themes." Australian Institute of Family Studies, prepared for the Social Inclusion Unit, Department of the Prime Minister and Cabinet, Canberra.

Jackson, C. 1999. "Social Exclusion and Gender: Does One Size Fit All?" *European Journal of Development Research* 11 (1): 125–46.

Kabeer, N. 2000. "Social Exclusion, Poverty and Discrimination towards an Analytical Framework." *IDS Bulletin 31* (4) 83–97.

Levitas, R. 2003. "The Imaginary Reconstitution of Society: Utopia as Method." Paper presented at the University of Limerick/University of Ireland, Galway, as part of the Utopia-Method-Vision project led by Tom Moylan, February.

Powell, F. 1995. "Citizenship and Social Exclusion." *Administration* 43 (3): 23–35.

Sen, A. 2000. "The Discipline of Cost-Benefit Analysis." *Journal of Legal Studies* 29 (S2): 931–52.

Silver, H. n.d. "Social Exclusion." In *Encyclopedia of Sociology*. Oxford: Blackwell.

Stewart, A. 2000. "Social Inclusion: An Introduction." In *Social Inclusion: Possibilities and Tensions,* ed. P. Askonas and A. Stewart, 1–16. London: Macmillan.

Stewart, F., M. Barrón, G. Brown, and M. Hartwell. 2006. "Social Exclusion and Conflict: Analysis and Policy Implications." CRISE Policy Context Paper, Centre for Research on Inequality, Human Security and Ethnicity, Oxford.

Vleminckx, K., and J. Berghman. 2001. "Social Exclusion and the Welfare State: An Overview of Conceptual Issues and Policy Implications." In *Social Exclusion and European Policy*, ed. D. Mayes, J. Berghman, and R. Salais, 27–46. Northampton, U.K.: Edward Elgar.

World Bank. 2011. "Social Safety Nets in Nepal." Draft report, World Bank, Washington, DC.

Zeitlyn, S. 2004. "Social Exclusion in Asia: Some Initial Ideas." Department for International Development, London.

APPENDIX B

Recent Measures of Well-Being

Table B.1 Recent Measures of Well-Being

Measure/author/URL	Calculation	Number of indicators[a]	Dimension (number of indicators)	Indicators
Better Life Index OECD http://www.oecdbetterlifeindex.org	Defined by user (dashboard)	24 (4)	Housing (3)	Rooms per person, dwellings with basic facilities, housing expenditure
			Income (2)	Household net adjustable disposable income, household financial wealth
			Jobs (3)	Employment rate, long-term unemployment rate, personal earnings, job security
			Community (1)	Quality of support network (P)
			Education (3)	Educational attainment, student skills, years of education
			Environment (2)	Air pollution, water quality (P)
			Civic engagement (2)	Voter turnout, consultation on rule-making
			Health (2)	Life expectancy, self-reported health (P)
			Life satisfaction (1)	Life satisfaction (P)
			Safety (2)	Assault rate, homicide rate
			Work-life balance (2)	Employees working very long hours, time devoted to leisure and personal care
Multidimensional Poverty Index Sabina Alkire and James Foster (Oxford) http://www.ophi.org.uk/policy/multidimensional-poverty-index/	Weighted average; equal weights by dimension and within dimensions	10	Health (2)	Child mortality, nutrition
			Education (2)	Years of schooling, child school attendance
			Living standards (6)	Electricity, improved sanitation, improved drinking water, flooring, cooking fuel, asset ownership

(*continued next page*)

Table B.1 Recent Measures of Well-Being *(continued)*

Measure/author/URL	Calculation	Number of indicators[a]	Dimension (number of indicators)	Indicators
Human Development Index United Nations http://hdr.undp.org/en/statistics/hdi/	Geometric mean of dimension indexes	4	Long and healthy life (1)	Life expectancy at birth
			Knowledge (2)	Mean years of schooling, expected years of schooling
			Living standards (1)	Gross national income (GNI) per capita
Social Progress Index Social Progress Imperative (Michael Porter) http://www.socialprogressimperative.org/data/spi	Weighted average; equal weights by dimension, PCA within	52 (6)	*Basic human needs (18)*	
			Nutrition and basic medical care (6)	Undernourishment, depth of food deficit, maternal mortality rate, stillbirth rate, child mortality rate, prevalence of tuberculosis
			Air, water and sanitation (6)	Deaths attributable to indoor air pollution, deaths attributable to outdoor air pollution, access to piped water, rural/urban access to improved water source, access to improved sanitation facilities, access to wastewater treatment
			Shelter (2)	Satisfaction with housing (P), access to electricity
			Personal safety (4)	Homicide rate, level of violent crime, perceived criminality, political terror
			Foundations of well-being (18)	
			Access to basic knowledge (4)	Adult literacy rate, primary school enrollment, secondary school enrollment, women's mean years in school
			Access to information and communications (4)	Mobile telephone subscriptions, Internet users, fixed broadband subscriptions, press freedom index

(continued next page)

Table B.1 Recent Measures of Well-Being *(continued)*

Measure/author/URL	Calculation	Number of indicators[a]	Dimension (number of indicators)	Indicators
Social Progress Index *(continued)*			Health and wellness (6)	Life expectancy, obesity, cancer death rate, deaths from cardiovascular disease and diabetes, deaths from HIV/AIDS, availability of quality health care
			Ecosystem sustainability (4)	Ecological footprint of consumption, CO_2 emissions per capita, energy use per $1,000 GDP, water withdrawals per capita
			Opportunity (16)	
			Personal rights (5)	Political rights, freedom of speech, freedom of assembly/association, private property rights, women's property rights
			Access to higher education (2)	Total and female tertiary enrollment
			Personal freedom and choice (4)	Basic religious freedoms, contraceptive prevalence rate, access to child care, freedom in making life choices (P)
			Equity and inclusion (5)	Equity of opportunity for ethnic minorities, women treated with respect (P), community safety net (P), tolerance for immigrants (P), tolerance for homosexuals (P)
Indices of Social Development Institute of Social Studies/World Bank http://www.indsocdev.org	Matching percentiles	169 (40)	Civic activism (33)	Indicators in the areas of social norms, organizations, and practices that facilitate greater citizen involvement in public policies and decisions
			Clubs and associations (36)	Indicators for community ties that allow individuals to better weather the impact of sudden hardship

(*continued next page*)

Table B.1 Recent Measures of Well-Being *(continued)*

Measure/author/URL	Calculation	Number of indicators[a]	Dimension (number of indicators)	Indicators
Indices of Social Development *(continued)*			Intergroup cohesion (11)	Indicators for relations of cooperation and respect between identity groups in a society
			Interpersonal safety and trust (42)	Indicators on how much individuals in a society feel they can rely on people they have not met before
			Gender equality (21)	Indicators for the extent to which women and men face same opportunities and constraints within families, the workplace, and society at large
			Inclusion of minorities (26)	Indicators for the degree of discrimination against vulnerable groups such as indigenous people, migrants, refugees, and historically disadvantaged caste groups
Human Opportunity Index World Bank http://go.worldbank.org/A9Z0NUV620	Estimated coverage rate minus penalty for inequality of opportunity among circumstance groups		One index per dimension; can be aggregated using a weighted average in the case of several dimensions	Any dimension for which coverage can be measured (for example, education, housing, electricity, water, sanitation)

(continued next page)

Table B.1 Recent Measures of Well-Being *(continued)*

Measure/author/URL	Calculation	Number of indicators[a]	Dimension (number of indicators)	Indicators
Social Institutions and Gender Index OECD http://www.genderindex.org	Weighted average; equal weights by dimension (squared), PCA within Also defined by user (dashboard)	14 (1)	Discriminatory family code (4)	Minimum legal age of marriage, prevalence of early marriage, parental authority, and inheritance
			Restricted physical integrity (3)	Prevalence of female genital mutilation, extent to which women can exercise reproductive autonomy, and violence against women (existence of laws against domestic violence, the prevalence of domestic violence, and attitudes toward it [P])
			Son bias (2)	Gender bias in mortality and fertility preferences
			Restricted resources and entitlements (3)	Women's access to land, credit, and property other than land
			Restricted civil liberties (2)	Freedom of social participation of women, including access to public space and political voice

Note: P denotes indicator that captures perceptions. PCA = Principal Components Analysis.
a. Number in parenthesis in this column represents number of indicators that capture perceptions.

APPENDIX C

Illustrative Examples of Policies and Programs That Address Social Inclusion

Table C.1 Illustrative Examples of Policies and Programs That Address Social Inclusion

Domain of inclusion	Instrument/intervention	Examples
Markets		
Land	Titling of land	• Giving women titles to land under Barrios de Vereda (Real Neighborhood), an urban infrastructure project (Bolivia)
	Establishment of gender parity in inheritance laws	• Ensuring that titles are in the name of both spouses under the resettlement plan for the Yemen Flood Protection Project • Rwanda, South Africa
	Redistribution through land reforms	• Brazil, Costa Rica, parts of India
	Dissemination of information about land rights to excluded groups	• Dissemination of information to women about ownership of property under Complementing EU Support for Agricultural Restructuring Project in Romania (CESAR)
	Accommodation of communal land use patterns	• Sarawak Land Code (Vietnam) • Ley (Law) 70/1993, which seeks to protect the rights of Afro-Colombian communities (Colombia)

(*continued next page*)

Table C.1 Illustrative Examples of Policies and Programs That Address Social Inclusion *(continued)*

Domain of inclusion	Instrument/intervention	Examples
Housing	Housing projects for slum dwellers, the poorest, people with disabilities, and migrants	• Inter-American Development Bank's (IDB's) Urban Rehabilitation Program (Haiti) • Allocation of 10 extra preference points to people with disabilities who apply for housing programs (Chile) • Million Programme has built new homes in Sweden to ensure widespread access to housing • Minha Casa Minha Vida (Brazil)
Labor	Affirmative action/quotas	• India, Malaysia, South Africa, Uganda
	Training on employability skills	• Adolescent Girls Initiative (Liberia) • New Opportunities for Women (Jordan NOW) • Jovenes (Latin America)
	Short-term wage subsidies to firms	• Adolescent Girls Initiative (Nepal) • New Opportunities for Women (Jordan NOW)
	Enforcement of anti-discrimination laws	• U.S. Equal Opportunities Commission
	Maternity, paternity, and child-care benefits	• Maternity and paternity leave and state-sponsored child care; cash benefits for children under age of three not enrolled in state-sponsored child care (Denmark, Norway, and Sweden)
	Coaching and mentoring programs for youth from excluded groups	• The Mentor Network, under the Danish Centre for Information on Gender, Equality and Diversity, facilitates path to employment and society for young immigrant women living in Denmark
Financial	Preferential credit	• Central bank directs public sector banks to give a certain percentage of credit to women's self-help groups (India)
	Mobile phone banking	• Sub-Saharan Africa, where mobile banking reaches 16 percent of the market

(continued next page)

Table C.1 Illustrative Examples of Policies and Programs That Address Social Inclusion *(continued)*

Domain of inclusion	Instrument/intervention	Examples
Services		
Health	Conditional cash transfers	• Benefits of Opportunidades go disproportionately to indigenous communities, who are overrepresented among the poor (Mexico)
	Subsidized health insurance	• Ghana
	Integration of cultural norms and values of the excluded into service delivery	• SEARCH (Society for Education, Action and Research in Community Health), an NGO in tribal areas of Maharashtra, India, has developed a Home Based Neonatal Care (HBNC) model to reduce infant mortality
	Raising awareness on HIV/AIDS in infrastructure projects	• Western Africa HIV/AIDS Project for the Abidjan-Lagos Transport Corridor
	Transport vouchers	• Rural Transportation Voucher Program for People with Disabilities (United States)
Education	Affirmative action/quotas	• India, Malaysia, Uganda
	Tuition and other cost exemptions	• The government, the Open Society Institute, and DROM (a Roma NGO) provide transportation, shoes, school lunches, and other goods and services to integrate Roma in mainstream schools (Bulgaria)
	Multicultural curriculum	• National school textbook program to promote diversity of society (Brazil)
	Teacher training in inclusive education	• Ethiopia
	Bilingual/alternative teaching	• Maori universities in New Zealand
	Accessible teaching methods and flexible curriculum	• Provision of services to children with disabilities in educational institutions
Information/ information and communications technology (ICT)	Distance/online learning for the excluded	• e-Rwanda, e-Lanka programs

(continued next page)

Table C.1 Illustrative Examples of Policies and Programs That Address Social Inclusion *(continued)*

Domain of inclusion	Instrument/intervention	Examples
	Use of ICT to disseminate information on inputs and prices	• TradeNet, Africa, a service designed to provide market information through mobile phones • E-choupals, India, a service designed to provide real-time information on agricultural inputs and prices to farmers through village kiosks linked by satellite
	Mobile phone applications to monitor outcomes and perceptions	• Listening to Africa program
Social protection	Social pensions	• South Africa's old-age pension, which was reformed to include more black beneficiaries
	Disability pensions	• Australia, Brazil, Germany, Nepal, and other countries
Water and sanitation	Separate toilets for girls in schools	• All secondary schools in rural areas of Bangladesh have separate toilets for boys and girls
	Assurance of women's access to irrigated land and water	• World Bank's Land Conservation and Smallholder Rehabilitation Project (Ghana) • Spaces for women in water user associations and women as managers of water points (Tanzania)
Infrastructure	Women-only transport services	• Belarus, Brazil, Arab Republic of Egypt, India, Japan, Mexico, and the Philippines
	Accessible transport, buildings, and curb cuts for people with disabilities	• Building and roads protocols in most countries have accessibility as a criterion; best enforced in OECD countries
	Improvement of safety through street lighting, pedestrian walkways, and crossings	• Urban Infrastructure Project (Bolivia)
	Involvement of communities in maintenance of local infrastructure, disaster management, and environmental planning and conservation	• World Bank's Third Rural Transport Project (Vietnam) • Asian Development Bank's Coral Reef Rehabilitation and Management Program (Indonesia)

(continued next page)

Table C.1 Illustrative Examples of Policies and Programs That Address Social Inclusion (*continued*)

Domain of inclusion	Instrument/intervention	Examples
Spaces		
Physical	Establishment of safety in public places	• Safe Cities Free of Violence Against Women and Girls Project, UNIFEM (India)
	Training on gender-based violence (and recourse to it), including separate training for men and women to reduce gender-based violence	• World Bank project for rape survivors (KOFAVIV) in Port-au-Prince, Haiti, run in cooperation with a community-based organization and international women's rights organization (MADRE)
		• World Bank project on institutional capacity building to follow up on Brazil's federal law against domestic violence
	Reservation of spaces in markets	• Asian Development Bank's Rural Infrastructure Development Project (Bangladesh) • World Bank's Integrated Coastal Zone Management Project (India)
Cultural	Recognition of multiple languages, customs	• Australia, where aboriginals are referred to as "indigenous custodians of this country" • People's Association of Singapore, which embraced the motto "enhance cultural difference, promote national harmony"
Social	Institutionalization of different forms of family life, such as same-sex marriages	• Malawi's move to legalize homosexuality
	Information campaigns to change stereotypes	• Theatrical performance by Lotus Integrated AIDS Awareness Sangam in a number of South Indian villages portraying the stigma and discrimination that prevents men who have sex with men from accessing services • HIV/AIDS awareness campaigns in high-prevalence countries in Botswana, Zambia, Zimbabwe, and other countries in Southern Africa, run jointly by governments and NGOs
	Passage of anti-discrimination laws	• Racial Discrimination Act 1975 (Australia) • Americans with Disabilities Act of 1990 (United States)

(*continued next page*)

Table C.1 Illustrative Examples of Policies and Programs That Address Social Inclusion (*continued*)

Domain of inclusion	Instrument/intervention	Examples
	Raising awareness among excluded/stigmatized groups/individuals about their rights	• Advocacy events by Project Baduku in Bangalore; work with police and health workers to discourage stigma; work with families and neighbors of female sex workers
	Advocacy by public figures on behalf of stigmatized groups/individuals	• Anti-stigma project in India targeting hospital managers, who use checklist of indicators to determine how well their hospital serves people living with HIV and identify ways to improve
	Fostering of critical thinking by general public or stakeholders whose discriminatory behavior is particularly harmful, such as health care providers, police, the judiciary, journalists, and educators	• Roma Education Fund programs promote desegregation of the education system, through the Good Start Project and other efforts (Eastern Europe)
	Promotion of interaction between excluded and non-excluded groups	• All Together in Dignity Fourth World Movement (Bolivia, Guatemala, Haiti, Mexico, Peru, the Philippines, Thailand)
	Public celebrations of heroes of oppressed; building of memorials	• Black History Month celebrations (United States)
	Official apologies	• U.S. government's "Apology to the Native Peoples of the United States"
	Arts and culture	• Put Music to Your Rights (Argentina) • Urban development initiatives in Medellín (Colombia), which created new public spaces for social interaction, such as the Parque Biblioteca España and cable cars that link two communities previously at war
Political	Affirmative action/quotas	• India, Malaysia, Rwanda, Tanzania
	Counting in official statistics	• National identification cards • IDB's *Everyone Counts* program • Decision by Nepal and South Africa to collect survey data disaggregated by ethnicity and/or race

(*continued next page*)

Table C.1 Illustrative Examples of Policies and Programs That Address Social Inclusion *(continued)*

Domain of inclusion	Instrument/intervention	Examples
Institutional	Separate entities for enforcement	• Department of Social Development (South Africa) • Special Secretariat for Policies and Promotion of Racial Equality (Brazil) • National Council to Prevent Discrimination (CONAPRED) (Mexico) • Parliamentary Commissioner for Ethnic and National Minorities (Hungary) • Te Puni Kōkiri (Ministry for Maori Development) (New Zealand) • Equal Employment Opportunity Commission (EEOC) (United States)

ECO-AUDIT

Environmental Benefits Statement

The World Bank is committed to preserving endangered forests and natural resources. ***Inclusion Matters: The Foundation for Shared Prosperity*** was printed on recycled paper with 50 percent postconsumer fiber in accordance with the recommended standards for paper usage set by the Green Press Initiative, a non-profit program supporting publishers in using fiber that is not sourced from endangered forests. For more information, visit www.greenpressinitiative.org.

Saved:

- 6 trees
- 3 million BTUs of total energy
- 569 lbs. CO_2 equivalent of greenhouse gases
- 3,085 gallons of waste water
- 207 lbs. of solid waste